Traps Embraced or Escaped

**Elites in the Economic Development
of Modern Japan and China**

Traps Embraced or Escaped

Elites in the Economic Development of Modern Japan and China

Carl Mosk
University of Victoria, Canada

World Scientific

NEW JERSEY · LONDON · SINGAPORE · BEIJING · SHANGHAI · HONG KONG · TAIPEI · CHENNAI

Published by

World Scientific Publishing Co. Pte. Ltd.

5 Toh Tuck Link, Singapore 596224

USA office: 27 Warren Street, Suite 401-402, Hackensack, NJ 07601

UK office: 57 Shelton Street, Covent Garden, London WC2H 9HE

British Library Cataloguing-in-Publication Data
A catalogue record for this book is available from the British Library.

TRAPS EMBRACED OR ESCAPED
Elites in the Economic Development of Modern Japan and China

ISBN-13 978-981-4287-52-4
ISBN-10 981-4287-52-0

Printed in Singapore.

For Damon, Dane, Maeve, Sera and Simon

Preface

Scale matters but only up to a point.

Carved out of massive glaciers long since vanished into oblivion, Pender Island is a pair of islands joined by a tiny wooden bridge part of an archipelago chain of small gulf islands nestled between Vancouver Island and the mainland of British Columbia. It is not an island of great geographic expanse. Nor is it populous, its permanent resident population running into the thousands. The same can be said of Victoria on Vancouver Island, home of the University of Victoria. The greater Victoria population falls short of 350 thousand individuals, most residing in suburbs sprawling out to the north of Victoria's oceanic coastline. In these two tiny communities — buffeted by the sprawling windstorms and pounding rains sweeping across the Pacific Ocean — and in the small inland university town of Davis, California with a population of 63 thousand persons this account of the modern economic development of two very large, populous and powerful nation states was conceived. The scale of the locales analyzed and the scale of the locales in which the analysis was nurtured bear no connection one to the other.

The same can be said of the scale of the account itself. *Traps Embraced and Escaped* deals with China, home to over 1.3 billion persons and Japan — with a population around a tenth of China's — but a far larger income per capita. Taken together these are two of the largest economies — arguably two of the most complex and strikingly different economies — in the world, one a high income per capita nation that is a fully functioning democracy, the other a low income per capita nation ruled by a single political party. To offer a credible account of what drove economic development in these two gigantic economies over the last century and a half would seem the height of hubris. Still this book takes this tack, advancing a simple hypothesis concerning surplus labor, arguing there are remarkable similarities between the economic development experiences of these two nations. The principal thrust of this book is expressed within the compass of a few words. But it is the hope of this author that from the seeds planted here a bountiful harvest will eventually spring forth.

A Note on Transcription

There are two major transcription systems used to represent Mandarin Chinese in English: Wade-Giles and pinyin. Following the practice that has become increasingly popular in the English literature, this volume uses pinyin. Thus Mao Zedong appears in the text, not Mao Tse-tung; Lin Biao not Lin Piao; Yuan Shikai not Yuan Shih-k'ai; Li Hongzhang not Li Hung-chang; Guomindang not Kuomintang; Yangzi not Yangtze; and so forth. This said, a few exceptions appear in the text due to the widespread use of non-pinyin transcriptions in the general literature: the most prominent exceptions are the names Sun Yat-sen and Chiang Kai-shek. In addition in referring to Japan's Kwangtung Army the name Kwangtung appears.

I am grateful to Daniel Bryant for his assistance in clarifying the two major transcription systems for Mandarin Chinese.

Names for Japanese and Chinese individuals are given in the following order: surname first, given name(s) afterward.

Contents

List of Charts and Tables

Charts

Tables

Part I
Introduction

1

The Argument

It would seem the height of folly to argue that there is a striking similarity between the economic development of Japan and of China over
the period 1850–2000. After all contemporary Japan is a high income
per capita country, a multi-party democracy with intense political
competition heavily relying upon market forces in allocating goods
and services including those flowing from the factors of production.
By contrast China is a much lower income per capita nation, nominally a Market Socialist economy characterized by one-party rule of
the Communist Party, market forces being strongly tempered by a
legacy of command and control directed central planning embod-
ied in state owned enterprises and collectively owned town and village enterprises that still play a significant role in the contemporary
Chinese economy. Yet the existence of remarkable similarity is the
core of the argument I advance in this volume.

The common challenge faced by both countries overshadow-
ing many of the salient differences between them is how to with-
draw surplus labor from agriculture by raising the number of hours
worked — and by raising the efficiency of each hour worked — by
workers in farming.[1] True each country went about addressing this
problem in different ways. Still the stark reality of coping with the
same basic transformation problem is so fundamental — constraining
and shaping politics, policies, and markets — that the overall

contour of economic development is remarkably similar in the two nations.

Increasing hours worked per worker and the productivity of each hour worked augments labor. Each worker expends more effort and makes each hour of effort count for more and more in terms of actual realized output. It is useful to express the flow of augmented labor input per worker in terms of a simple algebraic equation, namely:

$$l^* = h \, e(h), \qquad (1.1)$$

where h, $e(h)$, and l^* stand for hours worked per worker, for the productivity of each of those hours, and for total per worker augmented labor flow, respectively.

Given l^*, it is easy to compute the total augmented labor input for an economy. Let W be the number of workers. Then the total augmented labor force is:

$$L^* = l^* \, W = h \, e(h) \, W. \qquad (1.2)$$

For example in panel C.1 of Table A.10 in the statistical Appendix appear estimates of the growth of augmented labor force in China between 1952 and 2005. These numbers are based on estimating growth for L^*, in this case augmented only by education and not health, as defined above.

In a farm sector awash in surplus labor a typical worker puts in relatively few hours of labor, hours which sadly count for little in terms of crops harvested, animals tended, soil that is properly irrigated then drained. Why? While a host of specific factors account for this dismal performance they do fall into three categories: (1) constraints on physical work effort stemming from inadequate nutrition, frequent bouts of illness, and atrophy of vital organs due to degenerative disease or accident; (2) inadequate education limiting the ability of the worker to solve elementary problems in economic management that hinders the worker from informing soil and animal management tasks with a basic grasp of the elements of physics and chemistry; and (3) a perverse set of incentives stemming from being isolated from alternative opportunities — say in manufacturing — or from an unattractive set of rewards for hard work.

To see how to augment farm labor turn these negatives on their head: improve the health and physical robustness of the farming population; improve the educational capacity of individuals directing the workers in their tasks and/or the educational attainment of the workers themselves; and bolster the incentives faced by workers, either by opening up opportunities for using their labor in other income generating activities (encouraging them to economize on the effort they put into farming tasks) or by restructuring the matrix of carrots and sticks that spurs on a worker to undertake their tasks with greater intensity.

To be sure the flow of grains, vegetables, fruits, and industrial crops like cotton, cattle, and poultry generated annually from a farming community depends on more than the augmentation of farm labor. It also depends upon the augmentation of land and the augmentation of physical capital — planting and harvesting machinery, ploughs, tractors — that are combined with augmented labor to generate output. Independent of education, health, and incentives output per farm worker tends to increase when land is improved — say with more potent fertilizers or enhanced irrigation — or when more and better equipment is made available to the worker. In short, productivity of farm labor increases when it is directly augmented or when the land it toils on is enhanced or when it has access to equipment, mechanization being substituted for labor flow.

In a land scarce labor surplus rural environment there is a natural progression to land augmentation and mechanization of farm tasks, natural in the sense that it corresponds to real resource constraints.[2] In a so-called "cheap labor" environment in which real earnings in terms of food production per farming worker are low and land is scarce, supply of and demand for the two factors of production dictate whether land is expensive relative to labor. Moreover, because arable land is scarce trying to convert wasteland or woodland or the perimeters of lakes or steep mountains is costly, perhaps prohibitively so; the only way to increase arable in a cost effective manner is to augment existing farmland through more concerted use of fertilizers, planting more robust higher yield seed varieties, and more systematic irrigation. We can describe this situation by saying land is relatively dear and inelastically supplied while labor is relatively cheap and elastically supplied. Increasing agricultural output tends to drive up land rents. Augmenting land tends to counter land scarcity. In effect each acre of scarce arable is made more productive through the so-called Green Revolution package of better seeds, more water, and fertilization. Technological progress in agriculture reflective of real resource constraints commences with land augmentation, only later on shifting toward mechanization after the real cost of labor has risen substantially relative to the real cost of land.

The implication of our analysis for countries like Japan and China that commenced industrialization under conditions of "cheap surplus labor" in agriculture can be conveniently summarized in terms of two propositions: (1) to industrialize workers must be withdrawn from farming; (2) withdrawing labor without seriously cutting into farm output is most efficiently achieved by (2a) augmenting labor through improved health, formal education, and enhanced incentives and/or by (2b) augmenting land through expanded irrigation, employing better seed varieties, and by applying greater volumes of fertilizer and/or more potent fertilizers.

An important social problem endemic in surplus labor agricultural settings is landlordism. It is endemic not because most landlords own vast tracts of land — this was not the case in pre-World War II Japan or China — but because the ratio of wages to land rents was low. Acquiring land through hard work was a protracted arduous task.[3] Resentment against landlords is a common theme in both countries, landlords often accused of being parasitic, not working hard and living off the fruits of their compatriots. This was not always the case: for instance Waswo (1977) argues that during the 1870–1910 period Japan's rural landlord elites played an important role in securing infrastructure for their communities, promoting rice improvement associations and pushing the best seed varieties in Japan. In so far as they made positive contributions to their tenants and their communities they were tolerated and respected. However, absentee landlordism became increasingly common in Japan after 1910 and was a major problem in China before the 1950s. Even though many of these landlords were far from prosperous, they were often reviled because they were not toiling in the fields.

A key part of my argument concerning effort levels for farm workers involves incentives. One incentive facing farm households is the opportunity to dispatch one, perhaps several, household members to factory employment perhaps on a short-term contract say in a textile factory. If a farm household does so it has two options: reduce the total amount of farm output; or increase the work effort — through some combination of bolstering h and/or $e(h)$ — of at least some of the household members who remain on the farm.[4] In turn the opportunities to send household members into factories depend on the capacity of rural households to tap into nascent industrial employment.

A key part of the thesis of this book is that opportunities outside of the rural village depend heavily on the development of infrastructure coupled with the pace of industrialization. In this book the term "infrastructure" includes three types of infrastructure: physical infrastructure (e.g., roads, railroads, harbors, telephones, and telegraphs), human capital enhancing infrastructure (e.g., schools, hospitals, and public health clinics), and financial infrastructure (e.g., banks advancing loans to factories and postal offices offering postal savings opportunities).[5] In interwar Japan the density of this infrastructure was already well advanced; in China it was not. In Japan opportunities to diversify into nonfarm employment, perhaps on a short run contract offered by a textile mill, opened up for rural communities all over the country, especially in central Japan but even in far-flung communities in Northern Honshū and in southern Kyūshū as roads and railroads penetrated the hinterland. Factories sprang up because the density of banks increased mediating between growing numbers of savers and businesses seeking loans in order to invest in plant and equipment. But in China, as Skinner (1995) demonstrates, most marketing opportunities for the rural Chinese family were circumscribed within a fairly narrowly defined geographic compass.

To be sure the assertions made about the contrast between the pace of industrialization and the buildup of infrastructure in pre-1950 Japan and pre-1950 China only serve to raise another query: why did this divergence occur? The answer offered by this book is simple: elites.

Greed, the sex drive, and aggrandizing power rule human behavior. In pre-industrial agrarian economies with relatively average low standards of living only a small number of individuals can be movers and shakers in shaping cultural agendas, only a small number can exercise political influence, only a small number can secure sexual favors from a large number of potential partners, only a small number can amass great riches. These are elites. It is important to realize that elites in one dimension are not necessarily elites in the other dimensions. To be sure overlap occurs. Still in low income per capita settings there are many key figures in the cultural elite who are impoverished and some of the richest families may wield relatively little political power.

With the rise of income per capita there is a tendency of elites to surrender their influence over political power, the cultural agenda, and their capacity to secure sexual favors. This is a process that most elites do not welcome, do not embrace. Why should they? But they cannot overcome the force of competition. Indeed both competition and cooperation exist even in the low income agrarian setting. Individuals within specific elite groups compete with each other. They also cooperate with each other, partly for strategic reasons, partly because they may harbor altruistic feelings toward other members of the elite. The same applies to members of different elite groups, for example, military and political elites may cooperate in some arenas while bitterly contesting power in other arenas.

Industrialization, rising income per capita, and the spread of literacy does tend to dissipate elite influence. In countries that move along the path of democracy, political competition erodes the ability of elites to dominate the political arena though there are plenty of examples of attempts to resist this deterioration in status. As literacy spreads and income per capita increases, a middle class emerges, exercising its growing clout over the cultural agenda by flexing its demand in markets, by questioning values and doctrines held sacrosanct by elites in the agrarian past. Indeed, in the long run it is possible to argue that there is an "iron law" of political evolution, democracy ultimately spreading with industrialization. Whether this proposition is applicable to contemporary China, or to a future China, is a controversial point to which this book turns at the close of Chap. 10.

It is useful to summarize the crux of my argument concerning the role of elites within specific economic regimes with a stylized description. I discuss my schema in Chapt. 2 where I present matters in terms of discrete "stages." I concede that I present matters in this way out of convenience not conviction. Far from it for me to deny the importance of intermediate transitional phases between one regime and the next one (indeed revolutions and military conflict may be the hallmarks of these transitional phases, their bitter legacy lingering on for many decades). Rather I adopt the schematic approach because I am focusing on relatively stable regimes in which the nature of elites is relatively easy to characterize, transitions between regimes often being chaotic.

As well I am not making any claims that there is a universal set of stages that all societies move through as they industrialize. I do believe path dependence matters. Indeed it is crucial to my argument since societies can make the transition from one stage to the next more quickly and more smoothly provided the old elites are able to assume a prominent role in the formation of the new elites, transforming themselves.

A crucial part of my argument concerns the differences between the political/military and economic elites in China and Japan during the period following their initial "opening up" by the industrializing Western powers in the mid-19th century. A short summary of the key differences regarding elites during the period following "opening up" is provided in the following four points:

(1) In China there was a long transition — over seven decades — between the initial "opening up" and the collapse of the Qing dynasty; in Japan the political transition was very short, basically taking place in less than two decades. This can be explained in terms of the nature of the incentives facing political/military elites in the two countries.

(2) In China the vast bulk of the political elite consisted of the gentry who exercised power at the local level, lived in rural areas, often owned land, and were literate. Those gentry who excelled on the higher levels of the civil examinations might become rich by securing an appointment as an imperial official. But the bulk of the gentry were not especially wealthy. The examinations were standardized and a bureaucracy staffed by successful high level officials was a meritocracy. In Japan the bureaucracy/political elite mainly consisted of *samurai* warrior-bureaucrats, literate but — because their status in the pecking order of the fief bureaucracies was largely hereditary — generally constrained, denied the opportunity to advance status through ability and hard work. A typical *samurai* elite was poor and did not own land.

(3) In China the military and political elites tended to be separate. In Japan they tended to be identical.

(4) Because it took seven decades for the Qing dynasty to collapse a merchant elite emerged in China whose economic interests were strongly tied up with the Western imperialist powers and mainly operated in the treaty ports, especially in Shanghai. This did not happen in Japan.

Testimony to the efficiency of the civil examination system in China as an instrument of administrative control is the fact that the Qing dynasty fell only after it abolished the civil examination system, thereby denigrating the accumulated knowledge of vast numbers of the gentry who had devoted years to studying for the examinations. By contrast, a typical *samurai* was poor and did not anticipate climbing out of poverty through prodigious feats of study and hard work. Hence, having invested far less in the old regime, and expecting far less from it in terms of opportunity, there were many *samurai* fully prepared to topple Tokugawa rule. Moreover, because they were trained in military techniques they were perfectly equipped to organize a military campaign aimed at overthrowing the Tokugawa shogun. This they did soon after the Tokugawa regime signed the humiliating, unequal, treaties that set up a group of treaty ports in which Westerners enjoyed extraterritorial rights. An ambitious lower *samurai* did not have much to lose in the event of Tokugawa collapse and much to gain in a revamped political regime that did away with the *samurai* class itself.

Proof of the fact that the Tokugawa elites did not have much to fear in terms of lost opportunities can be gleaned from the following facts:

(1) According to Hirschmeier (1964: pp. 248–249) of the 50 leading entrepreneurs of the early Meiji period, 23 (46%) were former *samurai*, 12 were merchants (24%), and 13 (26%) were peasants.

(2) Two of the major financial cliques (*zaibatsu*) emerged out of merchant houses already powerful during the Tokugawa period (Sumitomo and Mitsui); the new Mitsubishi *zaibatsu* was the creation of a former *samurai*.

(3) Most of the paid-in capital for the new national banks consisted of bonds that had been issued to former *samurai* during the early Meiji period.

(4) Landlords were crucial in promoting rice improvement associations, Encouraging the diffusion of the best practice planting and irrigation techniques and the traditional seed varieties that generated the highest per hectare yields; as well they lobbied for the construction of roads and railroads leading in and out of their districts.

(5) The Meiji oligarchs were former *samurai*.

(6) Former *samurai* were active in the newly created Army and Navy.

(7) The political parties were largely peopled by wealthy farmers and headed up by former *samurai*.

(8) Many of the bureaucrats during the Meiji period were former *samurai*.

(9) *Samurai* were active in the "Dutch learning" phase at the close of Tokugawa Japan and many became ardent advocates for integrating Western values and knowledge with their Japanese cultural heritage.

(10) Former *samurai* were numerous in the ranks of students of higher education for instance at the University of Tokyo.

It is important to keep in mind that a key ideology that operated to create a "big tent" political consensus in Meiji Japan was *fukoku kyōhei* ("enrich the country, strengthen the military"). This was clearly particularly catered to secure the loyalty of potentially dangerous former *samurai* many of whom either went into the newly created Army and Navy where they could exploit their military skills, or into business, education or government where they could exploit their literacy and administrative skills. Coupled with the cult of the emperor the *fukoku kyōhei* agenda was central to the nationalism that emerged in Japan in the aftermath of the Western onslaught, a nationalism that forged a consensus — albeit contested — around nation-state building and incipient industrialization. By contrast a coherent consensus building nationalism failed to develop in China in the aftermath of the collapse of the Qing dynasty. Chapters 3 and 4 are devoted to making these points.

In the divergence of elite behavior of Japan and China lies the tragedy of Republican China. The fact that no major elite groups — outside of the relatively small warlord/military elite — emerged in late Qing China eager to revamp China, providing leadership for a post-dynastic regime, consigned China to ongoing internal conflict, exemplified by civil warfare between rival warlords, a relatively weak Republican Nationalist government and a nascent Chinese Communist movement, the latter two organizations both highly dependent on military leadership. This was the problem on the Chinese side of the equation. On the Japanese side the problem was military adventurism, fueled by the fact that the *fukoku kyōhei* ideology gave the Army and Navy a prominent role in political decision making. Indeed under the system of quasi-parliamentary government set up with the Meiji Constitution, the Army and Navy were not controlled by civilian politicians. Their leaders reported directly to the emperor with whom they made military decisions. An Imperial Army and Imperial Navy bent on pursuing their geopolitical interests in the East Asian theater — basically committed to making Japan the hegemonic power of Asia — became increasingly aggressive and adventuresome after securing a imperial base in Taiwan and Korea that they built on in taking over Manchuria in the early 1930s. With military cabinets in Japan desperately trying to control the Japanese army the stage was set for Japan's all out invasion in 1937 of Northern China and the Chinese coastline.

The legacy of the diverging behavior of elites in Tokugawa Japan and Qing China was full scale war in China. Pitted against the Japanese Army were the combined forces of Republican Nationalists and Chinese Communists fighting against a foreign aggressor under the umbrella of a fragile uneasy alliance of convenience that broke down as soon as Japan surrendered, concluding a Pacific War brought on by Japan's military onslaught in Asia. Chapters 5 and 6 focusing on the period between 1910 and the later 1930s deal with economic developments in the two countries. Chapter 7 focuses on military matters that increasingly dominated the period 1930–1955.

Out of the maelstrom of World War II and the Communist victory over the Nationalists in 1949 emerged a new China and a new Japan, both purged of many of the elites who had brought on the military tragedy of the 1930s and 1940s. In Japan the ranks of landlords and militarists were decimated and the *zaibatsu* dissolved during an American Occupation which was largely directed by liberal Japanese bureaucrats who escaped being purged by the Occupation authorities. In China Confucian officials, warlords, compradors and capitalists, and the landlord gentry were brought to heel in the aftermath of Communist victory. In both countries language reform was carried out, denigrating the acquired skills of cultural elites. In the place of these elites, new elites emerged in both countries. Chapter 8 deals with the issue of elites in decline.

There is little doubt that the new elites that emerged in the postwar Japan and postwar China had very different agendas. Their foreign policy agendas were radically different. China joined a vast Eurasian Communist bloc stretching from the Iron Curtain in Europe to the South China Sea. Japan became a key ally of the United States securing the protection of the nuclear umbrella. As an ally of the Soviet Union the Chinese leadership was committed to promoting heavy industry under the logic of command and control. In Japan a political leadership freed of the meddling of militarists who favored command and control, renewed its commitment to the market, albeit tempered by industrial policy exercised by the Ministry of International Trade and Industry.

Still there are important similarities. In both countries absorbing surplus labor was paramount in the structural transformation of their labor markets. In both countries foreign technology was tapped, the Chinese securing it largely from the Soviet Union (before Soviet advisors were withdrawn in 1960 signaling growing tension in the alliance between the two Communist giants) the Japanese securing it mainly from the United States and Western Europe. In both countries heavy industry was promoted. In the Japanese case a combination of industrial policy and the natural evolution of the economy drawing upon Japan's considerable pre-Pacific War achievements drove the rapid buildup of iron and steel, chemicals and machinery manufacturing. In the Chinese case the Soviet model provided a blueprint initially followed by central planners, subsequently jettisoned in favor of Maoist inspired utopian Communism. In both cases the dominant political party relied on a rural agricultural base for the perpetuation of its power: in Japan the Liberal Democratic Party depended heavily on voters in rural jurisdictions to retain power; in China the Communist Party elite tended to have peasant origins.

In Japan Miracle Growth between the mid-1950s and the early 1970s was heavily driven by total factor productivity growth especially in heavy industry, transport equipment, and machinery (especially electrical machinery). The sources of Japanese productivity growth are clear enough: (1) technological and organizational change; (2) scale economies, some geographic and external to firms, some internal to firms; and (3) structural shift in the labor force away from low productivity agriculture towards higher productivity manufacturing. Foreign technology import and adaptation, innovation, and the internalization of blue collar workers in large and medium sized firms were crucial. Urbanization played a major role in generating geographic scale economies.

Draining surplus labor out of rural districts was crucial during the 1950s and early 1960s. Profit rates in manufacturing were high because the wage bill did not rise rapidly in the wake of labor productivity growth. After the mid-1960s the refinement of the Spring Offensive collective bargaining system set wage increases throughout the Japanese economy in line with labor productivity growth for low productivity growth industries, the spill over shaping wages elsewhere in the manufacturing sector, feeding profit growth in industries and firms enjoying outstanding labor productivity growth. To be sure policy played a role. But the process of marshalling high rates of total factor productivity growth and capital accumulation was heavily market driven, competition between firms playing a crucial role in separating the wheat from the chaff. Miracle Growth and its aftermath are the subject of Chap. 9.

During the period when Japan's per capita income soared upward with Miracle Growth, the Chinese economy moved forward under command and control central planning that largely set the growth agenda for the period 1950 and 1978. Much attention is given to the impact of the reforms on China's growth that commenced in 1978, but it is important to appreciate that important advances were made under the command and control regime that freed up labor from the farm sector. These centered around raising h and $e(h)$ in the rural sector and promoting the augmentation of land largely through the expansion of domestic fertilizer production and the expansion of irrigation. Collectivization of agriculture begun in 1955 was crucial here. By rewarding workers on the basis of hours worked, workers were given incentives to increase h. Scale economies ushered in with the implementation of the commune and brigade system facilitated the marshalling of labor to build irrigation ditches, construct dams, and shore up the banks of rivers. The commune and brigade system brought public health and medical care into the countryside, a typical unit staffing midwives, doctors, and advisors knowledgeable about antibiotics and antiseptic techniques. This improved health bolstering $e(h)$. All of this contributed to the freeing up of workers from agricultural tasks.

To be sure that China experienced significant mortality decline during the 1960s was a double-edged sword. One result was rapid population growth that put considerable pressure on the agricultural sector hence the massive increase in conversion of land to irrigated land during the 1960s and 1970s. A combination of policy and market forces — the relatively high cost of space in urban centers, the formulation of the One Child system that gave strong incentives to reduce fertility — eventually slowed the surge in population growth.

It should be pointed out that the Great Leap Forward and the Cultural Revolution had a mixed impact on China's long run economic growth potential. Developing rural manufacturing — a priority during the Great Leap Forward — was a factor leading to the great famine during 1959–1962; at the same time it laid the basis for the development of town and village enterprises that have played an important role in China's post-1980 manufacturing growth. Again the Cultural Revolution is much criticized in the Western literature. True it spawned chaos that was ultimately suppressed by the People's Liberation Army. True it depressed returns to investment in urban education, as city cadres were dispatched to rural communes to both learn from and to educate the rural masses. True the Cultural Revolution was partly driven by an anti-Confucian agenda, a hatred of urban intellectuals. True it was the purest expression of militant Chinese nationalism now harnessed to the cult of Mao. But the Socialist Education Movement was part and parcel of the Cultural Revolution. At a purely practical level it dramatically improved rural education. In short the Cultural Revolution ultimately contributed to improvement in $e(h)$ in rural areas. In so far as it did so it contributed to the release of rural workers from agricultural pursuits, freeing them up to work either in rural or urban manufacturing. Since migration to cities was tightly controlled during the command and control period, much of this surplus labor was tapped by the rural manufacturing sector.

While this discussion of economic advance in China under the command and control system suggests that considerable progress was being made, it is clear that there were limits to growth under this regime. One major problem was total factor productivity growth in state owned enterprises (S.O.E.s) in manufacturing. This was a source of embarrassment to the Communist Party leadership. It was particularly galling because of the much better records achieved by Japan, by South Korea, and by Chinese populations in Hong Kong and Taiwan. While the Communist Party's propaganda machine worked hard to censor the foreign press it could not completely deny to a potentially restive Chinese population snippets of information about rising living standards in these neighboring nations. In order to justify and retain their elite political status the Communist Party leadership bowed to the inevitable and began launching reforms. Necessity was the mother of invention.

Because of the overriding importance of absorbing surplus labor it is not surprising that the reforms commenced with the de-collectivization of agriculture under a program that gradually phased in the household responsibility system in farming providing farmers with long term leases on land. Giving farmers market driven incentives bolstered $e(h)$. The next step was to tap foreign technological and managerial knowledge and practice, inviting in foreign investment, especially from more successful Asian neighbors — from Taiwan, Hong Kong, South Korea, and Japan — by developing Special Economic Zones. Doing this absorbed surplus labor; doing this exploited geographic scale economies, thereby giving a fillip to total factor productivity growth. Following these reforms, the Communist Party began countenancing domestic private enterprises, albeit many operating behind the facade of being a town and village enterprise. The command and control economy and its dismantling are the focus of Chap. 10 of this volume.

Taking a long-run view it is apparent that there are remarkable similarities between these two Asian giants. Both economies struggled with the problem of withdrawing surplus labor from the rural sector. In both cases collision with the Western powers ultimately endangered the activity of elites that had dominated economic and political affairs prior to being challenged by the West. In both countries virulent nationalism emerged, associated with the cult of the emperor in the case of Japan and with the cult of Mao in the case of China. Finally in both countries, new elites committed to absorbing foreign technology and applying it to domestic industry emerged. While this book does not fail to point out dramatic differences between Japanese and Chinese economic modernization the main thrust of this volume is that in the intertwining of elites and surplus labor is the making of a remarkable commonalities between these two great Asian powers.

Endnotes

1. I do not employ the term "surplus labor" in the sense employed by Arthur Lewis — see the classic Lewis (1954) article for a statement of his version of the surplus labor thesis — according to which the marginal product of labor is zero. Rather I mean by "surplus labor" the capacity to reduce the number of workers W in farming without reducing the level of agricultural output.

2. In both Japan and China during the period of early industrialization land that could be converted to arable purposes was scarce. Indeed this is a major reason why so-called "cheap surplus labor" existed in both economies prior to industrialization. Other things equal when labor is abundant relative to farm land food output generated per worker — in terms of calories, protein, and vitamins per day — tends to be low, the poor level of nutrition depleting the physical work capacity of the farm population and their capacity to fight off the ravages of infectious diseases. Moreover the absence of opportunity in the form of lands that ambitious youth can develop into fresh arable depresses the incentive to work hard. The opposite situation is a frontier setting, population densities being low and land readily available. When land that can be turned into productive agricultural fields is available in abundance land rents tend to be low relative to the earnings a worker can generate reflecting the relative supply and demand for each factor of production. In this case improving agricultural output is most efficiently achieved by mechanizing tasks thereby increasing the ability of each worker employed to plant and harvest over an increasingly large acreage.

3. An important difference between the Japanese and Chinese family systems plays a role in the acreage held by typical landlords: in China assets including land were commonly divided up amongst inheriting sons; in Japan farmland was typically passed to one inheriting child, usually but not always the eldest son.

4. This reasoning is based on the assumption that the farm household is managing its farm whether it consist of owned or tenanted land or some combination thereof. With a bit of modification it can also be applied to the communes set up in China after the mid-1950s that employed a work points system in determining the incomes of commune households, the idea being that the commune as a whole reallocates labor input from farming tasks to those manufacturing activities it carries on. The incentives for household members of communes are discussed in Chap. 10.

5. For an account of Japanese industrialization emphasizing infrastructure build-up as a driving force, see Mosk (2001). On the role of the public health, medical and compulsory educational sectors in promoting improvements in health see Mosk (1996). On the slow growth of physical infrastructure in pre-1949 China see Skinner (1995).

2

Elites and Traps

2.1. The Fundamental Transformation of Labor Surplus Economies

Behind great opportunities lurk great obstacles.

Consider surplus labor in pre-industrial economies existing in a world in which other countries have already industrialized. Exploiting the technologies and institutional innovations that were painstakingly arrived at by dint of trial and error experimentation, economic actors operating in a labor surplus environment can dip into the foreign reservoir of knowledge. In imitating they can leap into becoming domestic innovators at relatively low cost. Wedding this knowledge with domestically supplied cheap labor yields a second great advantage: the possibility of out-competing firms in the more advanced countries where wages — and living standards — are higher.

One of the great opportunities that economies following this path to industrialization can take advantage of is total factor productivity growth. Total factor productivity growth is a technical concept that can be explained in commonsense language. Suppose it is possible for economic actors — managers, entrepreneurs, and bureaucrats — to apply a mix of theoretical knowledge and practical experience to a production process, thereby extracting more output from a given combination of land, labor, and capital. This is total factor productivity growth. For instance doubling the yield of rice from two farm workers toiling on one hectare of paddy is an example of total factor productivity growth in agriculture. The growth rate at which this occurred depends on the number of years required to achieve the improvement in yield. The shorter the period the higher is the growth rate.

At the aggregate level of an economy there are three major sources for total factor productivity growth: technological and organizational progress within a particular field of endeavor; shifts in the use of the factors of production from a lower to a higher productivity field of endeavor (e.g., industrialization involves the shift of resources out of farming into manufacturing); and scale economies realized through the expansion of economic activity. Scale economies are either internal to production units like factories or organizations or external to them. Concentration of economic activity within the confines of a specific geographic region, for instance a city or neighborhood, is a good example of a scale economy external to a specific economic agent.

For the reader comfortable with a technical discussion of this concept, I provide details concerning total factor productivity growth in appendices: in the appendix to this chapter and in Appendix Table A.1 appearing in the Statistical Appendix to this book.

Total factor productivity growth is crucial to economic development because it is one of the major sources of growth in income per capita, hence the standard of living. This can be seen if we express income per person (y) in terms of output per worker (q), the average productivity of labor, that depends on the level of output (hence on total factor productivity growth) as follows:

$$y = Y/P = Q/P = (Q/W) * (W/P) = q * (W/P), \qquad (2.1)$$

where Y is the flow of income (equaling the flow of output Q), P is population, and W measures the total number of workers in the labor force (the use of national income accounting used to estimate income and output is discussed in the Statistical Appendix to the volume). In so far as economic development is calibrated in terms of raising income per capita it is clear that total factor productivity growth is crucial to economic development.

As important as total factor productivity growth is it is not the only source of growth in labor productivity and the standard of living. The other sources are augmentation: of labor; of land; and of capital. The importance of augmentation — for land and labor in the context of farming — has already been hinted at in Chapter 1. In this juncture it is useful to expand on this discussion using the idea of a production function. Consider a production function for agriculture:

$$Q_A = A f (L^*, K^*, LA^*), \tag{2.2}$$

where Q_A is total agricultural output, A is an index of total factor productivity, and L^* = augmented labor (service flow); K^* = augmented capital (service flow), and LA^* = augmented land (service flow). Since a key part of the argument in this book concerns how augmenting labor and land is crucial to releasing labor from farming it is useful to decompose both augmented labor and augmented land flows into their components.

Consider labor. The decomposition discussed in Chap. 1 yields:

$$L^* = h \, e(h) \; W = l^* \, W \tag{2.3}$$

where h is hours worked per worker, $e(h)$ is the efficiency with which a worker toils during each of those hours, l^* is per worker augmented labor input, and W is the number of workers. It should be noted that there are two ways — operating directly on labor only — to release labor from farming: raise h so that it requires less worker units W to generate a given number of hours of work in farming ($H = h \, W$ is the total number of hours worked); or increase $e(h)$, largely accomplished by improving the health or educational experience of each worker W, or by offering the worker more attractive incentives for working hard.

It is useful to work through a highly stylized but simple numerical example in order to see exactly what is going on in concrete terms. Let us consider a farm household that generates 480 units of output — a mixture of rice, potatoes, radishes, tea, and so forth — over a week's production period (a typical average weekly production period for the year). Imagine the household consists of four workers, each working 60 h a week, the average output per hour worked being 2 units. For instance each worker might toil 10 h a day, six days a week, resting on the seventh day. Now suppose the opportunity of working in a factory that is not too distant from the farm — given transport in the region — opens up. In principle sending one worker to the factory where he or she generates wages some of which are remitted to the farm household increases the total income that the household can garner.

The household can respond to this opportunity without loss of farm output if each worker increases his/her work hours from 60 h to 80 h a week in response to the reduction in the number of farm workers from four to three. For instance each worker might now work 13.3 h a day, six days a week; or work 11.4 h a day, seven days a week.

We can describe this process as the incentive effect reducing the incidence of surplus labor in rural areas. The incentive is the potential improvement in income farm family income generated by the remittances.

Now consider the labor quality effect stemming from improvements in education and health. Suppose the net impact of this form of augmentation is to increase output per work hour from 2 units of output to 3 units of output. To generate 480 units of farm output under these conditions only requires 160 h a week, not 240 h. At 80 h of work per week only two farm workers are required to generate 240 units of output. Another worker can depart the farm, securing employment in a factory, sending back remittances to his/her family of origin.

It should be noted that the reasoning here applies to all forms of farm organization: to rented land; owned land; to share cropped land; to collectivized land in a commune where work assignments are determined by a committee, say by a group of cadres in charge of a commune during the heyday of command and control in China (see Sec. 10.2 in Chap. 10). For instance in the Great Leap Forward in late 1950s China, the labor input of workers was reallocated from farming to the manufacture of iron and steel and chemical fertilizers. The key point is that the number of hours worked in total for the commune as a whole was reduced in farming at the expense of an increase in work hours in manufacturing. For farm output to not fall labor augmentation is required in the agricultural sector.

This is the basic logic of labor augmentation.

Now consider land. Land already in arable production is augmented — its inherent productivity per hectare enhanced — by irrigation, by the application of fertility, and through the introduction of more robust seed varieties like the Green Revolution Modern Varieties developed in the post-World War II period. In agrarian economies like those of Japan and China that had highly unfavorable ratios of population to arable land — hence surplus labor in the sense that worker units W could be withdrawn from farming without changing agricultural output — there is a natural progression to technological progress: the ratio of hourly wages to land rents (w/la_r) is low, hence technological progress tends to be directed in a market oriented economy toward enhancing the scarce, relatively expensive, inelastically supplied factor of production, namely land. The result is land augmenting technological change that makes heavy use of variable capital like fertilizer, land productivity increase being the main engine for growth in output per worker in farming. Only when the ratio of wages to land rents rises sufficiently do market forces promote the substitution of fixed capital — machines like power tillers, tractors, threshers, and harvesters — for labor, raising the productivity of labor but not necessarily the productivity of land.

Evidence on the Japanese and Chinese agricultural sector — the withdrawing of workers, labor augmentation (hours and days worked), labor and land productivity, and land augmentation — appear in the Statistical Appendix to this volume. At this juncture it is imperative that the reader study Appendix Tables A.7 and A.8, including the text describing the various panels in the tables.

That the augmentation of the factors of production, especially for labor and land in the case of agriculture, is important for economic development brings us back to the issue of opportunities and obstacles. Unlike securing total factor productivity growth through the importing and adapting of foreign technology and organizational innovations that in principle is relatively costless, augmentation requires costly investment by economic actors. In particular investment in infrastructure — schools for the educational sector; medical clinics and public health programs for enhancing health; banking and stock market institutions in the field of financial intermediation that links savers and investors; and physical infrastructure like harbors, roads, airports, and hydroelectric grids — is required. This is expensive. More importantly infrastructure investment of the sort described here tends to yield social benefits that may not be captured by private party investors. In this case private parties may not undertake the infrastructure investment since they cannot capture all of the rewards flowing from it. Hence infrastructure investment typically involves government intervention. In turn the nature of government intervention depends on both politics and policies.

In the economic realm there are six major avenues through which government intervenes in the economy. These are briefly described in Chart 2.1. Two involve economic stabilization also known as aggregate demand management: monetary and fiscal policy. One is a keystone of the welfare state namely transfer policy. These three are embraced by liberal democracies that mainly rely on the private market to allocate goods and services. In addition to these three approaches, regulation is also commonly

Chart 2.1: Government involvement in economic affairs: modes and examples.

Mode	Examples
Command and control	Military organizations relying on hierarchy and direct commands; central planning in which bureaucrats set production targets and quotas for farms and manufacturing firms
Stabilization — fiscal	Government spending for goods and services and for capital formation; setting taxation levels; collecting revenue from tariffs and user fees
Stabilization — monetary	Money supply management in which a central bank serves as a lender of last resort for other public or private banks; reliance on reserve ratios for, and/or the setting of discount rates offered to, member banks; open market operations involving the sale or purchase of bonds, and informal pressure; participation in the international economic order, for instance by adhering to the gold standard
Transfer	Welfare benefits and social insurance
Regulation	Setting standards for, and monitoring activities in, labor and capital markets; setting quotas on imports or quality standards for products consumed domestically
Facilitating/coordination	Mediation and arbitration; industrial policy (monitoring cartels, subsidizing selected sectors or firms); promulgating rules for the enforcement of patents and the diffusion of technology; working together with firms or local groups in developing infrastructure; assisting firms in negotiating technology licensing agreements

Source: Mosk (2008: p. 39).

utilized in the liberal democracies. Two other approaches are less commonly used in the liberal democracies except in select sectors like the military: command and control and facilitating/coordination approaches. Command and control was the main policy approach utilized by the Communist government of China during the period 1950–1978; facilitating/coordination policy was an approach pioneered by the Japanese government after 1870.

That governing is important for infrastructure investment and that it involves both politics and policies, brings up one of the chief obstacles to economic development: the fact that unhealthy politics and/or misguided policies may hinder augmentation, hence serve as a major impediment to economic development, consigning a national economy to a low income per capita trap. It is in this context that the nature of elites dominating politics, culture, and economic affairs becomes crucial.

2.2. Elites Competing and Cooperating

By elites I mean those individuals or families/households that exercise substantial influence in political, military, economic or cultural affairs. It is important to grasp that elites of a specific type are not a homogeneous social class. This is a myth. Competition sometimes brutal and unrelenting takes place within a particular elite group. For instance military warlords may fight one another or political contenders may devise complex strategies to overcome other contenders for influence. Competition also takes place between individuals that have secured elite status within different elite groups. For instance warlords and high level political officials may contend for power, engaging in elaborate Byzantine cutthroat politics in the halls of an imperial court. At the same time elites cooperate with one another, partly for strategic reasons, joining coalitions when they believe it serves their own individual interests, partly because they are motivated by altruistic sentiment.

With the fundamental shift out of agriculture into industry the nature of elites changes typically dramatically. The landed elite including landlords tend to lose influence. Politicians whose vested power base is rooted in the rural community tend to see their power dissipate. In so far as educational expansion accompanies industrialization — and in the long run it always does — the status of old cultural elites as the defenders and bastions of traditional wisdom and knowledge dissipates. At a more general level any major shift in the nature of economic activity within a country tends to shake up elites, eroding the influence of some while rewarding other individuals including those who were not elites in earlier economic regimes.

We can characterize the dynamics of elites in a country experiencing economic change by delineating four types of response to the change: resistance, disappearance, transformation, and creation. By resistance I mean the process by which elites whose vested interests are likely to be eroded through change attempt to prevent or slow down the process of change. Elites whose opportunity cost to losing status stemming from change — who have invested considerable resources of time and money in securing status within the pre-change regime — are likely to resist change, throwing up impediments when and where they can muster resources to do so. Other individuals who enjoy elite status prior to change may be resigned to losing that status, disappearing. A third type of elite may be able to successfully manage transformation becoming elite in the new regime. Finally change always throws up new elites from the ranks of those who were not elites before.

From these remarks I believe it is apparent that the transition from one economic regime to the next involves messiness in designating who are elites. Still, I feel it is useful to summarize the nature of key elites in Japan and China exercising influence during their economic development with a stylized description. My summary appears in Chart 2.2. I would like to stress that this schema is highly stylized. I present matters in terms of discrete "stages." I concede that I present matters in this way out of convenience not conviction. Far from it for me to deny the importance of intermediate transitional phases between one regime and the next one (indeed revolutions and military conflict may be the hallmarks of these transitional phases, their bitter legacy lingering on for many decades). Rather I adopt the schematic approach because I am focusing on relatively stable regimes in which the nature of elites is relatively easy to characterize, transitions between regimes often being chaotic.

As well I am not making any claims that there is a universal set of stages that all societies move through as they industrialize. I do believe path dependence matters. Indeed it is crucial to my argument since societies can make the transition from one stage and the next more quickly and more smoothly provided the old elites are able to assume a prominent role in the formation of the new elites, transforming themselves.

Given the differences between elites in Qing China and elites in Tokugawa Japan apparent from Chart 2.2 it is important to emphasize

Chart 2.2: Key elites in the industrialization of Japan and China, 1850–2000.

Elites	Comments
Tokugawa Japan, circa 1850	
Samurai, daimyō, and *shogunate* (military/bureaucratic/political/cultural elites)	Fundamentally hereditary not a meritocracy; competition between fiefs and between fiefs and shogunate; strong incentives to create and maintain infrastructure; lower *samurai* poor, thereby willing to jettison the system; relatively high taxation due to the costs of maintaining *samurai* and infrastructure; *samurai* as warrior-officials.
Merchant house owning families and managers (economic/cultural elite)	Internal labor market system of recruitment; merit important
Rural landlords and merchants	Local elite; limited political clout outside of immediate jurisdiction
Japan, 1870–1945	
Zaibatsu owners and their high level managers; other entrepreneurs establishing a national presence (economic elite)	Some former *samurai* join the ranks of this group; some former merchant houses of late Tokugawa also join these ranks (the *fukoku* faction of *fukoku kyōhei* "consensus agenda"); declining status during the 1930s as the militarists promote "command and control" policies, especially in the empire, promoting the *shinzaibatsu* (new industrial groups like Nissan)
Military commanders	Former *samurai* play an important role in promoting *military* agenda (the *kyōhei* faction of *fukoku kyōhei*); during the 1930s they become increasingly important in policy making

(Continued)

Chart 2.2: *(Continued)*

Elites	Comments
Meiji oligarchs and architects of party system	Competition between oligarchs an important factor in the promotion of party government; oligarchs become a declining elite as democracy spreads with the extension of the franchise during the 1920s
Landlords	Play an important role in the diffusion of higher yield seed varieties and the promotion of rural infrastructure improvements (irrigation, railroads); after 1910 increasingly disengaged from rural affairs, becoming "parasitic" absentee landlords during the 1920s and 1930s, therefore finding their interests and landlord status under attack by tenant unions
Imperial officials	Bureaucracy factionalized into conservative and liberal wings; responsive to political pressure from oligarchs, party leaders, and military commanders; cognizant of bureaucratic practices abroad, especially in Europe and North America
Japan, 1945–2000 Economic elite	*Keidanren* and *Nikkeiren* leadership; high level managers of *keiretsu* (corporate groups) and major owners/managers of highly successful companies like Toyota, Honda, Sony

(Continued)

Chart 2.2: *(Continued)*

Elites	Comments
Major politicians	Highly factionalized; during the period of so-called "Miracle Growth" (1955–1970) leaders of factions in the Liberal Democratic Party strongly entrenched in rural Japan; declining status of the Liberal Democratic Party in the post-"Miracle Growth" period, in part due to political scandals, in part due to a shift of voting power from rural to urban districts
High level ministry officials	Highly factionalized; declining status in the post-"Miracle Growth" era; responsive to political pressure from major politicians
Qing China, 1850–1911	
Imperial officials (political/cultural elite)	Few in number; selected on the basis of intense competition in examinations; meritocracy though ranks of imperial officials largely drawn from gentry; economic and cultural elite as well as political elite committed to Confucian style government; very high opportunity cost to jettisoning Confucian based rule; benefit relatives through sharing of resources and influence in lineages; of declining importance in the final years of the Qing dynasty with changes in the examination system; officials as scholar-officials

(Continued)

Chart 2.2: (*Continued*)

Elites	Comments
Gentry (political/cultural elite)	Relatively numerous, often but not always a local economic elite owning and renting land; expected to mobilize resources to suppress local rebellions and banditry and to build and maintain infrastructure; due to competition and free-riding amongst gentry, infrastructure maintenance an on-going problem in a low taxation environment; committed to Confucian rule because gentry members tended to participate in the examination "lottery" to gain imperial official status for at least one member of their lineage
Compradors and treaty port entrepreneurs (economic elite)	Employees of foreign owned enterprises active in the treaty ports; mainly located on China's coastline, especially in south and in the Yangzi delta region (e.g., Shanghai)
Military commanders, heads of banners, and warlords	Military officers defending the dynasty's interests mainly but not exclusively Manchu; warlords operated at the regional level
Manchu Court	Seat of imperial power; foreign dynasty exercising power primarily through imperial official bureaucracy and military garrisons

(*Continued*)

Chart 2.2: (*Continued*)

Elites	Comments
Republican China, 1911–1949	
Officials (cadres)	Operating with a combination of Confucian values and Western learning especially in science and engineering; factionalized
Landlords	Former gentry many still committed to Confucian values due to the importance of Confucian values for promoting local consensus and lineage practices; limited commitment to investing resources in financial institutions outside of their lineages
Warlords	Many committed to Confucianism; some aligned with Nationalist (Guomindang) politicians; some aligned with anti-landlord/anti-Confucian Communist Party, some aligned with the Japanese Army (in Manchuria after 1931, in Northern China after 1937)
Major entrepreneurs	Especially concentrated in (former) treaty ports, especially in Shanghai; typically allied with Nationalist politicians although reluctantly due to onerous *lijin* taxation imposed on them by the Nationalists

(*Continued*)

Chart 2.2: (*Continued*)

Elites	Comments
Communist China, 1949–2000	
Officials (local and national level state officials)	Distrusted to a degree throughout Maoist period (1949–1976) and subjected to extreme criticism during Cultural Revolution with its strong anti-Confucian/anti-urban intellectual ideology
Communist Party political leadership, "leading cadres" and rural cadres	New elite, factionalized along ideological and regional lines; after the late-1970s increasingly becoming both an economic and political elite; rural cadres instrumental in promoting the development of rural infrastructure, increasing hours worked, and attempting to enhance efficiency per hour worked in agriculture during the Maoist period (beginning with the attack on landlordism and the collectivization of agriculture during the 1950s)
Managers of state owned enterprises and commune/brigade (Town and Village) enterprises	Managers of state owned enterprises a declining elite after the late 1970s; mangers of town and village enterprises a rising elite after the late 1970s
Military leaders	Play an important role in determining the outcome of factional political struggles
Major private sector entrepreneurs	A new elite sparse in numbers, emergent in the 1980s and afterwards, encouraged to join the Communist Party in recent years

that these differences existed despite tremendous similarities between the two societies. Similarities include income per capita (see Panel B of Appendix Table A.2), the regionalization of military and political power, the existence of an emergent merchant elite that was subjected to taxation by governing authorities, the existence of craft or proto-industry, the stockpiling of grain, the suppression of peasant rebellions, the existence of Neo-Confucianism as an official ideology, the private ownership of land, and a monetized economy. To be sure differences existed: infrastructure was better developed in Tokugawa Japan than it was in Qing China. And the logic of demographic change was not precisely the same in the two societies, a stem family system based on transmission of assets to one favored child becoming strongly entrenched in Japan during the 18th century while equal division of assets among males was the norm in China.

The thrust of my remarks is that the most salient difference between the two agrarian economies lay in the nature of the elites, more specifically in the degree to which their vested interests were tied to maintaining the old regime. In Qing China the political elite, the bureaucracy was basically a meritocracy while the Japanese bureaucracy was not, heredity being crucial to *samurai* status during the Tokugawa era.

To appreciate the significance of the fact that the Chinese bureaucracy was a meritocracy while the Japanese bureaucracy was not it is important to understand how the Chinese civil examination system worked, what were the rewards associated with success in the examination tournament. Several points should be emphasized: there were many levels that had to be passed through to reach the apex of the system, the palace examination; the success rate at the higher levels of the examination ladder were extremely low; and successful performance on the examinations required arduous feats of memorization, hence for the typical aspirant years and years of study.

A detailed account of the system is given by Elman (2000). At the foot of the hierarchy of tests was the apprentice test, often given in lineage schools managed by lineages amongst the gentry. Above this level in ascending order were the (1) country/department/prefecture licensing examination (passed by most members of the Chinese gentry); (2) the triennial qualifying examination; (3) the triennial provincial examination; and (4) then the triennial metropolitan examination leading up the palace examination. Feats of study and memorization required to do well on the examinations was demanding to say the least. Elman (2000: pp. 261–262) comments on the initial set of examinations:

> "*The oral and written went together in the examination regime, enhancing both literacy and memory .... Classical learning was formed through ... (1) memorization of Chinese graphs; (2) reading the Four Books, one of the Five Classics ... and the Histories; (3) and composition.*"

As the student proceeded up through this examination ladder — dubbed by Miyazaki (1976), who has made quantitative estimates of the volume of memorization required, an "examination hell" — the study required, the opportunity cost in terms of time devoted to this endeavor that could not be devoted to alternative activities — rose and the success rate fell. Indeed some individuals were in their 80s when they sat for the metropolitan examinations!

Why devote such time resources to this endeavor? The answer is that the number of high level officials in the vast sprawling Chinese empire was minuscule hence the reward in terms of remuneration and power was great. Chang (1962: p. 7) comments on this fact:

> "*An official's position was also one of great power and prestige ... the official represented the absolute power of the emperor. This position offered also the greatest opportunity for the rapid accumulation of wealth. Of all the activities open to the gentry, the holding of office was ... almost the only way to amass a large fortune.*"

Drawing upon figures in Chang (1962: p. 42) it is possible to estimate the approximate average incomes of selected elites in late 19th century China as follows:

Position	Number	Average income (in Taels)
Key provincial and local officials	1701	36918
Court officials	2622	3110
Military officers	7464	1257
Educational officials	5043	1500
Other provincial and local officials	6000	4500

In short the rewards for exemplary performance in the examination hell were great. If they were not, it is hard to understand why some many individuals spent so much time preparing for the tests, generating simultaneously a low success rate and a very high opportunity cost to the gentry as a group.

Was a system that devoted such immense resources to study of the Confucian classics a waste of resources? Not necessarily. The examination system created a tiny elite bureaucracy devoted to imperial stability. It kept the gentry in line. It perpetuated Chinese culture and administrative continuity through a number of dynastic changes. It lasted for over five centuries both Ming and Qing rulers relying upon it. It can be argued that it was a remarkably efficient system for managing a vast empire with considerable ethnic and cultural diversity at least in the western reaches of the empire where Moslems and Tibetan Buddhists resided. Even though the stipends for the elite bureaucrats were high the overall cost for administrating the empire — the cost imposed on the coffers of the imperial center — were quite low as the local gentry was marshaled at the local level to assist in government and to squelch rebellion on the part of nonelite groups. As a result Qing China was a low taxation regime. By comparison Tokugawa Japan had considerably higher taxes since the *samurai* elite — over 5% of the Japanese population — was supported on rice taxes extracted from villages by fief governments.

While the difference between Qing meritocracy and Tokugawa heredity is the most crucial to my contrast between the political elites in the two countries, two additional differences are worthy of mention: the Chinese bureaucratic elite was almost exclusively drawn from the ranks of the rural gentry who usually owned land in the countryside while the *samurai* usually did not own land; and the *samurai* were both an military and political elite while the typical Qing official was primarily a political elite (there were prominent exceptions during the late Qing period that will be discussed in Chap. 3). But the chief difference lay in the fact that the Qing bureaucratic recruitment system relied upon highly competitive examinations rooted in the Confucian literary tradition, automatically rendering the Qing political elite a cultural as well as a bureaucratic elite.

2.3. Traps

One of the modern concomitants of industrialization is the harnessing of the inorganic economy, breaking away from organic — wind, water, fire, and human or animal generated — energy sources. In severing the relationship between energy and organic energy there is a fundamental break between the expansion of economic activity and land area. For instance no longer must water be diverted from its natural flow in rivers and streams or woodlands slashed down to generate mechanical energy. Organic economies are trapped in the sense that there is a limit to the average levels of income per capita that can be generated in organic economies and limits to the rate of population growth that can be generated in organic economies. Perusal of Appendix Table A.2 bears this point out. For instance estimates for circa 1500 A.D. suggest that no region of the world enjoyed income per capita exceeding $800 (measuring in international Geary–Khamis dollars). Moreover over the period 1500–1820 the highest population growth rates were achieved in the region with the highest per capita income — namely Western Europe — and even so population growth in that favored region was relatively desultory, especially in light of the much higher population growth rates achieved in the post-1820 era.

Harnessing the inorganic economy is associated with the systematic application of modern science and engineering — in physics, in chemistry, in biology, in genetics — to a broad range of economic and social phenomena. These include the use of mechanization of production in both manufacturing and agriculture; the harnessing of energy first with steam power, later on with hydroelectric power and the internal combustion engine; the elaboration of the germ theory of disease and its application to public health and medicine; and innovations in transportation and communications that have dramatically conquered the tyranny of distance.

Societies that remain mired at relatively low income per capita — as was true of Asia in 1870 according to the estimates in Panel B in Appendix Table A.2 — are said to be trapped in a low level equilibrium trap. The figures in Table A.2 suggest (1) that the world as a whole was trapped in a low level equilibrium trap prior to 1500; (2) that Western Europe (and the Western offshoots that were settled by colonists migrating from Western Europe after 1500) was the first region of the world to break out of this trap; (3) as a result a gap grew between Western Europe and the Western offshoots, combined regions enjoying sustained upward growth in per capita income, and the rest of the world including Asia, a gap that can be characterized as the great divergence; and (4) some regions of the world — notably Asia beginning with Japan in the late 19th/early 20th centuries — have dramatically closed the gap that was created by the great divergence.[1] Overcoming traps is crucial to the success or lack of success of societies in effectively harnessing the inorganic economy through the systematic application of modern science and engineering to economic and social concerns.

To summarize: the great divergence envisions a key turning point in global economic history. Prior to the harnessing of the inorganic economy

the possibility for appreciably increasing the standard of living above $2 a day —
say around $700 a year when calibrated in international United States dollars
a measurement concept discussed in the Statistical Appendix — was severely
constrained by the fact that economic activity was largely limited by land; and
by energy sources and productive activities secured from the land's surface.

In the classic Malthusian trap model population growth presses up
against the limits of land. As it does so agricultural production is forced out
onto relatively poor marginal land, reclaimed from forest, waste, marsh,
lakes, and ocean. The average standard of living falls. Reflecting diminished opportunities to secure land on which new families can eke out a subsistence living, marriages are postponed, fertility falls; and mortality rises
as food intake plummets. Population growth falls off until it is completely
extinguished. The standard of living remains mired at a culturally defined
subsistence level, culturally defined in the sense that marriage customs vary,
societies in which marriage is earlier and more universal ending up with
higher population densities and a lower subsistence level of income.[1]

An economy caught in the webs of a Malthusian trap is the mirror
image of a pre-industrial organic economy. With the great divergence some
regions of the world broke free from the Malthusian trap, population, and
the standard of living soaring in a sustained fashion. Ultimately — as is clear
from the a variety of figures on population growth, notably for Western
Europe, appearing in Panel A.2 of Appendix Table A.2 — growth in human
numbers falls off. This is due to the demographic transition, birth and
death rates plummeted with industrialization. Going through the demographic transition may not guarantee escaping from demographic traps
impeding economic growth but it certainly helps. That said, an incomplete
demographic transition — the death rate plummeting in the face of fertility
remaining stubbornly high — can generate a second demographic trap as
potentially corrosive as a full fledged Malthusian trap. If fertility does not
fall in the wake of mortality decline population tends to grow rapidly, especially the population of young persons, putting pressure on human capital
enhancing infrastructure, for instance on the school system and on clinics
and hospitals struggling with combating the ravages of infectious diseases
from which children often suffer.

The demographic transition is intimately tied up with the expansion
of education that accompanies the spread of the inorganic economy. Think
of getting additional schooling or on-the-job training as investment in skills
or in the capacity to quickly acquire fresh skills. Induced by a change in
the demand for labor — brought on by an expansion in the bewildering

proliferation in the range of technical, professional, skills required to carry on inorganic economy activity — the rewards attached to securing a higher education increases. This encourages parents with an altruistic interest in the welfare of their children and the resources to support the academic aspirations of their offspring to invest more and more familial resources in each child, cutting back on the number of offspring they bring into the world in order to garner the resources to do so. The shifting composition of the relative earnings in the labor market matters. So does mortality. As income per capita advances and public health and medical technology is brought to bear on warding off death, especially from infectious and parasitic disease, life expectancy rises. Hence the payoff period to investing in education — bought at the expense of postponing or reducing work activity in the short-run so training in skills that benefit the individual in the long-run can be squeezed in — increases. This also stimulates the demand for schooling.

In short tapping the benefits of the inorganic economy within a country or region has vanquished the Malthusian monster that entrapped the globe consigning humanity to a dismal existence, life being "short and brutish," over most of human history: (1) by raising the standard of living as a widening range of technological discoveries are harnessed, made economically feasible, advances that break asunder the long-standing connection between population increase and the expanse of land; and (2) by inducing a long-run decline in population growth, namely the demographic transition. But once one region of the world — Western Europe and its offshoots — has broken free from the low level Malthusian trap is the rest of the globe fated to do so? Not necessarily. Indeed the notion of a great divergence assumes that the spread of the inorganic economy and its bountiful harvest is limited. Why?

One possibility lies in the changing nature of the international marketplace brought on by a region of the globe industrializing. With industrialization the demand for foodstuffs and raw materials — copper, zinc, magnesium, coal, rubber, and petroleum — soars. One response is the expansion of demand is to specializing in producing these products, the so-called raw material periphery selling them to the industrializing center of the globe. This is one option available to the people in the periphery. Another option is emigration the poor seeking a better life in the higher income per capita industrialized center, the most ambitious and capable leaving a sinking ship as it were. In both of these cases embracing the inorganic economy may not occur in a periphery economy, or only in a desultory fashion, on the margins. Of course a third option may be even worse: ignoring the rest of the world — most unfortunately ignoring developments in the dynamic zone enthusiastically embracing the inorganic economy — altogether. Remaining closed off, in a state of autarky, denies to a country the potential rewards stemming from global trade in goods and global movement of peoples.

A fourth response to the newly fashioned global marketplace is to emulate the center, to industrialize by borrowing and adapting technologies and institutional practices pioneered in the center. A country or region doing so must begin the process by substituting domestic manufacturing products for those products that can be purchased from the already industrialized center, for instance by generating cotton textiles from its own factories rather than by importing these from mills located in the center or in other newly industrializing regions in the periphery. This is called import substitution. Once a country achieved a foothold on the ladder of industrialization, its nascent manufacturing sector can either push its output onto international markets or it can advance up the ladder of industrial sophistication through further import substitution.

For many periphery countries — including Japan and China — the options of specializing in raw materials and/or exporting people, or remaining forever in a state of autarky have been cut off: most notably by resource constraints and global geopolitics, including military exigencies.[2] In practical terms industrialization initiated through import substitution has been the only viable, or at least has been the most attractive, response. In the case of Japan and China this has involved tapping a great potential opportunity: surplus labor. But doing so means overcoming traps, not just Malthusian traps.

Negative feedback is crucial to traps.

In the classic Malthusian trap case the negative feedback arises from diminishing returns experienced on a fixed amount of land in an agricultural setting. As population presses up against the fixed land resource (in the absence of land augmenting technological change), per capita farming output falls. Key is that fact that land area is fixed and technological change is nonexistent or muted at best. The fall in average standard of living depresses fertility and enhances mortality choking off further population increase. We can say that given an unchanging technological regime the carrying capacity of any region of the earth is fixed. When population pushes up past this carrying capacity, a demographic crisis ensues, marriages postponed, infanticide resorted to by starving households, the Grim

Reaper stalking through the land. Human numbers are depleted. Negative feedback reigns.

Other types of traps involve obstacles, most notably obstacles thrown up along the path of industrialization. These traps are either political/military traps (conflict traps), cultural or economic. An economic trap is called a poverty trap. Here is how Sachs (2005: p. 560) describes a poverty trap:

> "... *poverty itself can be a trap. When poverty is very extreme, the poor do not have the ability ... to get out of the mess ... poor rural villages lack trucks, paved roads, power generators, irrigation channels ... hungry, disease-ridden, and illiterate villagers struggling for survival.*"

In discussing Africa's development problems, Collier (2007) focuses on political/military traps. Salient among these is the conflict trap due to civil wars. Civil wars are born out of desperate economic circumstances that in turn serve as roadblocks to economic betterment. For example consider the following passage from Collier (2007: pp. 32–33):

> "*Now we reach the aspect of civil war that is crucial for the thesis of this book. It is trap ... once a war has begun, the economic damage undoes the growth achieved during peace. Worse ... the risk of further war explodes upward.*"

In this trap bad politics join bad economics becoming bedfellows in a down spiraling conflict trap.

Easterly (2001: pp. 166–167) discusses traps in terms of increasing returns, incentives and expectations being bottled up, their capacity to spread through leaks and matches being limited by geography, cultural isolation, nationalism:

> "*I have talked about poverty traps at different levels of aggregation: the neighborhood, the ethnic group, the province, the nation ... poor people face weak incentives to upgrade their skills and knowledge because their leaks and matches come from other poor people.*"

In short, escaping from a trap is difficult due to inertia brought on by ignorance being matched to ignorance, desperation and hopelessness being matched to desperation and hopelessness, conflict being matched to more conflict, and a self-generating, self-defeating spiral circling downward on itself.[3]

The central theme of this book is that properly motivated elites can lift a nation out of traps. By the same token poorly motivated elites can leave a nation mired in traps. In settled agrarian societies posed to industrialize the character, the vested interests, of elites becomes crucial to the capacity of the society to break out of the traps inducing negative feedback.[4]

2.4. The Erosion of Elite Status

Elites tend to resist change because it endangers their vested interests. This is why the capacity — and the incentives — to transform themselves into new elites is so important in breaking out of traps impeding industrialization.

In cases where elite behavior steadfastly impedes breaking out of traps there are a two possible outcomes: (1) the elites successfully cling to their status, jeopardizing the breaking out of the trap their society contends with; or (2) the elites are unsuccessful in preserving their status, their status washing away as new elites surge to power, perhaps through civil war or violence. In the second case erosion of elite status is an important and often discontinuous concomitant of change in economic structure.

Erosion of elite status also accompanies economic development in a continuous fashion. In countries experiencing sustained economic development over the long-run elites usually find their status eroded. In discussing this it is useful to distinguish societies that have become fully functioning democracies (e.g., Japan) from societies that are governed by a single political party eschewing political competition that is ultimately settled through the voting at the ballot box (China). Whether an "iron law" holds whereby all societies enjoying long-run economic development — substantial increase in income per capita, the spread of literacy and growth in the proportion of population that have completed high school and/or have attained more advanced education certification, and the emergence of a middle class able and willing to expend resources on acquiring the trappings of culture — automatically become democracies is a matter of considerable controversy.

At this juncture I will restrict my comments to discussing the erosion of status among cultural elites as a general feature of economic development and the erosion of political elite status in countries like Japan that have nurtured their commitment to democracy over decades as their economic development progressed. The mirror image of this process of erosion of elite status is the growing muscle of the middle class.

The middle class gains muscle for two main reasons: the income elasticity of demand expressed in markets; and the demand for voice in political and cultural affairs that accompanies educational attainment.

When a population's income per capita is low — say under $2 a day in international dollars — most of its households spend the bulk of their income on food, clothing, and housing, the basic necessities of life. In this setting only a small elite have incomes sufficiently generous so that they enjoy a substantial margin of purchasing power over goods and services far in excess of that required to satisfy the basic needs of life. The demand for cultural expression exercised in markets largely reflects the tastes of this elite group of consumers. The resulting culture is the "high" art preserved in museums in the form of tapestries or paintings or scrolls. In music it consists of pieces performed by performers trained to interpret and reconstruct scores handed down from the distant past. In architecture it consists of the imposing buildings commissioned by rulers and aristocracies or other members of the cultural elite designed as much to inspire awe as to meet the needs of shelter. Absent destruction in warfare or decay due to disuse this high art is preserved. By contrast popular art tends to disappear, only being preserved when the costs of preservation (due largely to technological progress) make its survival from one generation to the next economically feasible.

As per capita income rises a new tier of society is created that can afford luxuries including culture. The standard argument is that the income elasticity of demand — the percentage rise in demand associated with a 1% increase in real income — is above unity for luxuries but not for basic necessities essential for survival (for which the income elasticity of demand is positive but low for instance hovering in the range 0.2–0.4). As a growing percentage of a population finds itself able to purchase luxuries the market demand for these luxuries widens, no longer restricted to satisfy the tastes of a small cultural elite. Freed from restricting their expenditures to basic needs, an emergent middle class exercises growing clout in the cultural sphere, demanding the services of suppliers of culture — writers, painters, sculptors, architects, and movie directors — through the market. Popular art gains force, displacing high art. Possessing and consuming art no longer necessarily conveys elite cachet. The status of the cultural elite erodes.

As well the spread of higher education contributes to the displacing of elite tastes in the cultural realm. Other things equal — for instance holding per capita income constant — individuals who have acquired additional years of schooling are more efficient in seeking out cultural opportunities, partly because they receive greater exposure to the culture of past and present in the course of their studies, partly because they have more leisure time on their hands.

My arguments concerning the transformation of culture are sum-marized in Chart 2.3. It is worth emphasizing that Chart 2.3 focuses on economic forces eschewing political considerations. Politics — especially nationalism — do play an important role in shaping the transformation of culture and the influence of cultural elites clinging to traditional clas-sical values. A classic example of this is the Great Proletarian Cultural Revolution that exploded in China during the 1960s, its impact spilling over into the following decade. While factional fighting amongst leading cadres played set the agenda for many aspects of the Cultural Revolution, one of its agendas was the denigration of Confucianism, a wholesale rejec-tion of Confucian values as the basis for Chinese nationalism. Similar ten-dencies were at work in Meiji Japan. Rejecting may of the vestiges of the Tokugawa past — destroying castles, turning Buddhist temples into Shinto shrines, promoting Western architecture — was part and parcel of a nation-alist agenda in which culture was consciously, systematically, politicized.

In democracies enjoying political competition the emergence of a middle class not only threatens the status of cultural elites. Political elites — bureaucrats, elected officials — are also put on notice. As higher education spreads so does critical thinking. Responding to an informed public demand for news about the scandals and cover-ups in high places, the media — newspapers, magazines, television programs, and websites — investigates and reports on corruption amongst the rich and powerful. Instead of being venerated, political actors wielding power often find themselves the object of ridicule.

In sum, in democratic societies that successfully develop economically, elite status is eroded across the board. An excellent example is modern Japan. But in societies like Communist China where democratic institutions have failed to take root, cultural elites find their status eroded but political elites cling to exalted positions, corruption remaining endemic and socially corrosive.

2.5. Co-evolution

One of the major themes of this work is the interaction of evolution in the economy, political institutions, and cultural life of societies. This is an example of co-evolution, transformation in one arena impacting the other arenas.

Co-evolution can be a controversial topic. In sociobiology models evolution of genes interacts with evolution of cultural memes.[5] Scholars

Chart 2.3: The growing importance of popular culture and the merging of folk art with high art.

Variables	Influence of variables on composition of culture
Prior to transition away from elite dominated agrarian economy	
Wealth and resources amassed by elites	Most artistic productions (e.g., literature, music, architecture, painting, sculpture, scrolls) created to glorify the elite and to display their command over resources through conspicuous consumption
After the successful transition to industrialization	
Technological change	Reduction in cost of producing and conserving artistic productions (e.g., in music evolution in preservation of musical performances from player pianos to phonograph using vinyl disks to tape recording to compact disks)
The income elasticity of demand	Mass marketing: the growing participation of middle class first, then masses of lower socioeconomic status consumers in shaping the demand for art in the market promoting scale economies in distribution of art (e.g., serialized novels in magazines)
Spread of literacy	Growth in sophistication of mass audiences as expressed in the demand for artistic productions in markets
The artist as sponge	Folk artists working from a tradition handed down from previous generations absorb the techniques of artists that once produced art aimed at elites. Artists oriented towards producing for elites appropriate the techniques and themes of folk artists
Interference by political elites	Folk art often provides critical commentary on the influence of elites in social and political matters. Depending on the ability of the political elite to control and censor the artistic environment — and shape it, for instance through the creating of propaganda — folk art may or may not evolve into a legitimate expression of mass culture

reasoning along these lines have wedded the study of genetics to the analysis of the chemistry of the human brain, bringing to bear co-evolutionary processes on a diverse group of social behaviors including the development of spoken languages, brother–sister incest taboos, preferences for various sexual positions, conflicts over territory, even codes of ethical conduct.

This book does not make claims about sociobiology co-evolution. Rather it makes more modest assertions, advancing an argument about economic development in modern societies in which self-interested elite behavior exercised in the cultural, political, and economic realms drives co-evolution in the cultural, political, and economic realms. It is the goal of the remainder of this volume to use this framework in analyzing the industrialization of two economies for which absorbing surplus labor from rural communities has been both opportunity and obstacle to long-run economic development. It is this author's fervent hope that a recounting of principal quantitative and qualitative aspects of the modern economic development of Japan and China will put flesh on the theoretical bones put forward in this chapter. As with the interaction of kitchen and dining table, the proof of the cook's skills is in the eating.

2.6. Appendix: The Fundamental Growth Equation

In the first table appearing in the Statistical Appendix to this volume, Table A.1, appears a basic growth accounting formula widely utilized by economists. Using a multiplicative formula in which output is the product of an index of total factor productivity A and the three factors of production (each augmented and each raising to a power that is their share of output), one can derive a growth decomposition formula, namely:

$$G(Q) = G(A) + \alpha\, G(K^*) + \beta\, G(L^*) + [1 - (\alpha + \beta)]\, G(LA^*), \quad (2.4)$$

where the share of capital in income, $\alpha = (i_K K^*)/Q$ (the product of the rate of return on a unit of capital multiplied by the flow of services generated by augmented capital), and $\beta = (w L^*)/Q$ (the share of augmented labor in output) and $1 - (\alpha + \beta) =$ the share of augmented land in total output which equals $(la_r LA^*)/Q$, the flow of land rents times augmented land area used in cultivation divided by output. The point of this equation is to decompose growth into growth of the three factors of production duly augmented and an index of total factor productivity which captures improvements in knowledge, scale economies, and structural change.

In addition to a provided theoretical framework for analyzing, growth equations like that appearing in Eq. (2.4) serve as the basis for estimates of growth in labor productivity (output per worker), in land productivity, and in total factor productivity. Estimates of growth in labor productivity appear in Appendix Tables A.3 and A.8. Estimates of land productivity appear in Appendix Table A.8. Estimates of total factor productivity appear in Appendix Tables A.8 and A.10. The reader should study these tables at this juncture, reading through the appendix for a discussion of the various panels in the tables assembled there.

Endnotes

1. On the great divergence see *inter alia* Clark (2007), Pomeranz (2000), and Pritchett (1997).

2. Geopolitical constraints — for instance military threats that act as spurs to industrialization — are discussed at many points in the remainder of this book. Since neither Japan nor China enjoys a bountiful endowment of natural resources — at least as calibrated on a per capita basis — exporting natural resources has not been an attractive long-run development strategy. In addition there are a host of problems associated with relying on exporting of natural resources like minerals (e.g., diamonds, and zinc). It tends to engender civil conflict caused by fighting over which groups or regions within a country benefit from the export trade. This political fallout goes by the rubric "resource curse." As well it leaves a country vulnerable to swings in the terms of trade — the average price of exports divided by the average price of imports — that appear to be particularly wild and volatile in the case of natural resources. Regarding constraints on emigration from Japan and China imposed by the Western offshoots see Lewis (1978) and Mosk (2005).

3. For the importance of culture as an impediment to economic growth see Landes (1998).

4. In this book I do not consider hunting and gathering societies. Rather I focus on economies in which settled agriculture centered around the cultivation of crops — wheat, barley, rye, rice, and sorghum — and the breeding and tending of domesticated animals — like cattle, pigs, chickens, goats, and sheep — is well advanced, hunting and gathering being marginalized. For a discussion of the transition from hunting and gathering to settled agriculture see Diamond (1999).

5. See for instance Blackmore (2001), Dawkins (2006), Lumsden and Wilson (1983), Pinker (2007), Richerson and Boyd (2005), and Wilson (1999). In many ways the thesis developed by Clark (2007) about importance of elite reproductive behavior in England — the economic elite transmitting their cultural behaviors (e.g., the propensity to save and invest abstaining from current consumption for future rewards, industriousness) to their offspring genetically — is a variant of sociobiological reasoning.

Part II

Coping with the Western Challenge, 1840–1911

3

Qing China, 1840–1911

3.1. Elites in Qing China

Mirrors are important.

A commonplace of economic history is comparing the fates of China and Europe. The mirror of China is used to capture Europe's benighted performance during the Middle Ages when Roman infrastructure — roads, aqueducts, and grand cities — was allowed to atrophy and fall into disuse, when much of the classical technical literature developed by the Greeks and Romans was forgotten or only referred to as the apex of knowledge treated dogmatically, reverently, in a completely uncreative and uncritical manner. Then the images in the mirror reverse position. Europe's dynamic performance following the industrial revolution is used to delineate China's shortcomings during the 19th and 20th centuries. This chapter focuses on the later period, the 19th and 20th centuries, when an assertive West, fueled by advances in industry, science, and engineering, confronted a once proud China that it now humiliated through military and commercial prowess won through intellectual advances in science and engineering.

As the work of Needham on Chinese technology tells us, a host of inventions appeared in China first, spreading to Europe only after a long lag. Square-pallet chain-pumps, rotary winnowing machines, draw-looms, wheelbarrows, cross-bows, deep borehole drilling, iron casting, the canal pound-lock, all fit comfortably on a list headlined by the illustrious triumvirate of gunpowder, the magnetic compass, and printing employing moveable type.[1] But by the early 14th century all of this began to change, the pace of Chinese innovation and invention drying up, Europe springing ahead in navigation, agricultural improvements, mining, printing books for large markets, metal working, mechanical watches, and clocks.

More important, these inventions went hand in hand with the proliferation of cultural elites — scientists, engineers, political philosophers that ultimately paved the way for key ideals in classical liberalism including the principle of the "invisible hand" in markets wedded to a theory of social contrast based on natural rights — during the Renaissance in Italy. Emboldened by their successes this disparate elite, spreading throughout Europe, went on to foster the scientific revolution of the 17th century and the industrial enlightenment of the 18th century.[2] Practical tinkering, inventing in laboratories, and shops was increasingly linked to, informed by, theoretical ideas elaborated by physicists, chemists, and biologists, the language of mathematics playing an increasingly important role in advancing hypotheses that explained experimental results or that suggested experiments to be performed.

The new cultural elites increasingly came into conflict with older elites — in churches, in monasteries — clinging to a worldview formulated and refined during the Middle Ages. Out of the crucible of intellectual conflict between the views of those in the clergy who aspired to understand the workings of the universe through the lens of Aristotle's principles of natural philosophy and persons like Galileo who espoused experimentation was born a dynamic evolution, testable hypotheses formulated, perhaps discarded continually subjected to critical deconstruction that has moved modern science through successive waves of paradigm shift, a thesis pioneered by Kuhn (1962). For example, Newtonian physics gave way to Einstein's formulation of the theory of relatively and unified field theory in the world of the large objects, in astrophysics, while quantum mechanics — rejected by Einstein on philosophical grounds — became essential to unlocking the secrets of subatomic particles. Creative destruction increasingly took hold in the cultural world. The tearing down of intellectual paradigms espoused by old intellectual elites by those advancing freshly formulated theories became integral to a cultural dynamic that we think of as quintessentially modern.

It is against this mirror that we need to explore the world of Qing cultural and political elites. If rejecting orthodoxy was increasing becoming a cornerstone of Western culture, clinging to intellectual orthodoxy was increasingly becoming the cultural and political cement holding together the sprawling Qing Empire, populated by a diverse group of ethnic groups — the Han Chinese majority, Uyghurs, Mongols, Tibetans, Yao, Miao — ruled over by a non-Han foreign Manchu Imperial court that successfully invaded and conquered China during the mid-17th century.[3]

The administrative system inherited by the Qing was remarkable for its parsimony, a huge population and a massive land area governed by a relatively miniscule civilian bureaucracy backed up military garrisons. As a result the administrative system was highly efficient in the sense that the rate of taxation required by the central authorities in Beijing to pay its officialdom was remarkably modest.[4] For instance in 1469 it is estimated that China had about 1000,000 civil officials and 80,000 military personnel governing a population of around 100 million, a ratio of around one official per 1,000 persons.[5] A cause or consequence of this parsimony was a lack of depth in administration, the lowest level officials governing ether *chou* (department) or *hsien* (district), both being relatively populous. The *chou* and *hsein* were organized into prefectures or independent sub-prefectures or independent departments governed by higher level bureaucrats, who in turn took orders from provincial administrators. Ultimately through this chain of command, policy radiated out from the central court to the lowest levels of the government.

Prior to 1850 the military authority was maintained through the Eight Banners — originally Manchu in origin, the banners increasingly staffed by Han Chinese — that were garrisoned around the country.[6] The Eight Banners managed to suppress regional rebellions like the White Lotus Rebellion that gathered force in the mountains where the provinces of Hubei, Sichuan, and Shinxi meet during the late 18th century and the Triad (Heaven and Earth Society) inspired uprising of Lin Shuangwen with its pro-Ming/anti-Qing message.

Given the fact that a select few, a small civil and military elite, ruled over a vast heavily populated territory the question that naturally arises is how? The answer is through power sharing, the official civilian or military working hand and glove with local elites. These elites consisted of the gentry (consisting mainly of civil examination degree holders by the early 19th century) on the civil side and the *pao-chia* on the military side, the latter being 10 households organized into groups of 10 that were further organized into groups of 10 known as *pao* for the purpose of policing and maintaining law and order in communities including defense against banditry. With an eye to implementing a "divide and rule" strategy, the center tended to select commoners as heads of a *pao-chia*, not members of the gentry (though gentry were members of *pao-chia*) checking headstrong gentry abuse of power and influence at the local level. By astutely delegating authority over the day to day management of village and town affairs including policing functions to competing elites, the center managed to rule a vast empire with limited fiscal resources.

Key to making certain the gentry elite remained loyal and committed to rule by the center was the examination system used to select officials and military personnel. First utilized by the only female emperor in Chinese history, Wu Zetain (690–705) to choose officials, the examination system became the political centerpiece of dynastic rule after dynastic rule.[7] And key to the examinations was Neo-Confucian orthodoxy, the memorization and discussion of classical texts in elegant essay writing.

The founder of the Confucian tradition Kong Fuzi — also written K'ung fu-tzu — tried to secure political power in order to establish his own dynasty during the period 551–479 B.C. Although he left no texts written by his own hand, he had disciples like Mencius and Xun Zi who hammered out a philosophy of sorts that had far-reaching ethical and political implications in the form of written documents. The basic principles of classical Confucianism were: (1) internalization of ethical behavior through the pursuit of rituals governing daily life; (2) government of one's self through seeking virtue; (3) rulers selected on the basis of virtue, not heredity; (4) gift exchange namely the practice of mutually beneficial exchange of services and obligations between superiors and inferiors, superiors being benevolent, is crucial to maintaining harmony; (5) five hierarchical bonds — ruler to minister, father to son, husband to wife, elder brother to younger brother, and friend to friend — should be carefully cultivated at the level of family and state; (6) the "mandate of heaven" governs the fate of dynasties, a dynasty's right to govern arising from its commitment to virtue; (7) ethics should be governed by a kind of golden rule, individuals being admonished to treat others as they would treat themselves; (8) the rectification of names, language being carefully utilized to yield transparent meanings reflecting actual conditions; and (9) the cultivation of the life of the gentleman.

Part religion, part philosophy, part moral code designed to regulate behavior in the interests of making sure people get along with one another, social interactions generating a modicum of friction, classical Confucianism merged with other doctrines and religions introduced into or developed in China — Taoism, Buddhism, naturalism, and practical statecraft — to become a kind of holistic all-embracing creed that was treated as the essence of Chinese culture for centuries. This was the Neo-Confucian doctrine that lay at the heart of the examination system.

The examination system was complex, bristling with stages and parallel routes to success, basically boiling down to a three stage process yielding first degrees, second degrees, and third degrees, the highest degree being prerequisite for appointment to a high level official post. Those successful on the youth examination — involving memorizing over 400,000 characters in order in the *Analects, Mencius, Book of Changes, Book of Documents, Book of Poetry, Book of Rites,* and *Tso Chuan* — received a licentiate student certificate, securing *sheng yuan* status that carried prestige but harbored no realistic possibility of securing employment as an official. This allowed them to proceed to the next stage of the examination tournament, becoming either tribute students or imperial scholarship students competing in the provincial level examinations, the successful becoming *juren* or provincial degree holders that qualified them for appointment as officials. Finally *juren* could pursue the tournament competition even further, taking the metropolitan examinations — the successful becoming *gongshi* tribute scholars — looking to compete in the highest stage the palace examination that awarded the coveted *jinshi* degree.[8]

The sheer economic burden of managing the examinations was immense, a real drain on central government resources. In order to control the number of students taking the examinations and to maintain the basic fairness of the process, Qing officials placed yearly quotas on the number of examinees allowed each district or county, department, prefecture, and province. For instance according to Elman (2000: p. 236) by 1850 there were over half a million civil licentiates and over 200,000 military *sheng yuan* whose demand for higher level examinations and needs local officials needed to deal with. Keeping the tournament going was an expensive proposition pressing up against the capacity of officials to write and monitor examinations.

Competition in this tournament was brutal. Population growth — growth in the number of the gentry — in excess of growth in the number of official positions sought after only made it increasingly brutal during the course of the 17th and 18th centuries. Discussing the cohort of examination takers born in 1761, Man-Cheong (2004: p. 38 ff) estimates that the cohort devoted three decades to taking examinations in which the chance of successfully securing a provincial level (second) degree was 1 in 50 (or even worse perhaps as low as 1 in 80) yielding only a 1 in 10 chance of actually obtaining an official appointment. In short the combined probability of getting an appointment after 30 years of brutal examination competition lay somewhere between 0.2% and 0.13%. And these probabilities only deteriorated as population and the ranks of the gentry increased during the period 1770–1850.

Feeding students in the civil examination was the role of official and lineage schools. Securing admission to these institutions required competitive achievement on entrance and qualifying examinations. In such a world studying for examinations was a way of life in such a world.

Despite the stated ideology of Neo-Confucianism that emphasized meritocracy over heredity, the fact is that there was scant mobility in Qing China: almost all of those taking examinations were either gentry or sons of military officials (and by 1800 being successful at least at the first degree level was crucial to joining the ranks of the gentry). This is one major source of inconsistency between the stated philosophy of Confucianism and the reality of how it was applied in the real world of officialdom, one reason why many Chinese found hypocrisy in the way Confucian doctrine played out in the real world.

A second major source of inconsistency was corruption, the negation of virtue that was supposed to govern the behavior of officials entrusted with governing and setting an example for the great mass of people. Consider officials at the lowest level of the system: district and department magistrates. Under an department (*chou*) magistrate labored assistant magistrates, tax collectors, jail wardens, granary supervisors (the dynasties stored up rice in granaries for the purpose of staving off famine and stabilizing rice prices), fish tax collectors, sluice keepers, and other miscellaneous officials. Clerks operating under the magistrate could and did manipulate the scales used to weigh the silver used to pay taxes; clerks could and did duplicate the number of stamps used to access land taxes; the ability of clerks to delay the receiving of tribute grain was costly to the bearer of the grain required to meet a stipulated quota opening up further avenues for extraction of economic rents by officialdom. And so forth. The opportunity to extract bribes was great. Once more and more officials participated in taking bribes, the proportion of honest virtuous officials dwindled, thereby reducing the probability of getting caught and prosecuted for corruption.[9]

Reasoning along these lines Ni and Van (2006: p. 330) estimate the following ratio of potential corrupt income — rent seeking income in the language of economists — to actual salary income for officials as a group.[10]

Their estimates — albeit based upon a variety of assumptions that could be questioned on empirical grounds — suggest the following ranges for potential corrupt income to actual salaried income (note that the figures are actually ratios not percentages):

Year	Range (ratio)
1400	3.4–7.3
1600	33.6–83.1
1650	14.3–33.7
1750	8.7–17.6
1770	10.1–19.8
1850	15.0–26.9
1873	14.0–21.9

The ratios are high. For this reason Confucian official income was substantial, a great benefit to the official himself and to his family and lineage members. For this reason the opportunity cost of being an official in the Ming and Qing dynasties was great explaining why competition in the examination system was brutal. As well it explains why officials who espoused Confucian doctrine as an official line but practiced corrupt behavior were widely despised though feared by the great mass of peasantry. Population growth fed tension between doctrine and reality that policy makers at the center, intent on punishing corruption amongst officials, could shape by draconian purges of corrupt officials but not actually stamp out. The fluctuations in the ratio of corrupt to salary income testify to the inability of dynasties to control the problem over the long-run.

A third inconsistency between the tenets of Neo-Confucian orthodoxy and the actual reality of the examination system that perpetuated Confucianism in China was cheating by lineages and families on the examinations. One of the key ideas in Confucianism was the importance of family relationships — family hierarchy as expressed in relationships between fathers and sons, elder brothers and younger brothers, — for serving as a model, a mold, for general social behavior. Thus cheating by families and lineages was condoned to a degree, albeit frowned upon in official discourse.[11]

The importance for a lineage in the gentry of at least one member securing official status through the examination tournament is a principal theme of this chapter. Officials were the cultural and political elite of China, enjoying a tempting opportunity to extract substantial economic rents, corruption income, from their official positions. This focused the gentry on succeeding at the examinations, encouraging most of them to be loyal to the center albeit generating hostility amongst a disgruntled group within the ranks of those failing in the examination tournament. But the gentry diversified into other avenues yielding wealth: they were active in investing in land, becoming landlords, often absentee landlords; they diversified into merchant activities when they seemed profitable. They dabbled in banking particularly in lineage associated banking.[12] Nevertheless the rewards to being an official were so substantial that many lineages and families among the gentry successful in other endeavors encouraged members of the lineage to pursue the examination route or considered purchasing examination degrees or official positions. The merchant-official model that plays a major role in the post-1850 period emerged out of this nexus, merchant families investing in producing officials, officials broadening out into merchant activities.

Prior to 1850 two trends shaped the way the examination system leading to officialdom and diversification into merchant opportunities evolved: population growth and increasing penetration of Western commercial interests in China.

Why did population grow? In particular why did the number of gentry grow? Both controversy and consensus play a role in the discussion of Qing demography. There is general agreement that infanticide mainly directed at females played a significant role in shaping the population dynamics of Qing China (and continues to be important in contemporary China). There is also agreement the absence of primogeniture played a crucial role in the fate of wealth-holding amongst the gentry, property being divided up amongst the sons, dissipating fortunes, and reducing the value of land held by particular individuals. A third factor around which there is general agreement is importance of interregional migration, people in regions where population presses up against resources seeking a more prosperous existence in frontiers.[13] A study of the Tu lineage genealogy suggests that migrants to a frontier region had fairly high fertility and low mortality in the period immediately following their immigration into the frontier, fertility falling, and mortality rising thereafter.[14] If this genealogy is representative of a general trend, it is possible that fertility was higher and mortality lower in the early Qing period when frontier lands were being opened up — for instance in Southwestern China and in some coastal zones — than it was in the late 18th and early 19th centuries.[15]

A shift towards lower fertility might be explained by conscious regulation of reproduction within marriage or by an upward drift in ages of marriage and a decline in the proportion of women in the reproductive ages who are married. The evidence does not support the hypothesis that marriage customs changed in an appreciable fashion. Marriage of females in the second half of the Qing period appears to be early and universal. Where there is controversy and debate is the level of marital fertility which appears to be low, perhaps falling, during the 19th century. Campbell and Lee (2004, 2005) argue that the low reproduction within marriage is due to conscious birth control practiced amongst a sub-group of the Chinese population they designate as controllers. Engelen (2006) disputes this view, arguing that chronic malnutrition, untreated diseases, hard manual labor, and temporary spousal separation due to economic distress better explain the depressed levels of reproduction within marriage observed in lineage genealogies and registers for members of the Eight Banners.

In any event the figures assembled in Appendix Table A.6 do support the view that population was increasing throughout the Qing period up until 1850 when demographic disasters due to the great rebellions interrupted expansion in numbers. Given the absence of primogeniture population increase must have put pressure on the incomes of the gentry, pushing them increasingly into a vicious unrelenting competition for success in an increasingly competitive examination system. Working against this tendency, however, is the pressure of human numbers on land rents. Since many of the gentry owned land either directly managing it themselves or renting it out the economic benefits of holding onto the asset rose tended to improve. This said, it is likely that the overall impact of division of assets among inheriting sons was to reduce average gentry wealth, thereby encouraging more and more members of the gentry to try their luck competing in the examination lottery.

The second trend gradually reshaping the landscape of late 18th and early 19th century Qing — involving trade with the West — mainly impacted southeastern China, particularly Macao and Guangzhou (Canton). Trade between Western Europe and China began expanding during the 16th century, the Portuguese establishing footholds in India at Goa and in southeastern China in Macao. After the Spanish acquired the Philippines it began to carry on a brisk Pacific Ocean trade, bringing silver secured from its mines in Spanish America to Manila where a Chinese merchant community assembled to engage in trade exchanging silk, tea, and ceramics for silver (silver being used to pay land taxes in China).

Under pressure from a growing number of Western commercial interests — especially English — the Qing government agreed to open Guangzhou in southeastern China to trade with the West, licensing a Chinese merchant community of *hong* merchants assembled into a guild — a *cohong* — to carry on a restricted and circumscribed trade. The Qing regime agreed to tolerate this trade under its general policy of permitting tribute trade with other countries. Under this rubric the foreign trade community participating in this trade was required to *kowtow* to the Chinese emperor an act of humility irritating to a Western trading community enjoying growing expertise in managing global trade across both Atlantic and Pacific Oceans.

Aggressively moving into this trade over the course of the second half of the 18th century was the English East India Company exploiting the monopoly on the production of opium in Bengal that it enjoyed after the early 1770s. Unlike Spain that took plentiful cargoes of silver out of its sprawling American mining reserves stretching from Peru to Mexico, English merchant houses did not have ready access to silver bullion that the *cohong* demanded, only securing it indirectly from European continental powers like France. Casting around for commodities that were vigorously demanded in the Chinese market the East India Company hit upon opium traditionally used as a medicine in China. But Beijing officialdom, cognizant of the addictive properties of the opium narcotic opposed the import of opium, periodically attempting to ban it albeit without much success.[16] In fact the East India Company managed to smuggle in the opium on its vessels and the *cohong* managed to distribute it within China.

The economic prowess of the *cohong* was in the ascendancy. This was a preview to the clout exercised by the compradors — Chinese employed by Western enterprises in the treaty ports established after the Opium Wars — in 19th century China.

3.2. The Western Challenge

The key point about post-15th century Western Europe when it is viewed in the Chinese mirror is that it was competitive, aggressively so. Competition was endemic among cultural elites; military competition was endemic amongst emergent nation-states; competition was endemic in trade especially the global trade that developed in the wake of the European voyages of discovery in the late 15th and early 16th centuries. Consider the relative population sizes of China and Western Europe around 1700 and 1820.

According to the estimates in Maddison (2006: p. 42) the populations — in 1000s of persons — of China and Western Europe were:

Region/Year	1700	1820
China	138,000	381,000
Western Europe	81,460	132,888

Not only was China far larger. It was an empire ruled out of a metropolitan center administered by a bureaucracy trained methodically through a standardized examination system that hammered out a relatively homogeneous worldview. By contrast smaller Western Europe was divided intellectually — secular Renaissance views reviving classical teachings of the Greeks and Romans contesting with emergent Protestantism and a Catholicism committed to battling the Protestant sects after the Council of Trent of 1545 — and politically. Great Western European powers — France, Spain, England, the Netherlands, and Sweden — fought each other on land and sea, fashioning alliances of convenience with one another while resisting Russian and Ottoman threats to the East. By contrast China was a single political entity mainly concerned with threats from the North and West.[17]

The military implications of China's vast size and the divisiveness of less populous Western Europe can be readily grasped from the following function:

$$M = f(mY, p_{mf}),$$ (3.1)

where M is the military potential of a individual political entity (e.g., empire, nation-state), m is the rate at which income is converted to military purposes, Y is income generated by the entity, and p_{mf} is the price of exerting military force at home and abroad relative to other prices prevailing within the economy. It should be noted that:

$$Y = y * P,$$ (3.2)

where y is per capita income and P is population. Because military competition was endemic in Europe m was higher in a typical European state than it was in China. By the same token European scientists and engineers focused their efforts on developing military technologies because monarchs subsidized their efforts, showering them with status and money to reward their efforts. As a result p_{mf} was lower in Western Europe.[18] By contrast because China was so populous — P being large — China's level of income Y was massive, serving as a counterweight to most threats emanating from abroad. Indeed European expansionism in the Indian Ocean and the South China Sea went together with European military and commercial competition. In the 15th and early 16th centuries the European states vied for the services of Italian navigators who had honed their sailing skills in the Mediterranean Sea: John Cabot, who claimed Newfoundland for the British crown on a voyage to find a northwest passage to Asia was born in either Genoa or Venice; Amerigo Vespucci, an Italian Renaissance figure, sailing for Portugal landed on the coast of Brazil, claiming it for his benefactor on the basis of the Treaty of Tordesilla. The origin of the Spanish conquistadors — including Hernán Cortéz who defeated the Aztecs in Central America and Francisco Pizarro who defeated the Inca Empire ruled by Atahualpa in Peru — lay in a coterie of feudal knights who were instrumental in the recapture of the Moorish province of Granada at the behest of Ferdinand and Isabella.

The classic mercantilism of England and the Netherlands who eventually managed to sweep away most of the Spanish and Portuguese strongholds in Asia was predicated on chartering merchant companies like the East India Company whose ships bristled with cannons and sailors trained in military matters. Indeed the theory of mercantilism was rooted in aggrandizing the fiscal resources — precious metals that could be cast into coinage — that monarchies required so that they could hire professional soldiers dispatched to battlefields and sailors serving in naval contests. Under the logic of mercantilism chartered merchant companies established production facilities in the settled lands of Asia and colonies in the frontiers of the New World, managing these enterprises and the trade taking place between the colonial possessions and the mother country with an eye to generating a favorable balance of trade (exports exceeding imports). A favorable balance of trade yielded a positive inflow of precious metal into the mother country, filling the coffers of monarchs chartering the companies, thereby bolstering their capacity to purchase arms and personnel capable of mounting military campaigns at home and abroad.

Before the industrial revolution the global company operating under a mercantilist charter represented a massive institutional advance bringing together nascent stock markets financing companies, the commercial and managerial expertise of merchants, and the burgeoning military potential of the Western powers, particularly England and Holland.

Merchant activity played an important role in creating positive incentives that enhanced hours worked per worker, h, and the efficiency of each hour worked, $e(h)$, amongst the European peasantry. Merchants reached into rural communities for artisan and craft services. For instance in the putting out system textile merchants out-sourced spinning, weaving, and dying services amongst rural dwellers, farming out each stage of the production process, buying back semi-finished product from less finished goods that they had sold to the farming households (the difference between purchases and previous sale of raw material to be worked up equivalent to wages paid). Moreover the concentration of merchants and artisans — typically members of guilds — in cities increased the demand for food, thereby raising the prices that the farming population earned on the market. The industriousness of Western European populations — and their labor productivity — positively responded to the incentives associated with putting out and urbanization.

An additional factor that raised the productivity of agricultural labor in Western Europe was the Columbian exchange, the introduction of crops particularly from the Americas — corn, tomatoes, potatoes — that made their way into Europe as a result of European conquest and commercial expansion. While this fillip to agricultural productivity per worker in Western Europe might have eventually been wasted away, wiped out by population growth generated by the increase in the standard of living due to European agricultural productivity gain (note the rise in per capita income and population over the 1500–1820 period that occurred in Western Europe, evident in Panels A.1 and A.2 of Appendix Table A.2) it was soon followed by sustained industrialization permitting Europe to decisively break out of the Malthusian/inorganic economy trap that had constrained successful rise in per capita income everywhere prior to the 18th centuries.[19] One of the consequences of the favorable rise in food output per worker in Western Europe was the generating of a food surplus, the combined total of calories, proteins, and vitamins produced by a typical farmer exceeding his or her food consumption needs, thereby encouraging a further rise in urbanization linked to positive growth in putting out activity.

Into the world of mercantilist powers contending with the declining global colonial and trading empires of Spain and Portugal — and an expansionary French monarchy consolidating its hegemonic power within French territory — burst the technological advances of the industrial revolution disrupting forever the nature of global military competition.

Indeed, one of the most important implications of the industrial revolution of the late 18th and early 19th centuries was that it lowered p_{mf}. Iron hulled steamships, steam railroads, massive cannon made of cheaply wrought cast iron not only decreased the costs of moving soldiers and sailors. They also reduced the costs of delivering massive amounts of firepower in locales far from home. Consider the following quotation from Parker (1988: p. 154):

> "In February 1841, on here way to Canton during the first Opium War, for example, the two pivot-mounted 32 pounders of the ironclad steamship Nemesis destroyed in just one day, nine war-junks, five forts, two military stations and one shore battery .…"

Born out of the competition amongst cultural elites and emergent nation-states in Europe, the industrial revolution ushered in an era of military dominance by Western Europe and its offshoots in global affairs.

Not surprisingly the challenge posed by the West to China in a world in which industrialization was spreading throughout England, Western Europe and the United States was first and foremost military. But it was also commercial, political, and culture. Did the nation-state system of international diplomacy that was codified within the arena of Western Europe with the Peace of Westphalia in 1648 apply to China and East Asia accustomed to the tribute trade system? What approach was the Chinese cultural elite going to take in grappling with the cultural advances — the scientific revolution, the enlightenment, and the industrial enlightenment — of Western Europe that ushered in the industrial revolution?[20] How was China going to integrate its trade — its comparative advantage lying in craft products like silk and ceramic making — into a world in which industrial production occurring in factories was turning out substitutes for craft products aimed at mass markets, taking advantage of scale economies, thereby driving down cost?

Still the main challenge facing China was military. Various forces came together in the 1830s that led to the outbreak of war between China and England immediately precipitated by the seizing of opium by Chinese authorities in Guangzhou and the outbreak of rioting by British sailors in the summer of 1839. On the Chinese side was the attempt to control the opium market, maintain the tribute trade system, and apply Chinese law to foreigners carrying on trade on Chinese soil. On the British side was the dismantling of mercantilism, part and parcel of the rhetoric erupting in the nascent industrial towns of the English midlands — Manchester,

Leeds, and Sheffield — where factory owners increasingly made a fetish of unfettered market activity, arguing for the free unhindered exchange of labor services for wages paid. The East India Company was losing its monopoly on trade with China, British agency houses clamoring to get into the Chinese market. In short, the British wanted expansion of trade wrought through the dismantling of the rigid tribute trade system and the extension of a kind of quasi-diplomatic immunity to British merchants whereas the Chinese authorities wanted the opposite. The concrete dispute over opium was the powder keg setting off war between the two sides.

Defeated the Chinese signed the humiliating Treaty of Nanjing in 1842 that ceded Hong Kong to England on a long-term lease and designated five treaty ports where British subjects enjoyed extraterritorial rights, not being subject to Chinese law. In addition China agreed to grant most favored nation trade status to England, guaranteeing that China could not impose tariffs on a specific British good higher than the lowest tariff rate it imposed on the same good imported from any other country.

As soon as the British secured these rights, other countries with global commercial interests — notably the United States and France — opened talks with the Chinese authorities demanding equal treatment for their nationals, in effect expanding the foreign community allowed to operate in the treaty ports. Seizing on a strategy of using one group barbarians to counter the activities of other barbarians, Chinese negotiators agreed. This action spurred on the British to seek even more concessions including legalizing the opium trade and the stationing of a British diplomatic delegation in Beijing. The result of the ensuing breakdown in negotiations was the second Opium War that pitted English and French forces against the Chinese military between 1856 and 1860. Chinese defeat in the four year conflict led to the ratification of the Treaty of Tianjin — signed in 1858 — at the Convention of Peking in 1860. Under the terms of this Convention the British were allowed to open an embassy in Beijing, China was forced to pay an indemnity to England, and Protestant and Catholic missionaries were allowed to travel freely throughout China.

The Western challenge to China in the first half of the 19th century was sweeping in its scope. The Chinese response was remarkably tepid. Explaining why this was the case requires an examination of the actions of political, cultural, and military elites in the wake of the two Opium Wars.

3.3. Qing Response

From the first Opium War until 1911 when the Qing Dynasty collapsed — a period of seven decades — slow decay set in within the Chinese Empire. Terrible rebellions sweeping in their devastation broke out, military power became increasingly regionalized and fiscal resources were decentralized to a degree. A Self Strengthening movement aimed at promoting a "government-sponsored, merchant managed" model for nascent Chinese owned steamship enterprise and the creation of armories producing ships and weapons with which the Chinese military could fend off military threats both domestic and foreign failed. Remarkably the regime staggered on for 70 years, testimony to the allegiance of the gentry deeply invested in the examination system crucial to dynastic rule in China.

During the period 1850–1873 three major rebellions broke out in China, the death toll running in the millions, perhaps as high as 30 million: the Taiping Rebellion (1850–1864) mainly occurring in the Yangzi River delta; the Nien Rebellion mainly concentrated in northern China in the vicinity of the Yellow River (Huang He); and the Panthay Rebellion, a Muslim rebellion occurring in Yunnan province, in the Southwest. In addition less deadly rebellions took place elsewhere: the Du Wenxiu Rebellion between 1855 and 1873 and the Hui Rebellion, a Moslem inspired outbreak in Northwestern China, in Gansu and Shaanxi provinces.

Of these the Taiping Rebellion was the most devastating in terms of loss of life, in terms of threats to Chinese officialdom and the credibility of the examination system. The leader of the rebellion was Hong Xiuguan who failed the provincial civil examinations.[21] After study with a missionary, Hong became convinced that he was the younger brother of Jesus, declaring himself the ruler over the Heavenly Kingdom of Great Peace in 1851. The doctrine espoused by Hong included the following propositions: (1) strict separation of the sexes; (2) the ending of the practice of food binding women; (3) redistribution of land; (4) growing hair long; (5) suppression of use of opium, tobacco, alcohol, polygamy, slavery, and prostitution backed up with harsh penalties; and (6) the setting up of a new examination system based on the Bible. In general the Taiping rebels were not just hostile to the Manchu rulers of Qing China and their specific policies, rather decrying Confucian values, the Confucian official elite, and many Chinese practices predating the Qing period. For this reason the Taiping rebels had difficulty forming alliances with the leaders of the other rebellions breaking out in the wake of China's signing the humiliating treaties allowing extraterritoriality and the dismantling of the tribute trade system.

After the Taiping armies began their advance on Nanjing and threatened to take over Shanghai, both the center and the affected regions reacted: in Beijing a coup known as the Qing Restoration brought the Empress Dowager, Cixi (the concubine of the Xianfeng emperor) to power; and powerful regional officials organized their own militias, regions introducing the *lijin* tax in order to generate the required funding for raising armies. Typical of the latter officials were Li Hongzhang, the most powerful official in the second half of the 19th century, and Zeng Guofan who established a navy on the Yangzi River in order to methodically decimate Taiping power on the Yangzi. Li not only put together his own militia in his home province of Anhui. As well he worked closely with Frederick Thomas Ward in 1860 (after the second Opium War concluded) to establish the Ever Victorious Army, an army organized according to British military principles consisting of around 5000 soldiers trained in Western military techniques and armed with Western firearms.

Li and Zeng enjoyed remarkable careers that outlasted their activities in bringing the Taiping Rebellion to an end. Both excelled at the civil examinations, both being made members of the Hanlin Academy, an exalted elite academy at the apex of power within the world of the Confucian scholar–official elite, enjoined to supervise the examinations, perform secretarial tasks for the imperial court, and interpret the Confucian classics. After the Taiping Rebellion both played a role in suppressing the Nien Rebellion, Li ultimately replacing Zeng in that campaign. As a result of his success in beating back both Taiping and Nien rebellions, Li was appointed a vice royalty administrator in charge of the metropolitan Zhili province, taking on the additional responsibility of superintendent of trade.

To an important degree the military activities of scholar–officials like Li and Zeng were precursors to the descent of China into divided regional warlord territories that followed upon the death of Yuan Shikai who was appointed the commander of the first New Army — renamed the Beiyang Army — by the Empress Dowager Cixi at the end of the 19th century. All three men, Li, Zeng, and Yuan led modernizing armies that were more regional than national, were outside the Eight Banner system of the Manchus that remained entrenched in military technologies and strategies of the bygone past, and were more committed to their specific leaders than to supporting the Qing court, were more loyal to their commanders than to the center.

The movement that spawned the new armies that suppressed the Taiping and Nien Rebellions was an expression of the Self Strengthening movement that took hold in the wake of the coup that brought the Empress Dowager Cixi to power. In the economic realm the Self Strengthening movement involved the setup of the *lijin* tax, the building of armories like the Foochow armory, and the formulation of the "government-sponsored, merchant-managed" (*guandu shangban*) model for commerce and industry.

Under the "government-sponsored, merchant-managed" system officials were assigned to create a general outline of the activities of companies and monitor the profits and losses while participating merchants were expected to manage the day to day affairs of the enterprise. Modeled on the salt administration, sponsors of the concept like Li Hongzhang envisioned government becoming actively involved in the finances of the enterprises, through subsidies and grants. The grand experiment in this form of business was the Bureau for Recruiting Merchants that was chartered in 1873.[22] At first the Bureau for Recruiting Merchants was successful, moving aggressively into the steamship business competing head to head with foreign owned and managed enterprises. Between 1876 and 1878 it outmaneuvered in price wars the American owned Shanghai Steamship Navigation Company ultimately absorbing it. Then the rot of corruption, endemic amongst Confucian officialdom set in. The managers of the Bureau for Recruiting Merchants was impeached in 1880, the company ultimately being sold to the American Russell & Co. in 1884. Corruption and a lack of entrepreneurial drive stemming from excessive regulation did in the firm.

The failure of the Self Strengthening movement due to excessive reliance on a corrupt Confucian officialdom spread over into China's preparation for wars with foreign powers. Disputes over whether Japan or China would play a predominant role in Korean affairs led to the Sino–Japanese war of 1894–1895. The result was defeat for China — and personal defeat for Li Hongzhang who had sponsored the Beiyang Fleet considered the most powerful in Asian waters — and the ceding of Taiwan to Japan at the Treaty of Shimonoseki signed in 1895. Under the terms of the treaty Japan joined the ranks of countries enjoying extraterritorial rights in treaty ports and a clause was introduced allowing nationals of all countries enjoying extraterritorial rights in China the right to setup factories in the treaty ports. In addition Japan was given a lease over the Liaodong Peninsula including the strategically port at Port Arthur. A cynical intervention by Russia, Germany, and France applied pressure on Japan, forcing it to relinquish the territorial claim to the Liaodong Peninsula in exchange receiving an indemnity. Russia's subsequent move to sign a 25-year lease for the Liaodong Peninsula and to set up a naval station at Port Arthur in 1898 set the stage for the Russo–Japanese War of 1894–1895 as a result of which Japan strengthened its hold over Korea and acquired rights over the South Manchurian Railroad Zone and the railroad itself.

Defeat of China in the Sino–Japanese war precipitated the carving up the Chinese coastline and sections of the interior into regional blocs: by the end of the 19th century France had acquired a zone of influence in southern China; Britain had staked out two zones, one emanating out from Hong Kong including Guangzhou and a second major zone on the Yangzi River incorporating Shanghai; a Japanese zone around Fuzhou north of the British zone around Guangzhou; a German zone on the Shandong Peninsula in Northeastern China; and a Russian zone in Manchuria transferred to Japan after the conclusion of the Russo–Japanese war. It was this dismemberment of China that precipitated the Boxer Rebellion of 1899–1901 in which eight allies — Japan, Russia, the United Kingdom, France, the United States, Germany, Italy, and Austria–Hungary — defeated the anti-foreign, anti-Christian, Society of Righteous Fists of Harmony backed by the imperial court.

The defeat of the Qing Dynasty sponsored Boxer Rebellion forced the court to accede to the demands of reformers for a restructuring of the civil examinations, incorporating questions on world affairs, banking, police laws, and industrialization. In 1901 the reforms were passed and in 1902 the first set of reform examinations were graded. But as Elman (2000: pp. 596–597) the grading adhered to the old standard, the results being reported in the standard order, classical essays first, discourse essays second and policy questions (the new material covered) third. In the aftermath of Japan's success in the Russo–Japanese war the Dowager Empress acting at the behest of key military officials like Yuan Shikai agreed to the abolition of the examination system altogether, all degrees qualifying a student for placement in the civil administration to be earned by graduating from new schools set up in 1904.

In jettisoning the examination system the Qing Dynasty did itself in. With a stroke of the pen as it were — in early 1906 — the Dowager Empress signed off on a memorial that wiped out the value of years and years of schooling for the vast majority of the gentry. Not surprisingly the dynasty collapsed soon afterward. Ultimately satisfaction amongst — or at least the avoidance of a high level of dissatisfaction — the gentry elite was key to the perpetuation of imperial China. The abolition of the civil examinations wiped out a sacrifice involved mastering the Neo-Confucian classics — measured in terms of forgone opportunities, in terms of passing over other opportunities due to diligent study for the examinations — amounting on an individual basis to decades of lost potential earnings. Multiply this by the ranks of the gentry that ran into the millions — a group that was the backbone of local civic and economic affairs, whose existence was one of the main reasons why taxation rates were relatively low in imperial China — and the problem becomes clear. Doing away with the gentry's investment meant threatening to the core the cultural, economic, and political prowess that the gentry enjoyed in imperial China.

In the European mirror late Qing China appears wanting in the three dimensions of culture, economy, and politics. The European challenge to China forced China and Western Europe to observe each other in that mirror. A region once backward had soared to unprecedented global power due to characteristics that once — in the mirror of the late Middle Ages— might have seen as defects. Indeed prior to the 15th century focusing upon the achivements of two regions — China, and Western Europe — in a mirror would have yielded a comparison distinctly in China's favor. China was relatively peaceful, powerful by the dint of its sheer numbers, a technological leader over centuries. Europe was emerging from feudalism, culturally divided, politically and militarily contested. Ironically it was the defects of the past that became the strengths of the 19th century. This is not the first time that past glories presage contemporary failures. This is hardly the first time that the roots of future glory lie buried beneath a seemingly sodden and unforgiving soil.

Endnotes

1. For a summary of the sprawling work of Joseph Needham that examines Chinese technology, science, and invention in great (some would say excruciating) detail, see Ronan (1978, 1986a,b, 1994). On the development of science and technology in the West see Klemm (1964) and Hall (1966). For a discussion of paradigms shifts in Western science that treats the scientific community as an elite group erupting into intellectually opposed squabbling factions during periods of paradigm shift see the classic treatment of Kuhn (1962).

2. The phrase "industrial enlightenment" was coined by Mokyr (2002). Mokyr (2002: p. 35 ff) argues that the industrial enlightenment concerns that element of rational thought that involves "observing, understanding, and manipulating natural forces." In describing the development of the industrial enlightenment Mokyr puts heavy emphasis on the formulation of the scientific method by philosophers like Francis Bacon who argued that experimentation was crucial

to revealing natural truths that could be utilized by technicians and inventors to harness natural forces. First comprehend nature's deepest secrets, then enlist this knowledge in manipulating it with machines and chemical processes. For the expansion of educational institutions that educated and employed many of Europe's emerging cultural elite see Houston (1988) and Müller *et al.* (1987).

3. Dating the beginning and end of Chinese dynasties is tricky since new dynastic rulers did not necessarily secure control over all of the territory known as China at the commencement of their reigns nor were their successors able to maintain hegemonic power over all of Chinese territory throughout the dynasty they inherited particularly in the closing years of their dynasty when power was contested by rivals to the emperorship. That said, key dynasties in Chinese history are dated as follows: (a) Qin (221 BC–206 BC) widely considered to be the first dynasty unifying China; (b) early Han (206 BC–9 AD); (c) Sung (969–1279); (d) Yuan (1279–1368) founded by Mongul invaders; (e) Ming (1368–1644) founded by a peasant known who managed to overthrow the Mongul dynasty with his armies introducing an era of cruel and repressive despotic rule; and (6) Qing (1644–1911) founded by Manchu invaders who broke though Great Wall defenses defeating Ming armies with the assistance of Chinese military allies who opposed Ming rule.

4. The principal tax was the land tax. The center also secured revenue from various monopolies salient being on the sale of salt (the salt gabelle was a major moneymaker for the center authorities). During the post-1850 period local governments fighting off major rebellions throughout the country piled on additional taxes, notably the *lijin* — literally the term "*lijin*" means "one-thousandth unit of currency" — imposed upon the warehousing and transport for sale of commercial goods. The *lijin* tax was computed by applying a fixed rate — varying depending on the time period and locale but typically less that 10% — to the value of commercial goods.

5. This estimate is crude. Alternative population estimates suggest a slightly higher ratio of officials to people governed say around one official to 670 people. In any event there is little disputing the fact that the ratio of officials to populace was low.

6. Prior to their conquest of China the banners were established — around 1615 — by the Manchus. The three upper banners — plain yellow, bordered yellow, plain white — were directly loyal to the emperor, the others to various imperial princes. In addition to suppressing rebellions and fighting off foreign threats — like the *wakō* pirates of Japanese or Chinese origin that harassed the Chinese coastline from the 13th to the early 17th centuries — the banners had responsibility for public welfare. The provincial banner garrisons were typically situated in walled Manchu cities. On the banners see Elliot (2001).

7. The Mongol invaders who established the Yuan Dynasty in the 13th century were slow to reestablish the examination system that was used by the previous

dynasty, waiting four decades before realizing that examinations were crucial to securing the cooperation of gentry at the local level.

8. The military examination system was largely the same in terms of structure though it differed in terms of the skills required to be successful in the tournament. To become a military licentiate a man had to pass district, prefecture, and provincial military examinations after which he could compete at the metropolitan military examination level. Examinations tested both book learning and physical skill acquisition, the ability to excel at archery from horseback, weightlifting, and brandishing swords subject to intense testing in the competition. Cheating on the academic side of the tests was commonly condoned since academic learning was less important for a military career than it was for progress through the civilian official ranks.

9. Ch'ü (1962) gives many concrete examples of official corruption.

10. Rent-seeking income refers to income that is generated by dint of official or legal position. The point made by economists is that seeking rents uses up real resources (e.g., the time and effort of officials in soliciting bribes and the time and effort of those paying bribes to officials in actually arranging the bribes) that might be more productivity used in generating real output bolstering the economy as a whole.

11. Purchase of official positions and examination certificates was possible, obviating the incentive to cheat on examinations to some extent.

12. Mann (1987) provides a good treatment of gentry's wealth generating opportunities. Jones (1972) discusses the two main types of banking that developed in the Qing period: the so-called "native bank" system that appeared in the Ningpo area near the Yangzi River delta and the Shansi banking system that prospered in regions active in the silk, salt, and iron trades.

13. On migration and infanticide directed at female offspring occurring during the Qing period, see Ho (1959), Lee and Campbell (1997), and Lee and Tan (1992).

14. Umeno (2008).

15. On frontier areas see Giersch (2006) and Marks (1998).

16. Estimates of opium import into China suggest that it multiplied fivefold between 1730 and the early 1770s.

17. The dismantling of China's great naval fleet during the 15th century is an excellent illustration of China's focus on land threats not threats rather than those emanating from across the seas. During the first half of the 15th century the imperial court dispatched seven exploratory voyages of a massive fleet captained by Zheng Ho, the second voyage landing at Indian ports, the fifth landing on the Horn of Africa and exploring the area that is Kenya today. Official and gentry opposition to this expansionism ultimately led to the destruction of the fleet, the rump navy remaining largely being relegated to fending off Japanese and Chinese *wakō* pirates. For an interpretation of the contrast between the divisiveness of Western Europe and the vast continental

expanse of China rooted in geographic difference — emphasizing the nature of mountain ranges and rivers — see Diamond (1999).

18. On this point see Hoffman (2005).

19. The Columbian exchange was not the only factor underlying gains in Western European agriculture. Also important were the development of improved plows, the enclosure of open fields farmed by peasants in common, and convertible husbandry that involved the use of clovers and turnips that fixed nitrogen in the soil and slowed the pace of weed growth in increasingly sophisticated crop rotation schemes.

20. The Jesuits — notably Matteo Ricci — brought a number of concepts developed in Western science, notably astronomy, and mathematics to the Beijing court in the early 17th century. Having emerged as an offshoot of the Catholic renaissance known as Counter-Reformation that commenced with the Council of Trent, the Society of Jesus promoted establishment of universities and schools and encouraged its members to gain converts abroad by linking superiority of European science and mathematics to Christianity. However according to Elman (2006: p. 23) by the 18th century the knowledge of Jesuit missionaries in Beijing was becoming woefully out of date, not keeping pace with improvements in the manufacture of astronomic instruments and precision timepieces. Chinese intellectuals were unaware of the calculus prior to the first Opium War.

21. Hakka — a Han Chinese sub-group whose families did not practice foot binding of women freeing women to work in the fields — were heavily represented in the ranks of the Taiping rebels.

22. For details concerning the Bureau for Recruiting Merchants see Li (2001).

4

Tokugawa and Meiji Japan

4.1. In Two Mirrors

Casting China's experience in the European mirror helped us understand why Europe surged ahead of China after 1500, why Europe broke open China in the early 19th century instead of China breaking open Europe, why the West humiliated China in the 19th and early 20th centuries rather than vice versa. With this in mind, our discussion of Japan's response to the Western challenge commences by casting Japan's experience in both European and Chinese mirrors.

Viewing Japan in this light yields an interesting hypothesis: in many dimensions the Tokugawa Japan that was forcibly opened up by the Western powers in the 1850s was more similar to Western Europe than it was to China. To be specific:

(1) In terms of the productivity of the farming population, especially the farming population in south-western and central Japan, Japan appears to be more similar to Western Europe than to China. This is because infrastructure — roads, "canalized" rivers, urban centers — was well developed throughout Japan by 1700. The deep penetration of infrastructure throughout most of Japan provided farmers with positive incentives that bolstered hours worked per worker h and efficiency per work hour $e(h)$,

industriousness, the demand for education, and market orientation diffusing throughout most of the country during the 18th and early 19th centuries.

(2) In terms of demography Japan occupies a middle ground sharing important features with both China and the West. Marriage was early and virtually universal for females in Japan as it was in China. Moreover neo-Confucian values concerning the hierarchy of men, women and birth order were as entrenched in Japan as they were in China. That said, the stem family system — only one child, typically the eldest son, remaining with his or her parents when he or she marries, the other siblings leaving the household — rooted in the idea of not dividing the major assets of the family diffused throughout Japan among both elite and nonelite populations during the 18th and 19th centuries. The stem family system was characteristic of most regions of Western Europe, playing a crucial role in shaping inheritance and co-residence of children and their aged parents in France, England, and most of Western Europe north of Spain. However the diffusion of the stem family system in Japan is associated with a cessation of population growth at the national level between 1720 and 1850 while population did tend to grow in those parts of Western Europe that adopted the stem family system. In short, Japan is both similar and dissimilar to China, and to Western Europe, in terms of its demography. It lies in-between.

(3) In terms of elites, Japan is more similar to Western Europe than it is to China, despite elites in both Japan and China sharing a common neo-Confucian ideology. In part this is because Tokugawa Japan enjoyed many of the political and military characteristics of feudalism from which European nation-states and mercantilism sprung. Unlike China where the fate of the elite was increasing tied up with a meritocratic examination system that gave a strong bureaucratic cast to the country, the military–political *samurai* elite in Japan cultivated loyalty to feudal overlords, the *daimyō*. The *samurai* elite was not a meritocracy, nor did it tend to own land as did the Chinese gentry. Moreover, in 18th and 19th century Japan as in Western Europe after the 15th century, merchants had been increasingly influential in economic matters, many merchants rivaling the landless *samurai* warrior-bureaucrat in terms of elite status, though not political power. That said, the elite in Tokugawa Japan was not nearly as fragmented as was the elite in Europe where scientists and engineers contended for influence with

political and merchant economic elites. Again Japan is in-between Western Europe and China, arguably more like the West than China.

(4)   In terms of the penetration of infrastructure and the integration of a country into a putative nation-state, Tokugawa Japan is more similar to Western European countries like France and England than it is to China, a vast sprawling empire tied together politically through the Confucian bureaucracy and writing but not well integrated in terms of transportation and communications otherwise. Two of the characteristics of the early nationalism of emergent nation-states is that it is exclusionary, sharply defining national identity in both negative and positive terms, rejecting parts of its past in order to forge a nationalistic cement and that it goes hand in hand with integration of transport and communications. For instance nationalism in early modernizing England was associated with a rejection of Catholicism; in France rejection of the monarchy during the French Revolution was instrumental to the forging of French national identity. In both countries the development of roads and canals played an important role in setting the stage for nation-state integration under nationalistic banners. The same argument applies to Japan.

(5)   In terms of income per capita, Tokugawa Japan is more similar to China than it is to Western Europe. That said, Tokugawa Japan was largely closed to trade while Western Europe was open to trade. As we have seen, part of Europe's advantage in terms of per capita income prior to 18th and 19th century industrialization lies in European expansionism and the Columbian exchange.

4.2. Elites in Tokugawa Japan

The nature of Tokugawa period elites is intimately linked to the *bakuhan* system.[1] *Bakuhan* was a confederation system of government, sharing power between the *bakufu* — or military "tent-government" center under the control of the *shogun* — and the fiefs, or *han*, each ruled by a *daimyō*, a feudal warlord.

As fashioned by Toyotomi Hideyoshi at the end of the 16th century, and refined by the Tokugawa *shoguns* after 1600, the chief goals of the *bakuhan* system were (1) to eliminate warfare between rival warlords, ushering in a period of domestic harmony in which commerce and agricultural production — particularly rice cultivation — could prosper; (2) demilitarize the countryside by removing *samurai* farmer-warriors from rural villages, turning them into landless warrior-bureaucrats required to reside in a castle town that became the center of fief government ruled over by the *daimyō* warlord to whom they owed fealty and loyalty, *samurai* food consumption guaranteed by the fief that collected taxes in the form of rice distributed to the warrior-bureaucrats as stipends largely determined on the basis of hereditary rank (and not merit although some exceptions were made). Approximately 200 fiefs were created, the warlords assigned to each fief appointed by the *shogun* (the *bakufu* retaining control over the Kanto plain and key metropolises like Osaka designed to be the center of the rice market); and (3) prevent the European powers who were expanding their commercial activities throughout Asia from gaining a political and/or cultural foothold in Japan thereby threatening the integrity of the emperor system the *shogun* was committed to protecting.

Rice was the touchstone of the political economy of the *bakuhan* system especially during its early phase from 1600 to 1720. The economic fates of the *daimyō*, *samurai* and merchant elites of early Tokugawa Japan were completely bound up with the capacity of peasant producers to generate rice output in the villages of each fief. Two of the key aspects of early Tokugawa infrastructure — "canalized" rivers and the creation of metropolises like Osaka that were designed to be centers for the active exchange of rice — owe their creation to the drive to expand and handle surplus stocks of rice in order to keep the threat of famine at bay. By removing arms from the countryside through the forcing of warrior-farmers into castle towns, the frequency of disputes over water rights between villages closer and further from natural sources of irrigation plummeted. The tragedy of the commons — the failure to properly exploit a natural resource endowment (namely potential abundance of water for irrigation stemming from massive rainfall brought by the monsoon storms sweeping across Japan in the late spring/early summer) — was averted.

Building on demilitarization of rural Japan in order to further and aiming to further exploit the potential for converting land from forest or waste to productive rice yielding arable, fief and *bakufu* governments worked together to regularize the flow of rivers by bolstering their embankments and channels with rocks, thereby reducing the threat of flooding and making more predictable the flow of water along irrigation ditches carved out in the lands between one village and the next.

The incentives were clear. As a typical fief expanded the number of new villages through land reclamation and irrigation expansion, it increased its capacity to feed its *samurai*, permitting population increase among its

ranks, increasing the economic prowess, hence relative standing of the fief
in the pecking order of fiefs. In turn an expansion of rice output increased
the demand for merchants who had been expressly brought into Osaka by
Toyotomi Hideyoshi to handle rice surpluses, allowing fiefs suffering rice
output failures to secure foodstuffs that they could distribute to their desti-
tute populations.

The third aspect of early infrastructure creation — the laying down of
five major road networks connected to feeder roads linking individual castle
towns to the major road network — was closely linked to another key political goal of the *bakufu*: preventing domestic unrest. Under the *sankin kotai*
system refined by the Tokugawa *shoguns*, *daimyō* were required to provide
services to the *bakufu* on an alternating basis, making their way to Edo (later
Tokyo) the castle town of the *bakufu* along stipulated roads bristling with
checkpoints where they and their attendants could be carefully examined
for weapons and other suspicious paraphernalia. Moreover, each *daimyō*
was required to maintain a luxurious estate in Edo, where his wife and children resided, thereby guaranteeing that hostages could be taken by the
bakufu in the event of rebellion. To further intimidate *daimyō*, the *bakufu*
employed a veritable army of spies and informers whose job description was
ferreting out plots being hatched by restive *daimyō* and their retainers.

The *sakoku* or isolationist policy introduced in the mid-17th century
was also aimed at preventing the *daimyō* from mounting a successful rebellion, in this case by forming alliances with the Western powers. Unless specifically granted permission by the *shogun*, Japanese could not go abroad
and if he or she did so was subject to the death penalty. Commerce and contact with outside powers was almost completely monopolized by the *bakufu*
center (there were minor exceptions to the policy), that jealously guarded
contact with the outside. Indicative of this aim were two policies: the ban-
ning of Christianity and the forcible registration of families in Buddhist
temples and the creation of Dejima, a small island community of Dutch
traders, lying off the harbor of Nagasaki, an urban center controlled by the
bakufu in the southern island of Kyūshū.

One of the most important consequences of the infrastructure buildup
in the 17th century and the squelching of conflicts between rival *samurai*
in rural areas was a massive expansion of the area under rice cultivation,
hence villages and population. This extensive growth, the size of the economy blossoming while per capita income remains relatively unchanged, is
illustrated in Panel A.5 of Appendix Table A.6. Much of this growth is due
to an increase in arable due to the carving out of new rice fields (*shinden*)

from forest land, hills, hitherto un-irrigated valleys, and marshes surrounding lakes. As population increased so did the opportunity to carry on trade and putting-out activities similar to those that stimulated rural artisan activity in Europe. As in Europe population size was not the operative factor. Rather it was population size, population increase, and population density marshaled by relatively effective infrastructure. Creation of a road network and a system of "canalized" rivers and artificial canal waterways linked to rivers — most of Osaka's internal transport largely consisted of canals linked to the Yodo River that flowed into Osaka Bay — was as important as population expansion for extensive growth during the early Tokugawa period.

According to a basic principle of Adam Smith, the specialization and division of labor depends upon the size of the market. Merchant houses — Sumitomo and Mitsui are two famous examples — increased their activities diversifying out of dry goods (in the case of Mitsui) and silver production (in the case of Sumitomo) — into new endeavors, including the management of fief and *bakufu* debt. Rice wine, sword production, cotton textiles, fertilizer distribution (dried fish were an important source of fertilizer), *mikan* oranges, silk *kimono*, and the like were increasingly traded on the market. Major merchant houses developed systems of internal promotion of recruits, taking in apprentices at a young age (whom they housed), advancing those who were hard working to clerk and senior clerk status. Senior clerks might be allowed to open new outlets for the merchant house, in effect establishing franchises that operated under the insignia logo of the house. As in Europe a merchant elite emerged, one that sought practical education — use of the abacus, basic literacy — in order to carry on business.

Eventually extensive growth reached limits. The reason is deeply rooted in the organic nature of the Tokugawa economy its dependence on land intensive natural energy sources. It became increasingly costly to reclaim land turning it into arable. Fields were pushed onto the slopes of the coastline and up the sides of valleys, rendering further extensive growth uneconomic (the costs exceeding the likely benefits). Tree lined mountains were denuded of trees to build castle towns and major *bakufu* controlled metropolises like Osaka and Edo. Because Japan is volcanic — hence subject to earthquakes — fires were a constant threat during the Tokugawa period, districts of cities going up in conflagrations (in Edo some of these were deliberately set by *samurai* retainers living in the compounds of their fiefs who were bent on attacking the assets and personnel of rival fiefs).

Cutting down trees not only raised the price of wood, thereby imperiling future building or rebuilding of urban districts. It also removed one of the chief barriers to soil erosion, river beds silting up as mudslides brought dirt and debris into the beds of rivers and irrigation ditches alike.

In short by 1720 or so Japan had reached limits to growth. Most fiefs could not afford to increase the ranks of the *samurai* they were responsible for, despite providing relatively parsimonious stipends for many of their rank and file warrior-bureaucrats who were basically poor despite exercising power and enjoying high social status in the formal class pecking order (farmers and artisan/merchants in principle occupying lower rungs in the social ladder).[2]

Fiefs responded by requiring *samurai* to upgrade their skills in government and accounting, opening up fief academies in which *samurai* were required to study. This raised literacy and numeracy. Rational management of fief forest preserves became increasingly common, competent *samurai* or commoner attendants given the task of managing forest re-growth and culling of stands of trees that did not threaten the long-run viability of forest land. Fiefs spun off monopolies in certain craft products, assigning managerial duties to warrior-bureaucrats.

In addition *samurai* severely restricted their family sizes, aiming for one son who could exercise his natural inheritance, his birthright as it were. The possibility of in-adopting a fictive son from a family with two sons — even from a non-*samurai* household, an expedient condoned by fiefs that also allowed wealthier merchant/peasant households to buy *samurai* status under some circumstances — made adopting a low fertility strategy viable.

By the early 18th century many peasant households adopted a similar strategy. The diffusion of the stem family system went hand in hand with growing adherence to a low fertility strategy rendered palatable by the possibility of in-adoption of fictive sons. On occasion some households passed over feeble biological sons in favor of in-adopting a competent fictive son likely to keep the family's assets intake to be enjoyed by future generations in the family line. By limiting the number of children tension over the inheritance was minimized. The result — throughout central Japan — was fairly low marital fertility coupled with relatively long life expectancy, illustrating the Malthusian principle of a strong preventative check encouraging a relatively weak positive check. In southwestern Japan where the possibility of planting rice twice a year was good — due to a relatively benign climate — some positive population increase, albeit modest, continued during the 1720–1850 period. But in northeastern

Japan where the growing season was far shorter and volcanic eruptions that contaminated the air and prevented sunlight from reaching rice plants common, population seems to have declined. Overall, as suggested by the figures in Panel A.5 of Appendix Table A.6, population oscillated around a level of 26–27 million persons during the second half of the Tokugawa period.

Limitation of reproduction within marriage seems to have largely realized through infanticide. But unlike China, infanticide seems to have practiced against both male and female offspring.[3] Indeed, having a girl first was seen as an advantage as the girl could assist her mother in raising a brother born after her.

Amongst both elites and nonelites alike limiting fertility encouraged households to invest more resources in each child permitted life past infancy. Relatively long life expectancy and low fertility did contribute to a diffusion of literacy amongst both elite and nonelite Japan during the later half of the Tokugawa era. In the case of rural Japan *terakoya*, temple schools, proliferating in the latter half of the Tokugawa era.

The diffusion of rural numeracy and literacy was also a response to an increase in demand for the skills. Rice production had largely reached limits. Moreover other products of the land — fruits, vegetables, tea, mulberry plants for raising silk cocoons — were not subject to taxation at least in principle. Increasingly households diversified into products other than rice, and into services like participating in stages of putting-out in cotton and silk textile production. Managing a major silk operation from growing mulberry to tending the silk cocoons to reeling off the silk thread required substantial analytical skills including numeracy. The diffusion of craft or proto-industrial production into rural villages increased the demand for education in the vortex of the ensuing political upheaval.

The intensification of rural craft activity encouraged wealthy farmers to emulate merchants, to diversify into putting-out for instance. In turn this spawned a new rural elite, merchants and rich farmers who had successfully acquired land from their less able neighbors by dint of hard work and clever financial management.

In sum, Tokugawa Japan in the 1850s when it was forcibly opened up by Commodore Perry and the black ships of the United States was very different from Qing China when it was forcibly opened up as a result of the Opium Wars. In particular the nature of the Japanese elite was very different from the Chinese elite. Many of the *samurai* though literate, occupying positions of comparatively high social status and enjoying some power, were poor. They tended to be landless as well. Many a competent ambitious *samurai* was impoverished and stymied by a system that put heavy emphasis on inherited not earned rank. Prominent merchants both rural and urban were also members of the elite, increasingly literate and in many cases ambitious. In general literacy was fairly advanced among all sectors of the society.

The contrast with Qing China in terms of the diffusion of elite status and literacy is clear. So was the response of the elite.

In Japan the decision of the *bakufu* to accede to Western demands for the establishment of extra-territoriality along lines already established for China in the wake of the first Opium War immediately opened up deep political fissures among the ranks of the *samurai* elite, ultimately full scale rebellion against the *bakufu*, led by *samurai* committed to restoring rule by the Emperor through the destruction of the *shogun/bakuhan* system and — it should be emphasized — their own *samurai* status in the vortex of political upheaval that resulted.

Comparing *samurai* reaction to the Western intrusion with the behavior of the Chinese elite — Confucian officials rooted in the landed gentry — crystallizes one of the key arguments of this book in a nutshell. Amongst elites and nonelites alike, ambition and incentives matter. Overthrowing a regime whose perpetuation consigned them to relative poverty and stifled their drive to achieve power and wealth was in the interests of many, perhaps most, *samurai* constrained as they were by a system that linked status and wealth within the *samurai* pecking order to hereditary, that basically bottled up their ability to acquire land that had enriched many rural villages who had managed to become landlords and to engage in the truck and barter of commercial activity that had enriched many a merchant household.

Surely this logic did not apply to the China elite that usually owned land, who could and did diversify into commerce, and who had invested years and years of arduous study and interpretation of the Confucian classics in an unrelenting pursuit of high official status within the rule structure of an empire that had persisted for hundreds, indeed thousands, of years.

Ironically it was the flexibility and meritocracy enjoyed by the Qing elite that hampered China's economic development, China's political response to the Western threat. By contrast it was the rigid trammels of formal status and heredity constraining the samurai elite that propelled Japan forward into an embrace of Western technology and political institutions.

4.3. The Meiji Restoration

Between the forcing open of Japan in the mid-1850s, the abrogation of the isolationist policy and the creation of treaty ports where foreigners enjoyed rights of extraterritoriality until the overthrow of the Tokugawa regime was a mere decade and a half. Shortly thereafter the Tokugawa system of fiefs and social classes was abolished and a new government bent on emulating various aspects of Western commerce, industry and national policy making emerged.[4]

The contrast with China is striking. A process that took over seven decades in China took less than two decades in Japan. Within a matter of decades a nationalist ideology centered upon the cult of the emperor that united elites encouraging rapid industrialization linked to building up military security and later on a encouraging a drive to hegemonic power in Asia — *fukoku kyōhei* (wealthy country/strong military) — was fashioned.

At the root of Japan's comparative success in responding to the West in contrast to China's feeble success lies the elite of late Tokugawa Japan, an elite driven by an ambition to get ahead in personal terms, ready and willing to jettison the institutions and ideologies of the past.

The overthrow of the *bakuhan* system is known as the Meiji Restoration because in theory it restored the emperor to power. Two fiefs from southwestern Japan — Satsuma and Chōshū — played a particularly important role in the brief civil war that ended rule by a *shogun* who governed as the protector of the emperor in theory, and in practice as a substitute for the emperor and the emperor's closest advisors. It should be noted that these fiefs had never enjoyed access to the highest circles of *bakufu* power under the hegemony of the Tokugawa rule. The *daimyō* rulers of these two fiefs had been on the losing side of the cataclysmic battle that ushered in Tokugawa rule in 1600. Like many other *daimyō* on the losing side they were too powerful to be ignored, too powerful to be denied a fief. That said, they were assigned territory in the outlying districts of Japan where their capacity to meddle militarily and politically, threatening the Tokugawa strongholds in central Japan (defended in large part by fiefs whose rulers had allied themselves with the Tokugawa forces prior to 1600) was severely constrained, in the southwest of the main island of Japan (Honshū) in the case of Chōshū and the southern island of Kyūshū in the case of Satsuma. That these two fiefs had been denied respect in the Tokugawa system made it easier for rebellious *samurai* in these fiefs committed to ending the *bakuhan* system to enlist the assistance of their more conservative compatriots who might otherwise have been inclined to stick with a tried and true Tokugawa regime that had kept the peace for over 250 years.

Three features of the Meiji Restoration stand out: eclectic political reform based upon creating hybrids melding the practices of a diverse group of Western nation-states with Japanese traditions inherited from the Tokugawa period; the rapid expansion of infrastructure — physical, human capital enhancing, and financial — associated with the development of the inorganic economy in the West; and the simultaneous development of the agricultural and industrial sectors, that is balanced economic growth. In all three of these arenas, members of the old elite emerged as members of the new elite.

In the political realm the hybrids of the Meiji Restoration are striking. The fiefs were abolished on paper, but persisted in an attenuated form in the sense that they were incorporated into a Western style prefectural system, prefectures through amalgamation (after two major waves of amalgamation over 200 fiefs were packed into slightly less than 50 prefectures). The sentimental feelings of former *samurai* and *daimyō* toward their old haunts to which generations and generations of their ancestors had been loyal could not be completely disposed of by an oligarchy committed to centralizing government in ministries operating out of the new capital of Tokyo. Creating prefectures that retained a reasonable flavor of Tokugawa cultural regionalism but were actually embedded in a new political and fiscal reality in which regional government hardly mattered at all exemplified the pragmatic nature of early Meiji politics.

Again a wide range of Western institutions culled from visits by Japanese delegations to various foreign countries — constitutions, parliaments, administrative codes for legal matters (including the incorporation of businesses), draft armies and navies, central banks and American style national banks, compulsory educational systems — were studied by the new Meiji oligarchy that mainly consisted of former *samurai* from Chōshū and Satsuma (hence known as the Sat-Chō oligarchy). Out of debates within this oligarchy emerged experiments in government, some plans adopted, then discarded, in part because the Western practices of certain countries were more compatible with institutions inherited from the Tokugawa era, in part because some proved to be more workable than others. A good example of that latter principle is in the field of banking: first the Japanese rulers tried establishing a system of national banks without a lender of last resort central bank along the lines of the National Bank model exemplified by the United States, only to abandon this in favor of a bank system organized around a key central bank, the Bank of Japan, that operated under guidelines established by the Ministry of Finance.

In short, much of the political reform of Tokugawa Japan took the form of eclectic gradualism, cautious lest it overly offend the feelings of elites losing status and influence in the welter of change. Indeed one of the main rallying cries of the Mejji Restoration — *fukoku kyōhei* ("enrich the country, strengthen the military") — was a big-tent umbrella ideology bring together the interests of rural landlord elites and merchants primarily concerned with *fukoku* and former *samurai* enjoying extensive training in military matters primarily concerned with gaining positions in the newly established army and navy, hence concerned with securing resources for *kyōhei*.

However some political matters, the policies of the Meiji Restoration aggressively contended with — or at least tried to take on — the Tokugawa past. One area concerned the emperor, in particular the cult of the emperor; another concerned the economic and political fate of the former *samurai* as a group; a third involved the imposition of a land tax based upon the market value of land not on rice yield.

Molding their political capital around the restoration of imperial rule, the Meiji oligarchy was intent on building modern Japanese nationalism around the emperor whose status had been severely denigrated under Tokugawa rule. Because the emperor was the nominal head of the Shinto cult one tool at the disposal of the oligarchy was forcibly converting Buddhist temples into Shinto shrines, a policy that they eventually backed off on in the face of concerted opposition. Another was to embed the cult of the emperor into the textbooks studied by Japanese schoolchildren in the compulsory elementary schools that were set up by the Ministry of Education established in 1871. Promotion of this policy garnered additional muscle after 1900. A third prong to this policy was formulating a German inspired constitution — the Meiji Constitution of 1889 — that declared that the "Emperor is sacred and inviolable" exercising legislative powers "with the consent of the Imperial Diet" and "supreme command of the Army and Navy." The Meiji Constitution took military decision making out of the hands of the cabinet, leaving it in the hands of the Emperor and the high command of the Army and Navy; left the issue of whether a party enjoying a majority in the Diet or the emperor would appoint the cabinet rendering responsibility for the making of basic policy directions ambiguous; and denied the proposition that sovereignty rested with the people, the rights accorded to the populace being circumscribed.

The second arena in which the Meiji oligarchy decided to take a sharp break with the past concerned the funding of *samurai* incomes. The *samurai* were too powerful as a political lobby group and too dangerous (threatening the lives of foreigners taking up residence in the treaty ports that were established), to ignore. That said, the Meiji rulers had abolished the fiefs, making obsolete the old system of allocating rice stipends on the basis of position with the *samurai* ranks of fiefs. At first the new government tried to cope with this problem by converting the rice stipends to money payments paid by the treasury. But this proved to be an excessive drain upon the public purse. So, in an effort to kill two birds with one stone — reducing the fiscal burden of the former *samurai*, bolstering the new national banking system — the government eliminated the money payments, replacing these with bonds issued to the former *samurai*. The recipients were encouraged to use these bonds as paid in capital for the new national banks.

Imposition of this policy angered many former *samurai* leaders including Saigō Takamori who was also irritated over the refusal of the oligarchy to approve an expedition attacking Korea (for refusing to recognize the new imperial government in Japan but also for wishing to remain as a vassal of China). Infuriated by commutation of the stipends to bonds and what he perceived to be pusillanimous position on Korea, Saigō retreated to Kagoshima prefecture which had incorporated the old fief of Satsuma within its boundaries, organized a rebellion known as the Western War or the Satsuma Rebellion. With the defeat of the Satsuma rebels by the new army, the oligarchy shored up its credibility, putting to an end once and for all threats of civil war emanating from the disgruntled and discredited wings of the former *samurai* elite.

However formulation of a land tax policy with the Land Tax Reform of 1873 did raise the specter of rebellion emanating from a second source, the agrarian populace. Under the policy the old rice tax was abolished, each piece of arable land being assigned a market value — estimated as the capitalized net revenue from rice cultivation (deducting costs of seed and fertilizer from gross earnings) — upon which a flat tax rate was imposed. Concern over the political repercussions of imposing this tax that became the main source of revenue for the Meiji government forced the officials administering the system by enumerating land in cultivation and assigning it value to turn a blind eye to under-registration of arable. For this reason scholars working with the pre-1890 arable land input and yield figures — reductions in taxation rates and the formulation of a policy forgiving owners of land for concealing arable — generally make some kind of adjustment for concealment of arable during the first several decades of the Meiji period.

In short, the new Meiji government did take a hard line on three major issues: the elevated status of the Emperor; the economic plight of the former *samurai*; and the value of agricultural arable held by rural landowners, hence landlord elites. In some arenas sharp discontinuity between the Tokugawa past and Meiji occurred, albeit in limited number of arenas. In general, continuity trumped discontinuity facilitating the transition for old elites seeking to prosper in the new environment.

In the field of infrastructure creation, the emphasis characteristic of the Tokugawa period on fostering transport and communications, education and literacy, and financial interaction through infrastructure continued, now enriched by institutional models and technology developed by the Western powers after the 18th century. With the initial assistance of Dutch engineers, national government ministries allocated resources for the dredging of harbors to accommodate deep hulled steamships. Breakwaters were put into place in key ports like Yokohama, Kobe, and Osaka. Flooding was addressed through the use of concrete blocks and iron for the fashioning of breakwaters and piers strong enough to tame the violent surges in water flow accompanying the torrential monsoon rains. With the aid of British experts and equipment telegraph systems and railroad track were laid out. British rolling stock was acquired for the new steam railroads by both government and by private companies alike. Moreover soon after electrification began to spread in the United States and Western Europe, as early as the 1890s, private companies in cities like Osaka began to offer electrical power initially generated by thermal means. Physical infrastructure construction funded by both private and public parties but regulated by government administrators became a major economic priority in the early Meiji period, both for practical purposes and to set an example, to make a political point, about how progress could be achieved through harnessing the techniques of the Western industrial revolution.

The approach to modernizing education, spreading basic literacy and fostering the development of a new elite group of administrators, managers and technical personnel — engineers, scientists — was designed to mobilize the skills and ambitions of the former elites. Elementary school education — first four years, extended to six — was made compulsory, teachers being recruited from the ranks of old elites. This served as the publically funded — through the imposition of taxes on local school districts — base for what evolved into a system consisting of three main levels, the upper and middle levels initially mainly serving the old elites who could afford entrance for themselves and/or their offspring.

At the apex of the top tier was the imperial university system — initiated with the establishment of the University of Tokyo that relied heavily on recruiting faculty from the Western countries in its early years, the system expanding gradually thereafter with the creation of more imperial universities in major cities like Kyoto and Osaka — that was supplemented by private academies eventually upgraded to university status during World War I period reforms of education. To the University of Tokyo flocked former *samurai* intent on becoming officials in key ministries or engineers and managers mastering.

Occupying a middle group between the base designed to improve the literacy and numeracy of the masses and the apex principally aimed at the former *samurai* elite was a host of private and public schools — middle schools, high schools, and normal schools on the academic side, vocational schools focusing on agriculture, iron and steel making, electrical machinery in the early 20th century — designed to supply technical expertise of a practical sort to those engaged in farming, accounting, factory supervision, management and engineering. To these schools flocked the children of landlords and wealthier merchants.

In the field of financial infrastructure, the Ministry of Finance took responsibility for supervising the Bank of Japan set up in the 1880s and for creating specialty banks like the Yokohama Specie Bank. Moreover, with the passage of legislation allowing private banks to be established with the permission of the Ministry of Finance — operating under the lender of last resort umbrella of the Bank of Japan — a host of small banks sprang up in rural areas started by landlords and merchants. In cities two types of banks emerged: large banks with multiple branches that became associated with the *zaibatsu* financial cliques and smaller banks that typically had only a single branch. This financial infrastructure was supplemented by a stock market whose operation was legitimized under a freshly minted commercial code largely based on Western models.

The emergence of the *zaibatsu* illustrates one of the key themes of this chapter, continuity between elites in the Tokugawa period and the new elites of the Meiji period. Basically a *zaibatsu* is a combine, a group of companies in diverse fields — banking, real estate, marine transport, marine and general insurance, mining, textiles, iron and steel, machinery making, railroads — held together with the cement of family ownership and/or control by a holding company. Two types of *zaibatsu* sprang up during the

Meiji period: from the ranks of merchant houses that managed to survive the transition from Tokugawa to Meiji, a select group of *zaibatsu* — notably Mitsui and Sumitomo — came into their own as powerful financial entities enjoying close ties to the Meiji political oligarchy.[5] A second type of *zaibatsu* was freshly minted during the Meiji period. The most famous example of the second type is Mitsubishi, founded by a former *samurai* from Tosa fief, Iwasaki Yatorō. Mitsubishi owned its origins to the taking on of orders for the transport of munitions for the national Army during the Western War, gradually diversifying outward into general commercial shipping, iron and steel manufacturing, shipbuilding and machinery production.

Drawing upon entrepreneurial talent harbored by the former *samurai* and merchant elites of the Tokugawa period and access to financing encouraged by the establishment of a banking system backed up by the Bank of Japan, the *zaibatsu* played a crucial role in the development of both finance and industry in Meiji Japan. The success of *zaibatsu* like Mitsui, Sumitomo, and Mitsubishi stands in marked contrast to the fate of the Bureau for Recruiting Merchants founded by Qing bureaucrats like Li Hongzhang.

One of the most remarkable features of economic development in Meiji Japan is its balanced character: infrastructure expanded and so did both agriculture and steam using manufacturing. The expansion of agriculture was largely due to the diffusion of best practice technique from the southwest regions where yields were relatively high to central Japan and especially northeastern Japan where yields were far lower. Breaking down the barriers of fiefdom was important. Information could now flow more freely since the tendency of fief governments to jealously guard their secrets was done away with when the fiefs were done away with. But equally important was the landlord elite in Meiji Japan. It was the literate landlord and the wealthy farmer who aggressively drummed up support for rice improvement associations, who sought out recommendations on seed varieties and irrigation methodologies, who lobbied for the building of railroad lines into districts, who sent children to agricultural vocational schools to learn what government experimentation stations were discovering, what veteran farmers in higher yield districts had to say about seeds, fertilizer, and the draining of fields.

Harnessing of Western technology in early Meiji industry also owes a heavy debt to the former elites of the Tokugawa period. Consider the rapid buildup of the steam power using integrated spinning and weaving cotton textile industry centered in the Osaka region. Instrumental in this expansion was a former *samurai* Shibusawa Eiichi who was initially recruited into the Ministry of Finance, going on to take up the presidency of the First National Bank established in Japan. Determined to move into actual manufacturing, Shibusawa moved into the cotton textile industry, establishing the Osaka Spinning Factory in the early 1880s, hiring a Japanese engineer Yamanobe Takeo away from London to manage the machinery put into place in his new establishment.

In sum, the rapid political transition from Tokugawa to Meiji Japan is paralleled by an equally rapid economic transformation. Crucial to this speedy transition were the actions of old Tokugawa elites — *samurai*, merchants, and wealthy farmer/landlords — who were joined by new elites emerging from the less advantaged segments of Tokugawa society. While Qing China struggled for seven decades with the Western challenge, Japan moved rapidly to respond successfully marrying newly discovered Western technology and institutional forms to those that had flourished during the late Tokugawa era. The result was the laying of the groundwork for accelerating growth in the first four decades of the 20th century, the topic of our next chapter.

Endnotes

1. For more details concerning the *bakuhan* system, see Mosk (1996, 2001, 2008).

2. On the income of *samurai* see Yamamura (1974).

3. See Mosk (1983). During the Tokugawa period, births were registered at the Buddhist temple, their names placed into a register maintained for each family associated with the temple. Typically registration only took place once a year, at Chinese New Years, and this was when the infant was given a name. Hence births eliminated by infanticide usually do not appear as either births or deaths in the temple registers exploited by contemporary scholars as estimating fertility and mortality levels for Tokugawa Japan.

4. This section draws heavily from the more detailed accounts in Mosk (2001) and in Mosk (2008), especially Chap. 3.

5. The selling off of government owned and managed companies to the *zaibatsu* is a good illustration of the close relationships formed between the Meiji oligarchs and the managerial elites that took charge of the day to day operations of the *zaibatsu* companies. 16 companies — 12 mines, four cotton and silk mills, and two shipyards among them — were sold off, many at "fire sale" liquidation prices — to the private sector, principally to the *zaibatsu*. For details see Wittner (2008).

Part III

Traps, 1910–1955

5

Growth Acceleration in Japan, 1910–1938

5.1. Agriculture and the Decline of a Rural Elite

Early Meiji Japan experienced a classic case of balanced growth. This phase of Japan's growth ended around 1910, after which economic growth became increasingly dualistic, older sectors like agriculture stagnating while heavy industry began to surge. Unbalanced growth took over.

Under balanced growth three sectors — agriculture, manufacturing, and infrastructure — all expanded, bolstering each other. The expansion of roads, railroads, and harbors reduced the costs of securing raw materials and energy — especially coal — a major concern to factory managers attempting to hold down costs in a competitive market economy. In turn expansion of factory production, concentrated in rapidly growing metropolitan centers on the Pacific coastline — Osaka, Kobe, Yokohama, Tokyo, and Nagoya all bristling with harbors that were eventually dredged to accommodate steamships — created demand for more infrastructure.

Agriculture was also important on both the supply and demand sides. The opening up of job opportunities (and the expansion of demand for raw materials) in manufacturing — cotton textiles and silk production, the processing of tea and soy sauce, and match making were growth sectors throughout the early phase of Japanese industrialization — created opportunities for farm households. Now they could send a daughter, occasionally a son, to a factory on a one year contract negotiated with a job recruiter for a mill; now they could sell their raw silk to a filature, their cotton bales to a steam driven spinning and weaving establishment. Farm households responded by increasing hours worked, by sending children to vocational school to learn how to use their time and other inputs used in farming more efficiently. This response is essential in the fundamental transformation of labor surplus economies discussed in Sec.2.1 of Chap.2. It is documented with quantitative evidence presented in the Statistical Appendix, particularly in Appendix Table A.7 and the text dealing with that table.

Moreover, because farm households in central and northeastern Japan were able to expand their output per hectare through the application of techniques and seed varieties pioneered in southwestern Japan during the late Tokugawa period, the agricultural sector as a whole expanded food production at the same time it supplied increasing volumes of raw materials to the burgeoning light industrial sector. Urbanization and industrialization — the shares of both urban and nonagricultural population increasing — tends to put pressure on the capacity of a typical farm worker to generate output sufficient to meet both his or her food consumption needs and the needs of a remainder of the populace. But in Japan between the 1880s and 1910 the increases in yield per hectare coupled with the surge in hours worked per farm worker kept up with the surge in demand for food. This was true even as population resumed growth in the post-1850 period.

Eventually the well of established techniques ran dry. Diminishing returns to the diffusion of best practice technique set in, the capacity to either adopt lock stock and barrel or modify and improve upon the advances made in the southwest over the previous centuries exhausted. By the end of the first decade of the 20th century this was the case. Short of further improvements — for instance new seed varieties that government experimentation stations were devoting resources to develop — Japanese agriculture was running up against limits to expansion.

How was the expansion of demand for foodstuffs due to continuing population growth and on-going urbanization to be satisfied? In principle Japan could secure this on at competitive prices on international markets, companies in the business of selling rice in cities securing the needed rice in Southeast Asia, in Vietnam, Thailand, and Burma (that was to some extent a frontier region that was rapidly increasing its production with the encouragement of British buyers). But this type of rice was not the sticky glutinous variety favored by Japanese consumers. In any case another option was available: outsource rice production to Japan's new colony of Korea — formally incorporated into the Japanese empire in 1910 — and in Taiwan, secured from China as a result of the Sino–Japanese War.

Encouraging Taiwanese and Korean farmers to adopt the seed varieties developed in Japan was relatively easy to do since colonial administrations were set up in both countries providing Japanese government officials with policy levers that supplemented pure market forces of supply and demand. The outbreak of rice riots that spread throughout Japan in 1918 — demand outstripped domestic supply — was the decisive flashpoint, the wakeup call, cajoling the government into aggressively promoted the imperial option. After 1918 Japanese imperialism took on an increasingly economic cast, policy makers in Tokyo looking toward colonies on the Eurasian mainland as potential suppliers of food, cotton, coal, and — as time wore on — cheaply manufacturing clothing like silk or cotton. The end of World War I ushered in a new era, Japanese Empire building moving forward under the twin logic of geopolitics — guaranteeing security through the staking out of buffer zones in which Japan was hegemonic — and economics.

As rice imports from the empire streamed into Japan the upward drift in the price of rice relative to manufactured goods — the terms of trade faced by farmers — that was occurring due to the slowdown in domestic supply growth ceased. This fact — combined with an end to the diffusion of best practice technique — turned village Japan into politically contested ground, tenants who worked the land under fixed rent contracts aggressively demanding rent reductions. As long as prices for rice had been going up nominal rent increases demanded by landlords were acceptable. After all landlords were instrumental in promoting improvements in farming and the relative price of rice — its purchasing power in terms of other goods available for purchase — was improving. The drying up of technological progress and the downward pressure on domestic rice prices due to the expansion of imports did away with this state of affairs. Increasingly tenants joined agricultural unions, attempting to exercise clout and gain leverage through collective voice.

The landlord elite, once viewed as a group promoting progress in farming, was increasingly viewed as parasitic. In principle the Diet might have passed a land reform bill alleviating tensions between tenants and land owners. However attempts to pass land reforms ran into staunch political resistance. Elite landlords as a group enjoyed substantial political influence. Indeed many landlords had been elected to the Diet representing their rural districts. At first this state of affairs reflected the fact that voting was limited to the wealthy in the decades immediately following the setting up of the Diet, But even after the franchise was extended to all adult males in the mid-1920s unseating the landlords was difficult in part because landlords had played, and continued to play, an important role in bringing infrastructure to agricultural districts. As elected officials they could and did lobby on behalf of their districts, arguing for roads, post offices, harbors, and improved river embankments. Pork barrel politics was rampant in the Diet. As a result attempts to pass a land reform bill providing a modicum of relief to tenants failed.

During the 1930s landlords — under attack by tenant unions during the 1930s — became increasingly aggressive, terminating contracts, dispatching farmers from lands they had farmed for generations, combating the unions. In districts where job opportunities in factories for farmers who lost access to land were relatively good, this did not generate excessive unrest, the number of landlord/tenant disputes recorded by the authorities being minimal. This was the case throughout much of central Japan, particularly in the areas that fed into the labor markets for Osaka, Kyoto, and Nagoya. But in the northeast where population growth amongst the agrarian population was substantial and job opportunities in nonagricultural endeavors poor, tensions ran high and the number of disputes soared.

Landlords were a group in decline. Stave off as they might legislation to buy them out as set prices under some kind of sweeping land reform legislation, they were increasingly viewed as a spent force in terms of their contributions to farming. Under increasing pressure to create positive incentives to bolster food production during World War II, the government did bring into the floor of the Diet reforms bolstering tenant interests paving the way for the wholesale land reform that took place during the American Occupation.

5.2. Infrastructure and Urbanization

While agriculture entered into an era of desultory growth in the early 20th century from which it did not really recover until the 1950s, infrastructure expanded at a brisk rate, especially in the period 1904–1911. The driving force was electrification promoted by the development of intercity and intra-city electrical railroad and electric tramway networks.[1]

Throughout the period between the 1870s and the late 19th century politicians had been contemplating the nationalization of the steam railroad network in Japan. In 1906 a law that provided for the purchase of private steam railroad lines became law. By the end of 1906 over 65% of all track used by steam railroads was nationalized; further legislation in 1907–1908 basically completed the task, creating a Railroad Department elevated to full ministry status as the Ministry of Railroads in 1920. In carrying out this nationalization the government did not want to fully abandon a coordination approach that it had found useful during the early Meiji department, government investors working in tandem with private investors in developing infrastructure. Government bureaucrats and politicians alike viewed market competition as a good thing, a driving force behind successful industrialization in the Western countries. As a result legislation permitted a few steam railroads to escape being swallowed up by the Railroad Department. More important the government decided to allow non-trunk intercity — and intra-city — lines to be created and to be operated by either private companies or by local municipal governments. What made the trunk line steam railroad network especially attractive as a target for government management was its potential strategic military value, its latent capacity for moving troops and arms.

An important offshoot of creating a massive company Japan National Railroads with deep financial resources that it could tap is a famous reverse engineering project. Recounting it here helps hammer down a point made in the Statistical Appendix to this book, namely that the sharp dichotomy between total factor productivity growth and augmentation of labor is false. By augmentation of labor in this context is meant investment in the training of engineers. Relying on the fact that private companies like Hitachi and Mitsubishi Denki (Mitsubishi Electric) employed a substantial corps of competent engineers, the government promulgated a national self-sufficiency policy in 1909. Under its aegis it set forth specific guidelines creating a designated factory system that permitted the government to contract out projects to a select group of companies. With this system in place Japan National Railroads purchased steam locomotives from four different countries — American, British, and German — directing technicians to disassemble each locomotive down to its smallest components. Mingling the parts and components of the engines generated from this process, Japan National Railroads and the team of designated factory engineers created a design unlike that of any of the designs used in manufacturing the original locomotives purchased. Without fear of being sued for patent violation, the Japan National Railroads proceeded to order a host of "uniquely Japanese" locomotives to use as part of its rolling stock.

By redirecting a market oriented railroad sector hungry for exploiting opportunities in the transporting of passengers and freight into intercity arena, nationalization of the steam railroad network gave a strong push to electrification in Japan. Companies sprang up linking cities within a region to one another. For instance in the Osaka region, Kyoto was linked to Osaka by two electric railroad lines running along opposite sides of the Yodo River; Osaka was linked to Kobe with a line running parallel to the seacoast southward; Osaka was linked to Nagoya by a line running along the seacoast northward. To help cover the significant capital costs they incurred in building the rail and acquiring the rolling stock, these new electric railway companies naturally diversified into other arenas spun off from transport. They sold electricity to communities along the lines. They bought up real estate along the lines in relatively sparsely populated areas, later offering it for sale in the vicinity of stations that they opened up subsequent to purchasing the land. In this way they created satellite bedroom communities from which employees who worked in major metropolitan centers like Osaka could commute. They diversified into bus transport, providing private bus lines that commuters could use in getting to their train stations. They built department stores close to station complexes in major metropolitan centers; they opened up amusement parks and hot spring resorts along their lines; they even purchased baseball teams. In short they took on the character of regional *zaibatsu*.

Investment in the electric railroad network facilitated the creation of geographical scale economies particularly in the industrial belt stretching along the path traced out by the old Tōkaidō road created by the *bakufu* to facilitate and monitor the passage of *daimyō* and their retainers to and from Edo to meet their *sankin kōtai* compulsory attendance obligations. This region encompassed five of the six most important industrial and commercial metropolises of industrializing Japan: Tokyo, Yokohama, Nagoya, Osaka, and Kobe. The sixth major city, Kyoto, was not far distant from Osaka and linked to it with two electric railroad lines. As Japan's nascent industrial belt, the Tōkaidō region created geographic scale economies that contributed to total factor productivity growth. It is important to keep in mind that actual buildup of physical capital — train lines, hydroelectric delivery networks, and bedroom communities — was required to realize these scale economies. As with the reverse engineering project of the Japan National Railroads total factor productivity growth is inextricably linked to accumulation, in this case capital accumulation.

5.3. Manufacturing

The massive buildup of infrastructure — railroads, electrical power grids, dredged harbors — that took place in Japan between 1904 and 1911 fueled a surge in manufacturing between 1911 and 1919. Key to this was the distribution of electric power. Electric power is important because harnessing electricity fosters the unit drive system, machines in a plant operating independently of all other machines because each is plugged in separately to the factory's electrical system.

Steam power is completely different. In a typical steam driven factory characteristic of the 19th century one central steam engine provides power to a myriad of machines that run off it through a system of transmission belts and straps. The central steam engine for the establishment must be powered up in order for the machines to be powered up. Small factories cannot afford to mechanize because they cannot afford to utilize a huge steam engine to power a few machines. During the age of steam power most factories were not mechanized unless that were large; and because steam engines generated tremendous heat factories had to be multi-storied, constructed so that the steam could be siphoned off and dissipated through the top.

Once electricity became available to individual households and small and large factories alike, small plants — usually operating as subcontractors for larger factories to which they supplied components — could mechanize. To gauge the impact of electrification consider the following: in 1909–1910 when steam engines and turbines provided over 80% of the first mover power capacity in Japanese factories, less than 21% of factories employed under 30 workers were mechanized with inanimate power while over 88% of factories employing 100 workers or more were powered. By 1930 over 80% of factories with under 30 workers were mechanized (over 99% of factories with over 100 workers mechanized in that year). Electrification closed the gap between large and small plants, making subcontracting in both light and heavy industry possible.

By driving down the costs of energy supply and transport of raw materials the infrastructure boom paved the way for a massive industrial expansion. Between 1911 and 1919 industrial production soared. As a result income per capita surged, a fact evident in Appendix Table A.4. To some extent World War I contributed to the expansion of industrial production as most of the Western European countries were embroiled in the conflict, blockading oceanic trade including trade with Japan. As a result fledgling sectors of manufacturing — electrical machinery and shipbuilding — enjoyed temporary relief from foreign competition. To be sure, American firms continued to export to the Japanese market until the United States joined the European war in 1917. At the conclusion of fighting in Europe in 1918 foreign goods once more flowed into Japan but tariffs imposed on many manufactures continued to give a modicum of relief to Japanese companies that were moving down their cost curves.

Japanese firms moved down their cost curves for four reasons: absorbing and adapting foreign technologies acquired through licensing agreements; innovating (the creation of the Type G automatic loom developed at Toyoda Automatic Loom Works is a classic example of innovation); learning by doing, that is speeding up and streamlining production processes through experience; and exploiting scale economies both internal and external to individual firms. Many of the scale economies were external to firms that benefited by crowding together in metropolises like Osaka. In the big six cities firms locating near each other mutually benefited each other: through the selling of components produced by one company purchased by another (subcontracting is a classic illustration of this principle); through the joint creation of a labor pool that attracted migrants from rural areas thirsting for well paying job opportunities; through the driving down of costs for raw materials, say for raw cotton imported from India or the Middle East, or coal imported from the Eurasian mainland. There is no doubt that electrification — especially use of hydroelectric power — made a major contribution in the arena of scale economies, reducing energy costs, slashing back on demand for coal, cutting transport costs for domestic freight carried on trains, and giving a fillip to the mechanization of small scale firms that became subcontractors for larger gigantic enterprises including those spawned by the *zaibatsu*.

By channeling financial resources from already established profit centers (like textiles or mining) to new industries (like electrical machinery) the *zaibatsu* played a crucial role in pushing forward the product cycle characteristic of Japanese trade. The product cycle is easily described in terms of the ratio of net exports to domestic production in an industry or sub-sector: at first imports exceed exports, then — through the process of import substitution in which domestic output supplants imports — the net export to domestic output ratio comes up from negative figures to zero; then the ratio becomes positive; and finally, as the industry moves abroad to other countries where production costs — especially labor costs — are lower, the ratio becomes negative once again. Described as the "flying geese" pattern by a Japanese economist employed by the Japanese Imperial Army during the 1930s, Akamatsu Kaname, the idea is that the lead goose cuts the wind for the follower goose who draft off of the lead goose and off each other, the entire flock of geese moving in a V-shaped pattern.

In Japan's case the lead goose within manufacturing was textiles, the ratio of net exports to domestic output climbing from 0.04% in 1887–1897 to 3.1% in 1930–1938. Machinery production is an excellent example of a follower goose, the ratio climbing from –21.2% in 1887–1897 to –0.1% in 1930–1938. For manufacturing as a whole the ratio of net exports to domestic production climbed from –0.4% in 1887–1897 to 0.9% in 1930-output and exports of manufactures throughout the period 1887–1940.[2] This data well illustrates the product cycle at work.

The "flying geese" pattern is also an example of positive feedback, exports from lead goose industries paving the way for follower industries. Positive feedback also characterizes the relationship between industrial expansion and infrastructure expansion. During the 1920s the focus of the nonagrarian economy shifted back towards infrastructure — massive hydroelectric grids were completed that brought energy from the Japanese Alps to the great industrial conurbations of the Tōkaidō industrial belt; paved road networks supporting the use of internal combustion engine using trucks, buses, and automobiles were laid down; and higher education was revamped to increase the supply of technically trained professionals including engineers — mainly because the massive industrial expansion of the 1910s had put immense pressure on the infrastructure sector. In turn the infrastructure buildup of the 1920s paved the way for the massive industrial surge of the 1930s. The figures in Appendix Table A.4 bear out the hypothesis that periods of slower growth associated with infrastructure buildup — infrastructure output investment eating up resources in the short-run, setting the stage for subsequent industrial output expansion — set the table for faster growth that followed upon its heels.

5.4. The Demographic Transition Commences

Positive feedback also occurred in the arena of human resources, especially after the 1920s. This is evident in terms of heights, weights, and other physical characteristics of the Japanese population (see Panel B.1 in Appendix Table A.6).[3] It is also evident in terms of expansion of educational attainment (see Panels C.7 and C.8 in Appendix Table A.6). And more importantly it is evident in the decline of fertility and mortality — especially infant mortality — documented in Panel A.4 of Appendix Table A.6. The importance of the last of the three phenomena, the demographic transition, has already been discussed. This section looks at the commencement of the process that occurred during the period between World War I and World War II in Japan.

It is important to keep in mind that the demographic transition in Japan probably did not begin prior to World War I, or if it did so only isolated populations within the country participated in it. Indeed the quantitative evidence — unfortunately incomplete hence not fully trustworthy — suggests that birth and death rates rose in Japan from the late 1850s until the early 1920s. These trends are not wholly implausible. It is quite possible that both fertility and mortality rates rose. Four possible reasons stand out: the opening up of the country to intercourse with the rest of the world, bringing Japanese in contact with a number of infectious diseases that were generally absent in the Tokugawa era; the spread of industrial employment that spawned infectious industrial diseases, respiratory tuberculosis being an especially virulent problem in ill-ventilated textile mills in which cotton particles spread throughout the shop floor; urbanization that brought migrants from rural districts into rapidly expanding densely populated cities inadequately supplied with sewer and water treatment systems and host to a variety of airborne infections; and the diffusion of seed varieties from the southwest to the northeast, promoting the conversion of dry fields to paddy in the northeast, thereby increasing the number of farms and the demand for labor in these freshly staked out farming households, hence for children supplying this labor. A rise in birth rates — especially in the relatively isolated villages of the northeast that lacked adequate public health — may have generated an increase in infant mortality risks, lowering life expectancy under age one and raising overall mortality.

Urbanization was certainly a factor in any initial rise in mortality. Mosk and Johannson (1986) demonstrate that in 1908 age standardized mortality rates were highest in the industrial urbanized prefectures of Japan that also enjoyed the highest incomes per capita. The rates were lowest in the low income per capita rural districts in that year. By 1930 this pattern had been erased: mortality rates were largely the same everywhere. This is largely attributable to the spread of public health measures in the great cities — to sanitized water, the growing use of flush toilets, the building of sewer systems, the spread of health cooperatives with the encouragement of municipal, prefectural, and national health authorities, and to the lower costs per person for supplying medical facilities (large hospitals with a host of specialties) — in urban areas. Indeed by the 1950s, mortality rates were far lower in cities than they were in rural isolates.

Public health improvements go a long way to account for the falloff in both case rates for infectious diseases like cholera, typhoid, smallpox, and diphtheria. For instance in 1920–1929, the number of cases per 100,000 persons for cholera was 0.65; for typhoid 80.15; and for diphtheria 25.05.[4] In1960–1969 these rates were — respectively — 0.0; 0.85; and 4.85. Equally important were reductions in death per case, largely attributable to an improvement in the standard of living, particularly better nutrition, and more effective medicine, the medical profession after 1940 being beneficiaries of the development of the antibiotic drugs. For instance in 1920–1929 deaths per case were 64% for cholera, 36.9% for dysentery, 20.4% for typhoid, 18.9% for smallpox, and 23.9% for diphtheria. By 1960–1969 these percentages had fallen to the following: 0.0% for cholera; 1.0% for dysentery; 1.6% for typhoid; 0.0% for smallpox; and 1.9% for diphtheria. Applications of the germ theory of disease were pushing up life expectancies in Japan.

For fertility, the story basically hinges on the diffusion of control over reproduction as realized in the reduction in the incidence of high parity — high birth order — births. While marriage ages for women did tend to rise in Japan between the 1930s and the 1960s, partly driven by growth in the employment opportunities for young adult women outside of farming, the main reason for falling birth rates (see the declining gross and net reproduction rates in Panel A.4 of Appendix Table A.6) was an increase in the conscious control exercised by married couples over the number of offspring. Once couples had the number of children they wanted — say two — they stopped having children. Increasingly they regulated their reproductive behavior in terms of specific parity goals. The ultimate reasons for this change in behavior — evident for high-income urbanized prefectures in the 1930s — are clear enough, although assigning specific weights to the various factors is tricky: a shift in the control over children's careers from parents to state managed institutions like the compulsory educational system; the falloff in infant mortality; growing job opportunities for married women; a rise in the opportunity cost — earnings forgone — of raising children, especially for women; and growing social acceptance of restricting family size.

In short, that Japan began the demographic transition between the World Wars, reaching low levels for mortality and fertility by the 1960s, is a perfect example of positive feedback, economic development promoting changes in the demographic realm that contributed to further economic

development, especially to increases in the demand for advanced schooling. Interwar Japan was experiencing accelerating growth stemming from
positive feedback.

5.5. The Disintegration of the *fukoku kyōhei* Consensus

Crucial to Japan's escaping the trap of economic stagnation and subjection
to Western political and military intervention was the embrace by political, military, economic, and cultural elites of an ideological and political
umbrella *fukoku kyōhei* ("enrich the country, strengthen the military").
Beginning in the early 1900s commitment to this umbrella that emphasized
the common interests of economic, political, and military elites began to
erode. In the place of common, symbiotic, interests, elites began to per-
ceive that the idea of building military prowess conflicted with the idea of
improving national per capita income and economic success. Increasingly
elites conceived of policy in terms of tough trade-offs, strengthening the
military eroding rather than facilitating the drive to economic success.

During and after World War I the breakdown in the *fukoku kyōhei* consensus intensified. During the 1920s those elites putting "wealthy country"
priorities first had the upper hand, only to see the militarists promoting
"military strengthening" take charge over the political agenda during the
1930s. In many ways this state of affairs was the result of Japan's escaping
the traps China fell into when the Western powers broke it open in the first
half of the 19th century: in particular the success of the new political elite
in building up armies and navies that not only squelched internal threats
that erupted in domestic civil war, but also defeated China and Russia on
the international stage.

It is useful to formulate the issues in terms of a few simple equations.
According to Eq. (3.1) introduced in Chap.3, the military potential of a
political entity (M), an empire or nation-state is a function of its economic
size (Y), the rate it converts economic resources into military goods and
services (m, typically by taxing the population combining this with a draft of
civilians or the purchase of soldiers' services on the market) and the relative
price — compared to other prices prevailing in its economy — of exerting
military force with military goods and services available to it (p_{mf}). That is:

$$M = f(mY, p_{mf}) = f(myP, p_{mf}), \qquad (5.1)$$

where y is income per capita and P is population.

This general formula ignores geopolitics, namely the fact that it is more difficult to exert force across great distances than short distances, and it is more difficult to exert military force across the water than across the land. For two political entities i and j separated by distance d_{ij} the relative military potential of i with respect to j is a function of the following:

$$M_{ij} = f[\text{rat}(mY), \text{rat}(p_{mf}), d_{ij}], \tag{5.2}$$

where $\text{rat}(mY)$ is the ratio of the military potential of each country:

$$\text{rat}(mY) = m_i Y_i / m_j Y_j \tag{5.3}$$

and

$$\text{rat}(p_{mf}) = p^i_{mf} / p^j_{mf} \tag{5.4}$$

is the ratio of relative prices for military goods and services in the two jurisdictions.

Complicating the algebra a bit further is the fact that a home country enters into alliances with foreign powers in order to achieve a modicum of security through the commitment of allies to provide military support in the event that the home country is attacked.

Taking these equations into account we can express the trade-offs facing policy makers in Japan in terms of both domestic and international geopolitical considerations. As long as Japan was building up its infrastructure and military services in order to suppress domestic rebellion and speed up the transport of troops, the private business sector benefited. For instance nationalizing the railroads served both domestic military concerns — moving troops to the periphery of the country — and domestic economic interests. But once it acquired an empire requiring military resources in order to secure it — Taiwan, Korea, and the South Manchurian Railroad — the situation changed. Spending on infrastructure in Korea or Taiwan was not subject to the same domestic political log-rolling logic that applied in the domestic case.

In short whether the levels of m and government subsidy reducing p_{mf} should be high or low became an increasingly contentious issue after Japan's empire expanded onto the Eurasian mainland.

During World War I the fact that the European powers were embroiled in conflict with one another in the European arena and the United States was attempting to stay out of the conflict altogether reduced China's capacity to call on European or American support in the event that nearby Japan pressured it. The result was Japan's Twenty One demands delivered in secret to Yuan Shikai leader of the Republic of China established in the aftermath of the collapse of the Qing dynasty. Divided into five groups of demands, the fifth group gave Japanese advisors to the Chinese government virtual control over decisions about policing and acquiring military goods and services. Japanese diplomacy was exploiting three facts on the ground during World War I. Japan's economy had grown relative to China's (see Panel D in Appendix Table A.2). The relative price of Japan's military goods and services was lower that enjoyed by the Chinese political leadership (because Japan's heavy industries were beginning to produce military hardware that was comparable to Western military hardware in a technical sense and cheaper than imported equipment). The Western powers other than the United States (committed to an Open Door policy aimed at preventing one or a combination of foreign powers from dominating or carving up China) with interests in China (especially England) were embroiled in the European conflict, hence unable to counter Japan's designs on China by brandishing military force.

In short during World War I those elites in Japan — particularly in the Army — interested in expanding Japan's empire on the Eurasian mainland tried to force the hand of the political and economic elites in Japan wishing to maintain good relations with the Anglo–American powers. For instance the *zaibatsu* traded extensively with the British Empire, Western Europe, and the United States. They were an important lobby group enjoying influence and clout with key politicians. They tended to oppose the militarists wishing to beef up Japan's military presence in the Asian theater through direct government expenditure, tax breaks, and other subsidies for sub-sectors of manufacturing producing military hardware.

In the eyes of some Japanese policy makers, including some of the military elites, maintaining friendly relations with the United Kingdom and the United States was not only attractive from an economic point of view. It was also appealing in terms of military strategy. The United Kingdom had a vast sprawling empire throughout the Asia-Pacific. Its formal empire included Australia and New Zealand in the South Pacific; India; and Hong Kong. It also enjoyed considerable informal leverage in China, particularly in southern China and in the Yangzi River delta. It maintained a massive navy, allocated partly to the Atlantic, partly to the Pacific and the Indian Ocean. As for the United States, its commitment to naval buildup in the early

20th century meant that it was emerging as a major oceanic power capable of exerting force in both Atlantic and Pacific waters. American acquisition territories in the Pacific, as a result of the settlement of the Spanish–American War over the Philippines; as a result of the overthrow of the Kingdom of Hawaii the island archipelago of Hawaii — both events occurring in 1898 — forcibly echoed American claims to be a major Pacific power.

Putting matters bluntly in the terms set forth in Eqs. (5.2)–(5.4), the strategic logic of avoiding direct confrontation with the Anglo–American powers is clear (and must have been clear to informed Japanese military planners). In both the United States and the United Kingdom, the relative price of military hardware was low. In terms of distance, the Anglo–American powers were natural strategic rivals of Japan in both Asia and on the Pacific. Moreover, economic size was an issue, the United States, a major industrial power by the late 1880s, boasting the largest economy in the world; and the total economic size, the combined national incomes, of the countries in the British Empire was equally awe inspiring.

In the aftermath of World War I and the various treaties and agreements ushering out of it, the geopolitical environment shifted considerably. Ideological divisions opened up, Communism, Fascism, and liberal democratic ideals contending; old empires were broken up, creating a proliferation of nation-states intent on building their domestic economies behind protectionist tariff walls; the gold standard under which countries on gold maintained fixed exchange rates with one another collapsed; and the international body designed to stave off future conflicts between the major powers, the League of Nations, proved to be relatively powerless, in part because the United States Senate refused to ratify the treaty that would have guaranteed American entry into the League as a full member.

Ideological divisions became intense once Communism was established in Russia after a bitter civil war in which American, European, and Japanese troops intervened against the Red Army. Under Stalin, Russian Communism took on totalitarian and nationalist trappings, operating under the banner of Socialism in One Country while still promoting Communist and anti-imperialist ideals movements under the aegis of the Cominterm (the Third International). Countering the class warfare ideology of Marxist–Leninist inspired Communism was Fascism that promoted corporatism, bringing together labor, management, and government in national front organizations whose goal was national glory and aggrandizement. In Italy during the 1920s, later on in Germany during the 1930s, the establishment of Fascist regimes went hand in glove with the harnessing of radio and the mass media to totalitarian programs, glorifying Mussolini in Italy, Hitler in Germany. Opposing these totalitarian tendencies were the Anglo–American governments and their allies in Europe, the British Empire, and Latin America.

Adding to the international friction brought on by ideological divisions was the floundering of international trade that had expanded by leaps and bounds in the late 19th century, technological advances — the growing use of steam transport coupled with the telegraph — accompanying expanding adherence to a fixed exchange rate system under the British dominated gold standard. After World War I, European countries trying desperately to reduce the burden of their World War I war debts, resisted going back on the pre-World War I par ratios that fixed their currencies relative to gold bullion. So the gold standard system floundered, creating uncertainty in international financial circles, impeding the flow of international capital that had helped stimulate trade expansion prior to 1914. Economic nationalism amongst the fledging nation-states of Europe and the Middle East — the Austro-Hungarian and Ottoman Empires broken up — threw up additional barriers to trade expansion, tariff wars breaking out as countries adopted "beggar-thy-neighbor" policies.

This international background played into the politics of the Japanese Diet, increasingly taking the form of a two-party system, cabinets being established by the majority party. With both of the major parties dependent on campaign financing proffered by the *zaibatsu*, cooperation with the Anglo–American powers became a linchpin of foreign policy making during the 1920s. Indicative of this tilt is Japan's participation in the Washington Conference of 1922 that brought together the United States, the United Kingdom, France, Italy, and Japan, the world's major naval powers. Under the terms of the Washington naval treaty, total tonnages were established for the navies of the five powers. Japan's tonnage limit was set at 315,000 tons, far short of the 525,000 ton limits set for the United States and the United Kingdom (the French and Italian tonnages were set at 175,000 tons). The logic underlying these limits was that the United States and the United Kingdom were two ocean powers — requiring fleets on both the Atlantic and the Pacific — while Japan was a single ocean power, only requiring capital ships on the Pacific.

Throughout the 1920s and early 1930s opposition to the Washington naval treaty limits grew in the ranks of Japan's military elites. Adding fuel to the flames of anti-Anglo–American sentiment amongst both military and political elites was the growth of membership in ultra-nationalist secret societies that advocated Japanese domination of Asia under the aegis of the Japanese emperor. Representative of this ideological tendency were the views of Kita Ikki who advocated nationalization of key industries in Japan, radical redistribution of wealth, restrictions of the size of private landholdings in farming under a sweeping land reform scheme. Kita called for a military *coup d'etat* that would lead to a military government committed to creating a command and control economy within Japan and an aggressive military policy towards Asia. While the views of the ultra-nationalist fanatics did not amount to Fascism as was it was being practiced in Europe, they mimicked many basic Fascist principles. Japanese ultra-nationalism was definitely opposed to Communism and it was definitely skeptical about the virtues of Anglo–American liberal democracy. By the early 1930s, many of the younger officers in the Imperial Japanese Army and navy became converts to the ultra-nationalist line, seeing Japan's destiny as the true savior of Asia, driving out the Western powers under the banner of the Japanese emperor.

In sum throughout the 1920s, opposition to the pro-Anglo–American alliance grew stronger amongst Japan's military and political elite. When the United States slipped into the Great Depression of the 1930s, opposition to liberal democratic principles and adherence to market oriented doctrines further weakened. Military cabinets took over in 1932, remaining in place until 1945. Within the ultra-nationalist camp that exercised increasing sway over the military elite were two major factions, the Imperial Way and the Control faction. The Imperial Way faction was heavily influenced by right wing radicals like Kita. It was visionary, believing Japan's military effort should be directed against the main ideological enemy of the Japanese emperor, Communism, Russian Communism in particular. More rational in its thinking, the Control faction believed that Japan's destiny on the Eurasian continent was to solidify its hold over China. In early 1936, the Imperial Way faction struck, seizing control over the capital, executing the finance minister and the Privy Seal. Countering the revolt was the Control faction. Ultimately successful in squashing the rebellion and negotiating surrender of the rebels, the Control faction came out on top, seeing to it that the leaders of the Imperial Way faction were swiftly tried and executed.

By the mid-1930s the logic of Japanese militarism coupled with the deterioration of the international geopolitical and economic environment (the floundering of trade and the slipping of the United States economy into the Great Depression) turned its political leadership completely against the Anglo–American powers. Japan withdrew from negotiations in 1936 that were aimed at renewing the Washington naval treaty, guaranteeing its actions that the treaty would lapse in 1937. After the Control faction took over the foreign policy agenda in 1936, Japanese diplomacy became even more strident in rejecting the demands of the Anglo–American powers. Committed to expanding Japan's military presence in China, Japan's political elite directed the country's foreign policy toward active military confrontation with the United States and the United Kingdom. At the same time in an effort to bridge the gap between the Imperial Way and the Control faction, Japanese diplomats signed the Anti-Cominterm Pact with Germany that made public its desire to combat international Communism, while secretly laying the groundwork for an anti-Russian military alliance with Germany.

During the first four decades of the 20th century, Japan's economy experienced positive feedback, growth feeding on growth. The result was acceleration in growth. The interaction of the expansion of infrastructure and the expansion of industry exemplifies this process. So do the inception of the demographic transition and the improvements in height, weight, and educational attainment of the Japanese population. But the same era that saw Japan decisively escape the traps that China fell into after the mid-19th century, also saw the political consensus achieved in the early Meiji period under the *fukoku kyōhei* rubric break down. During the 1920s those advocating a policy of cooperation with the Anglo–American powers committed to liberal democracy prevailed, infuriating and alienating ultra-nationalists and militarists bent on expanding Japan's imperial reign over Asia in the name of the Japanese emperor. By the mid-1930s the ultra-nationalists and militarists had fully seized control over the policy agenda. Japan was inexorably moving towards full-scale conflict in China, a step that would eventually lead it to attack the United States at Pearl Harbor.

Endnotes

1. For details see Chap. 5 of Mosk (2001).
2. For these and related figures see Table 6.1, p. 184 in Mosk (2001).
3. Mosk (1996) analyses the so-called anthropometric characteristics of the Japanese population over the period 1900–1985 in terms of net nutritional

intake. Net nutritional intake is a mix of calorie, protein, vitamin, and other nutrient food input (gross nutritional intake) minus decrements due to fighting off infectious disease and decrements stemming from physical work. The argument developed in Mosk (1996) is that net nutritional intake is especially crucial for children, youths, and young adults prior to their reaching terminal heights, weights, and muscular capacities.

4. The figures in this paragraph are drawn from Table 9.2, p. 296 in Mosk (2008).

6

Agriculture and Industrialization in Republican China, 1911–1935

6.1. A Divided Elite

With the collapse of the Qing Dynasty, China became a republic. At least on paper its political elite turned its back on dynastic rule; or rather most of its political and military elite turned away from dynastic rule.

Perhaps it would be more accurate to say that China entered into a period of political instability and uncertainty, its elites deeply divided over how to elaborate a single set of unifying political principles that would serve as a vehicle for holding together post-imperial China as a single nation-state. Was Confucianism to be embraced as a unifying doctrine or rejected as the ideological foundation of a defunct dynastic system? If the Chinese political elite was to follow the example pioneered by the Meiji oligarchs who grafted Western political and commercial institutions and Western advances in the fields of science and technology onto indigenous cultural and political principles harkening back to the distant past like Shinto and the cult of the emperor, how was it to weave Confucianism into the new nationalist fabric?

If Western doctrines were to be followed which doctrines were most compatible with the economic realities of China? Communism as exemplified by Marxism–Leninism that advocated gathering political power in the hands of an anti-imperialist avant-garde party committed to the dictatorship of the proletariat? A variant of democracy for instance a presidential system (the American version) or a constitutional monarch developed either along British (strong parliament, weak king or queen) or pre-World War I German lines (strong rule by a Kaiser). Or would totalitarian rule built around the cult of a charismatic leader — for instance a preeminent military figure — developing along the lines that ushered in post-World War I Fascism be best for post-dynastic China?

With the fall of the Qing China's political, military, and economic elites split into factions promoting one or a mixture of these options. That Chinese elites failed to rally around a "big tent" umbrella ideology like *fukoku kyōhei* that (albeit only temporarily) served to create unity among Japan's Meiji era economic, political, and military elites is hardly surprising. During the long-era of post-Opium Wars Qing decline, virtually every elite group in China had fallen under suspicion and opprobrium. Military leaders had to call upon Western advisors and troops in order to quell uprisings like the Taiping and Nien rebellions; China's military had repeatedly suffered defeats at the hands of both Western powers and Japan. The social basis undergirding the prestige and power of the gentry in the countryside and the urban bureaucracy was deeply compromised with the collapse of the Confucian based civil and military examination system. With the prop of Confucian examination certification pulled out from under it, the class of landlords in rural China was increasingly seen as parasitic, in many regions of China no longer enjoying respect for its contribution to local political stability.

In the treaty ports the nascent entrepreneurial group of compradors found its interests deeply intertwined with the activities of Western and managed trading ventures and — after the Treaty of Shimonoseki — both Western and Japanese managed factories, banks, and merchant houses. Could government officialdom intent on developing a nationalistically oriented program of economic development work comfortably with compradors in developing a market oriented program of economic development that required massive infusions of capital for both infrastructure and industry? Could compradors enjoying close ties to British, French, German, Russian, and Japanese commercial interests be trusted to jettison these connections, throwing their energy and talent into wholly Chinese owned and operated activities?

The fates of Sun Yat-sen inspired republicanism and the May Fourth Movement illustrate this theme.

The disjoint between Sun Yat-sen's stated political philosophy — the intellectual foundation for the Chinese Nationalist party (the Guomindang) that he helped create as a vehicle for establishing hegemony over China — and the actual behavior he and his colleagues exhibited in promoting revolutionary agitation against the Qing and establishing the new republican government that took over from the Qing on January 1, 1912, illustrate how divided was the Chinese elite.

On paper Sun Yat-sen's philosophy was deeply grounded in American republican ideals. This reflected his actual experience. Born into a peasant family in 1866, Sun Yat-sen migrated to Hawaii to live with an elder brother. The elder brother had started his career on Hawaiian soil as a laborer, his fortunes blossoming ultimately when he became a prosperous merchant. Enrolling in schools in Hawaii, Sun Yat-sen became adept in English, eventually became an American citizen strongly influenced by American political ideals especially as espoused by Abraham Lincoln. Permeating Sun's political philosophy, notably his formulation of the three principles of the people were the loosely cobbled out of his versions of principles Lincoln eloquently summarized in his Gettysburg address: the principle of government "of the people" or civic nationalism uniting all ethnic groups in China under an anti-imperialist banner; democracy set out largely along Western style constitutional lines; and government "for the people," policy makers taking responsibility for equalizing economic opportunities and outcomes, achieved in part through the equalization of rural land holdings. In actual fact Sun's interpretation of these principles differed wildly from the interpretation given to them in the United States. Sun's version was enriched by Confucian concepts completely alien to 19th century American democracy.

Contradicting the three lofty principles Sun advanced were many of the concrete actions of Sun and his political allies. He joined a secret society, a triad, allying himself with those who specifically rejected transparent principles of democracy; eschewing calls for popular rebellion, he formulated plans for a *coup d'etat*; living abroad during most of period 1894–1911 (in Hawaii, Europe, the United States, and Japan), he devoted most of his efforts to fundraising for rebellions directed against the Qing.[1]

Named the president of the provisional republic — recognized by the southern provinces but not the northern provinces of China — lacking the allegiance of a strong military body, Sun was forced to transfer power to Yuan Shikai who was in charge of the Beiyang army that dominated northern China. Under the terms of this arrangement Yuan Shikai became the president of the new republic in exchange for directing his forces against the supporters of continuing Qing rule.[2] When Yuan Shikai became increasingly dictatorial — eventually deciding to be declared emperor (an effort that ultimately failed) — Sun organized an unsuccessful rebellion against Yuan, eventually returning to Japan where he secured asylum.[3]

Upon China's descent into military chaos after 1916, regional commanders building up their own armies upon the death of Yuan Shikai and contending for power, Sun returned to China, becoming the head — generalissimo — of a military government in Guangdong province in southern China and the chief spokesman for the newly established Guomindang party. It was in Guangzhou that he appointed his protégée Chiang Kai-shek commandant of the military forces that he hoped to use against the militarists in the north. In order to gain financial and military support from the newly established government in the Soviet Union and the Cominterm, he reorganized the Guomindang along Leninist lines in the early 1920s, forging an alliance of convenience with the newly established Chinese Communist party under the encouragement of Soviet advisors.

In short, time and time again Sun jettisoned his principles of republican democracy in order to further his political program through military means, forging alliances of convenience with secret societies on the right and Marxist–Leninists on the left willy-nilly as a matter of political expediency. To be sure, no successful politician is free of the taint of resorting to political expediency from time to time. That said, the actual behavior of Sun Yat-sen smacks of political opportunism of the highest order, ingratiating himself to each audience he addressed — to nationalists, opponents of landlordism, and militarists — as a modus-operandi. Given the deep divisions in the Chinese elite this was an excellent strategy for survival. But adopting it denigrated the basic principles that Sun espoused, to some extent making a mockery of the basic principles of Chinese republican nationalism. Securing power took precedence over principles

Reflecting the divisions and intellectual turmoil among the Chinese elite that Sun contended with and to some extent exploited is the May Fourth Movement or the new culture movement. The May Fourth Movement is named for demonstrations that commenced on 4 May 1919, in Beijing. These demonstrations were organized by students shocked at the weak-kneed responses of the Chinese government to the terms of the Treaty of Versailles, the German sphere of influence in China — a zone in Shandong province in North-eastern China — was transferred to Japan that, as an ally of England hence an enemy of Germany during World War I, had occupied the territory. This was a violation of the conditions under which China entered World War I as an ally of France and England. Anti-imperialist, anti-Western, and anti-Japanese sentiment that spread throughout China in the closing decade of the Qing dynasty was intensified by the agreements reached in the crafting of the Treaty of Versailles. This sentiment fuelled the flames that exploded in the May Fourth Movement.

In response to the anti-Western, anti-Japanese, and anti-imperialist focus of the May Fourth adherents were a combination of very specific political demands — the abolition of extraterritoriality, the canceling of the twenty one demands by Japan, the return to China of the German concession in Shandong — mingled with a more general expression of unease with Western values, Western and Japanese commercial activities taking place in the treaty ports, and attendant foreign military presence protecting non-Chinese communities residing on Chinese territory.

From the anti-Western sentiment sprang a variety of different intellectual and political stances, at least three of which completely contradicted one another or at least led to radically different conclusions about the direction Chinese politics, Chinese regeneration, should take. One line of analysis promoted neo-traditionalism, the search for indigenous Chinese values that owed nothing to foreign influence, the veneration of Chinese essence and national character as expressed in historical documents and folklore. But what was national essence? Proponents of those committed to seeking out a Chinese essence tended to argue that it was not Confucianism that they believed rationalized a family system that impeded individualism and subjugated women. A second line of analysis took a contrary tack recommending the promotion of science and engineering, therefore a policy of importing ideas from the West and from Japan. But was this a real rejection of the West? A third line of analysis was taken up by converts to Marxism — Leninism who focused on organizing peasants bitter against landlord elites in rural area, workers in the industrial sector that was mainly concentrated in Shanghai, Manchuria, and the treaty ports, and merchants interested in driving out foreign firms under the banner of anti-imperialism. But was Marxist–Leninism not an import from the West?

As a practical matter the main concrete expression of the May Fourth Movement was the organizing of boycotts of Western and Japanese goods and general strikes aimed at applying pressure on government officials involved in formulating foreign policy.

In short a plethora of views, a cacophony of competing ideals and political level venerating Chinese tradition contended with the view promoting science and engineering. At the level of practical politics and party organization, two main parties emerged: the Chinese Communist party and the Guomindang Nationalists. The ideological gap between the two parties created in the early 1920s — the Communists and the Guomindang — was immense. Adherents of the Guomindang did not reject Confucianism and were more favorably disposed toward compradors and landlords than were the Communists. Still both parties were backed by advisors from the Soviet Union intent on driving out Japanese and Western imperial interests from China thereby creating an important ally for the new Soviet government in the east.[4] As a result alliances of convenience could and were hammered out between the Communist Party and the Guomindang. However reflecting the fact that alliances were alliances of convenience not resting on a common set of principles, these alliances broke down periodically.

In short, by the mid-1920s three groups began contended for political and military hegemony within China: Communists, Guomindang nationalists, and regional militarists that controlled local armies. These three groups periodically coalesced in alliances, regional militarists being co-opted by the two main political movements, military logic increasingly trumping politics.

6.2. Landlordism and Surplus Labor in Rural China

Given the failure of the political, economic, and military elites to rally behind a common banner, governing China became a haphazard affair. One of the consequences is a dearth of publications issued by republican government agencies documenting conditions in village China. That said there are a few central government statistical volumes published between 1914 and 1921 that contain data for selected rural regions of China.[5] In addition there are some useful official publications reporting research carried out by local government agencies.[6]

The main documentation that we do have for Chinese village life largely emanates from special field-level surveys carried out by a variety of organizations. Of these three stand out and are widely utilized by researchers studying republican era village life: studies carried out by the National Research Institute of Social Sciences Academia Sinica during the 1930s published in English by the Institute of Pacific Relations; surveys of 2866 farms throughout China carried out between 1929 and 1933 by students of John Lossing Buck, an American economist teaching at the University of Nanjing; and surveys of Northern Chinese villages — in Shandong and

Hebei — carried out after 1938 by the Japanese South Manchurian Railway Company's survey division.[7]

Studies based on these surveys tend to support one of two contesting views about the principle structural problem faced by most Chinese farmers during the republican period. One view is that parasitic landlordism and money lending had so impoverished rural China that many peasants were pushed to the brink of starvation, flooding or drought leading to famine; the other view is that surplus labor was endemic throughout much of village China.[8]

Reflecting the focus of this book we consider surplus labor first. For China quantitative evidence is harder to come by than it is for Japan. Panel B.1 in Appendix Table A.7 testifies to the suspicion that there was redundant labor in both agricultural and nonagricultural communities in interwar China.[9] Qualitative evidence is more abundant as the following quote from a book by Mallory (1928: p. 19) based on direct observation suggests:

> *"There is a tremendous labor surplus. With only an acre and a half to an average family of 5.7 members hundreds of labor days per family are wasted in the course of a year."*

Again, a study by Huang (1985) zeros in on the same problem. Consider the following quote[10]:

> *"For a poor peasant family farm with surplus labor and struggling on the margins of hunger ... it made sense to continue using that labor as long as the marginal product of labor remained above zero. A person nose deep in water, we might say, would do almost anything to rise above the surface."*

And again[11]:

> *"The problem facing the poor peasants of the North China plain in the twentieth century, however, was not a scarcity of labor relative to employment opportunities, but the reverse: underemployment and an overabundance of labor."*

> *It is clear that the problem was far more acute in interwar China than in interwar Japan. Why?*

The answer lies in infrastructure: physical infrastructure (e.g., roads, railroads, harbors, telephones, and telegraphs), human capital enhancing infrastructure (e.g., schools, hospitals, public health clinics), and financial infrastructure (e.g., banks advancing loans to factories, postal offices offering postal savings opportunities). As is evident from Panel A of Appendix Table A.9 in interwar Japan the density of this infrastructure was already well advanced; in China it was not. In Japan opportunities to diversify into nonfarm employment, perhaps on a short run contract in a textile mill, were opened up for rural communities all over the country, especially in central Japan but even in far-flung communities in Northern Honshū and in southern Kyūshū as roads and railroads penetrated the hinterland. Factories sprang up because banks sprang up mediating between savers and lenders. This was not true to nearly the same degree in China.

What about landlordism? On this issue there is considerable controversy. Refuting the views of the "distributionist" school that argued that the distribution of land holdings and income was becoming increasingly unequal in China during the period 1900–1935, Myers (1970) provides estimates suggesting that both land holding and income were becoming more equal, rather than less equal, during the period leading up to Japan's full scale invasion of China.[12] He argues the land fragmentation was increasing over the period 1880–1935, suggesting most landlords were renting out smaller and smaller total acreages. Land fragmentation is certainly consistent with the fact that Chinese families practiced partible inheritance and population was growing over the period 1880–1930 as attested to by the estimates in Panel A of Appendix Table A.6 to this volume.

Still it is clear enough that landlordism was an issue. It is clear because the Chinese Communist Party was able to garner political support in rural China operating under the banner of radical land reform, taking land away from landlords without compensation. Why? Several reasons explain why landlordism was a bigger problem in late 19th and early 20th century China than it was in Japan. Because infrastructure expansion and industrialization proceeded at a far slower pace in China than they did in Japan, poor farmers lacking substantial acreage had fewer opportunities to escape rural distress by tapping into opportunities for employment in factories and in construction. Compounding tensions over rent levels and access to land was the legacy of the Qing dynasty Confucian examination system that awarded high status — and political influence — to the rural gentry who tended to be the landowning class.

This said, it is thrust of this section that surplus labor — rather than landlordism — was the principal problem festering rural village in republican China. The grim threat of famine that hovered over China, especially in the North, fomenting rural unrest and upward spikes in mortality, went hand in glove with the existence of surplus labor that was endemic throughout most of China.

6.3. Manufacturing Expansion in Shanghai and Manchuria

That surplus labor existed to the extent that it did in Republican China was closely linked to the slow growth of the manufacturing sector. This is apparent in Panels A.1–A.3 of Appendix Table A.3 and Panels C.3 and C.6 of Appendix Table A.9. Not only was Chinese factory production limited in scope — being largely confined to the light industrial sub-sectors of manufacturing (e.g., silk reeling, cotton spinning and weaving, and food processing) — it was also limited in geographical extent, mainly concentrated in the lower Yangzi delta (particularly in Shanghai and the southern sector of Jiangsu province and the northern sector of Zhejiang province spreading out from greater Shanghai) and in Manchuria. This geographic concentration is borne out by the estimates appearing in Ma (2008: 381) the location of Chinese manufacturing capacity in the late 1930s was as 16.6% in Manchuria for a total of 62.7%. Chinese factory activity was not only limited in scope it was also limited in geographic extension.

By comparison Japanese industrialization spread out geographically. Emerging as major industrial metropolises were the six big cities — Tokyo, Yokohama, Nagoya, Osaka, and Kobe that formed the backbone of the emerging Tōkaidō industrial belt along the Pacific coastline of the main island of Honshū and Kyoto — linked together through a network of steam railroad and intercity electrical railroad lines by the end of the World War I.

Moreover unlike the Japanese industrial belt that where economic activity was dominated by domestic enterprises in both Shanghai and Manchuria foreign commercial and political activity played a major role.[13]

Reflecting its geographic position — bordering Korea part of the Japanese Empire after 1910 and Russia to the north — foreign activity in Manchuria mainly revolved around Russian and Japanese economic and political/military interests. In the northern sector of Manchuria was a Russian zone of influence through which ran the Chinese Eastern Railway; in the southern section was a Japanese zone of influence secured that included the South Manchurian Railway guarded by troops of the Kwangtung Garrison of the Japanese Army that also defended the Japanese controlled Kwangtung Leased Territory. Japan had secured the South Manchurian Railway and the right to maintain troops in the aftermath of its defeat of Russia in the Russo–Japanese War of 1904—1905. Prior to the 1920s the main economic activities in Manchuria consisted of coal mining (the right to mine coal at Fushun transferred from Russia to Japan after 1905) and soybean production and processing although a number of Chinese and Japanese firms began to produce glassware in Manchuria using waste glass at first, switching over to processes exploiting Manchurian deposits of silica stone, sand, and limestone after World War I.[14] Prior to the 1930s Manchuria was basically a frontier economy exploited by three groups: Chinese, Japanese, and Russians.

Shanghai was different. It was urban, densely inhabited, a classic case of a treaty port city. Opened to foreign trade in 1843 by the British Shanghai grew to become a mighty conurbation in the Yangzi River delta as a divided city, one section exclusively reserved for foreigners mainly consisted of an International Settlement initially run by foreign merchants (a separate French Concession was administered by the French community resident in the metropolis), a second section including the original walled Chinese city reserved for Chinese residents and businesses.[15] Its growth facilitated by being located in the one of the most productive rice growing areas of China — during the Ming and Qing periods supplying vast amounts of tribute rice to Beijing that were poled up to the capital on the Grand Canal — Shanghai was a natural transport hub, connecting to major cities like Nanjing that were further up the Yangzi River by water, lying across from the southern Japanese island of Kyūshū on the East China Sea.

Drawing upon a rich legacy of handicraft silk production that had blossomed in the Yangzi River delta spreading throughout the two provinces of Jiangsu and Zhejiang, Chinese merchants dealing with Western commercial interests in Shanghai naturally began to aggressively outsource raw silk in the Shanghai hinterland. As a result China's raw silk exports jumped in volume.[16] Indeed during the period 1870–1905 Chinese exports of raw silk exceeded Japanese exports. However around 1909 Japan's exports spurted past those of China's: Japanese export volumes growing by leaps and bounds during the 1920s while Chinese volumes began faltering.[17]

Why did Japan's silk reeling exports supplant those of China? The evidence suggests that the Japanese industry was able to generate higher quality silk denier — or at least to standardize the quality of the output — while relentless driving down costs. Quality in the Japanese industry improved because well trained managers graduating from vocational schools and universities were able to develop a set of incentives — grading workers on the basis of both throughput and denier quality — managers induced improvements in quality coupled with increases in output volumes per worker.[18] The spread of compulsory education also helped. Evidence assembled by Hunter (2003) suggests that workers who could read were better able to acquire skills and more disciplined in the behavior, in short easier to train and manage.

Similar arguments apply to cotton textiles. The Japanese industry took off rapidly, employment in the spinning sector jumping from 8.2 thousand in 1889 to 250.1 thousand in 1920.[19] Productivity gains were associated with technological improvements to be sure — the introduction of ring spinning and high drafting was important as was the development of scientific cotton blending that mixed different types of cotton in order to produce a blend that was cheaper than the best staple but unlikely to break easily during spinning — but so were the improvements in education for managers and rank and file shop floor workers alike. Evidence in support of this argument appears in Panel C.6 of Table A.9 in the Statistical Appendix. Japanese mills operating in China — mainly in Shanghai — had a cost advantage over Chinese mills that was partly attributable to a lower wage bill per unit of output produced. To be sure avoiding the *lijin* tax was an advantage enjoyed by the Japanese mills. In addition the Japanese mill could raise funds for capital acquisition in Japan at lower interest rates than generally applied in China. But the Japanese mill was more efficient in utilizing labor, presumably because Japanese managers were better equipped to direct workers and fashion incentives designed to improve productivity.

Why did Japanese firms aggressively push into the treaty ports setting up factories in cities like Shanghai after the signing of the Treaty of Shimonoseki?[20] Securing access to the huge Chinese consumer market was a factor. Taking advantage of the fact that the wages prevailing in China were lower than those in Japan was a consideration. Driving down costs of carrying on import and export trade was another. For instance consider the import of cotton from India: ships sailing back from Bombay to Osaka would naturally stop in Shanghai, unloading some raw cotton, securing some cheap low count Chinese yarn for instance, before sailing on to Japan. In particular the trading company arms of the *zaibatsu* became very active in the Chinese treaty ports, making loans, carrying on trade between Japan, China, India, and Europe. [21]

During the republican period Chinese manufacturing the geographic expanse of Chinese factory nonhandicraft manufacturing was extremely narrow.[22] Bottled up in a few enclaves it was kept relatively insulated and protected from fighting between regional warlords that destabilized China between 1916 and 1928 leaving a legacy of resolving political disputes through the gun rather than through political compromise. Regional political fissures interacted with the highly restricted regional concentration of Chinese industrial activity creating an environment in which most of China remained pre-industrial and poor while a few districts managed to pull away, insulating themselves from the sea of poverty that lapped up against their shores.

6.4. Regional Fissures

The extremely low density of infrastructure — human capital enhancing (health and education), financial (banking), and physical (harbors, roads, hydroelectric power grids, railroads) — evident in republican era China was both cause and consequence of the regional political and military fissures within the country.

Between 1916 and 1928 hundreds of armed conflicts broke out throughout China. Regional warlords raised armies, extracted taxes from the peasants and merchants in the regions they controlled, constructed plants to produce arms and military goods, managed the opium trade.[23] The typical warlord either sought hegemony for himself or at a minimum wished to stake out a position of power that could not be violated when the country was finally reunified. To further their aims they printed worthless currency, undermining commerce; forced the cultivation of opium in place of producing rice or other foodstuffs, thereby contributing to famine; and encouraged banditry. Most of the warlords were conservative in their outlook — some were staunch advocates of Confucianism, others were nominally Christian — and generally devoid of ideology.

In many ways the lack of infrastructure contributed to warlordism. The lack of infrastructure enhanced the degree of labor surplus existing within most of rural China. Underemployed idle youth, poorly educated and lacking viable options for earning a respectable standard of living, is readily recruited into armies, is more than willing to form bandit gangs when conditions are chaotic. The lack of physical infrastructure made it harder to organize national level campaigns aimed at defeating warlords. The lack of a strong nation wide banking system made it harder for any government claiming authority over the nation as a whole to raise a military force sufficient to defeat regional warlords.

At the same time the existence of on-going internal fighting made it hard if not impossible to build and maintain railroads and hydroelectric grids, to create a stable currency, to enforce standards for a national compulsory educational system.

A case in point is the fact that both the Guomindang and the Communists co-opted on occasion and/or made alliances of convenience with particular warlords in order to generate sufficient military force to carve out regional enclaves of power. Taking over the mantle of power over the Guomindang upon the death of Sun Yat-sen (in 1925) — and taking on the title of generalissimo — Chiang Kai-shek hammered out an alliance of convenience with a group of 34 southern Chinese warlords, defeating some, absorbing others — putting together a military force consisting of six main armies during the years 1926 and 1927. Moving northward Chiang's forces took Wuhan, eventually moving onto Nanjing and Shanghai where the banks and wealthy compradors were located. Hence the financial resources that could be cajoled and coerced into providing funds required to mount an even more powerful military campaign ultimately aimed at securing hegemony over all of China. In a bid to stave off political competition over the complexion of a future national Chinese government from the Communist party Chiang took advantage of his entry into Shanghai to arrange a deal with the Shanghai underworld gangs who proceeded to kill thousands of Communist Party supporters within the metropolis.

With the military success of the Northern Expedition Chiang Kai-shek was able to set up a Nanjing based government that operated under a five power model of Republican government formulated by Sun Yat-sen prior to his death.[24] Two of the key agencies set up under this new government was the Control Yuan aimed at combating misfeasance and corruption and the Examination Yuan aimed at standardizing the conditions of recruitment for civil service positions, promoting efficiency and honesty in governmental affairs.[25] In actual reality one of the principal motivations for setting up the Control Yuan was to use it as a device for weakening the power bases of warlords who had been co-opted by the Guomindang, attacking them for corruption or misuse of public monies if they proved too difficult to work with.

It is clear that securing control over funding both for future military campaigns and for establishing a state managed enterprise system consisting of national companies managed by government bureaucrats was a key goal of the new republican government set up in Nanjing.[26] With this in mind the government decided to create new banks and nationalize several existing ones. It was struggling with the problem of a lack of financial infrastructure. As late as the 1930s the density of banking remained low in China despite modern banking building upon a mixed legacy of banks set up prior to the collapse of the Qing dynasty: Shanxi or ticket store banks that were government oriented and mainly operated in the Yellow River zone of northern China; business oriented "native" banks that mainly functioned in the Yangzi River delta; government managed banks like the Imperial Bank of China set up in 1897; and foreign banks, particularly British and, after 1895, Japanese.[27] The upshot of the banking reforms carried out by the Nanjing government in the early 1930s was a massive shift in the private/public balance of bank assets away from the private sector to national banks. Building on this program of reforms designed to increase government control over the monetary and credit system the Nanjing government carried out a currency reform in 1935, formally taking the Chinese currency off of the silver standard, nationalizing all silver in circulation against payment of legal notes issued by national government institutions.[28]

By the mid-1930s a republican government operating under principles laid down in the Guomindang Party claimed hegemony over China. It was not a strong claim. It had managed to take control over a relatively undeveloped banking system, carrying out currency reform. It was attempting to control and constrain the actions of warlords who were loosely affiliated with it through the Control Yuan. It was attempting to recruit dedicated and honest public officials through the Control Yuan. Despite limited success in these areas, the challenges it faced were immense. It faced a bitter political rival in the Communist Party, and domestic military opposition at the hands of warlords who still operated in many regions of China. In addition it faced a fearsome foe in the Japanese Army entrenched in the South Manchurian Railway zone. Moreover, the threat of famine amongst the peasantry in the countryside hovered over the economy, darkening the political landscape. Addressing rural problems was not a strong suit of the new republican government that was focusing its main attention on building up the urban industrial economy that was highly regionalized. As the Guomindang was to learn to its chagrin, mobilizing political support among the peasantry not garnering support in the cities was to prove the true key to fashioning a viable program of nationalism for modern China.

Endnotes

1. Sun turned towards fomenting revolution after he failed to gain a hearing from Li Hangzhang regarding moderate proposals for a national reform program that Sun drafted in 1894. Li's snub of Sun was partly due to Sun's lack of classical Confucian education, Sun having been educated abroad. In late 1894 Sun created his first secret organization which aimed at overthrowing Qing rule, the Revive China Society, in Hawaii. Throughout much of the period

when he was organizing rebellion against the dynasty he lived abroad, notably in England and Japan. Arriving in Japan after 1897 he was lionized by Japanese Pan-Asianist "men of determination" even taking on the name Nakayama ("central mountain"). For an excellent brief account of Sun's activities see p. 148 ff. in Fairbank (1986).

2. The actual arrangement of transfer of power was hammered out between competing governments for post-Qing China, one formed in the north and the other in the south. The negotiators arranging a peace between the two competing governments thereby creating a single republic were persuaded to support Yuan over Sun by dint of Yuan's military experience suggesting force was more important than principles in the setting up of the new Republic. Yuan Shikai began his ascent to power as a protégé of Li Hangzhang. His advance was largely based on his military expertise, in particular his modernization of the new North China army. While his knowledge of civil affairs was limited, he did attempt to carry out significant reforms during his brief presidency lasting from his assumption of the presidency until his death in 1916. Among other things his government pioneered the use of local levies to fund modern schools and local police forces an initiative that garnered only partial success during the republican era in part due to constraints on funding. Funding at both the levels of central and local government was an on-going problem during the republican era — see Panels A.1 and A.5 of Appendix Table A.3 — as it had been during the Qing period and before. In order to raise funds to "defray the costs of the revolution toppling the Qing dynasty" the new government sold off the granaries that had been maintained by the Qing rulers, thereby increasing the probability that famine would break out, especially in northern China. On this point see p. 68 of Mallory (1928).

3. Sun did leave an important intellectual legacy for the republican government established in Nanjing in 1928: a model for a five power constitution for the Republic. Under this model citizens of the Republic were guaranteed four rights — suffrage, recall, initiative, and referendum — the fifth power accorded to the state granting the state the functions of administration, legislation, adjudication, examination, and censorial control. Sun's model was laid out in a speech he gave in 1924. See pp. 81–83 of Thornton (2007) and p. 29 of Strauss (1998).

4. Beginning in 1924 — and reflecting the principles laid out by Sun Yat-sen albeit in a watered down form — the Guomindang did adopt a moderate program of land reform for the peasantry, adopting policies designed to open up arable to poor distressed farmers and advocating a 25% reduction in land rents. On this point see p. 98 of Tawney (1964). This program fell short of the more radical attack on landlordism advocated by the Communists particularly after the Maoist faction of the party committed to building its base amongst the mass of peasantry took over control of the Communist movement in China.

5. See p. 28 of Lin (1997).

6. For use of data published by the Shanghai Social Affairs Bureau see Faure (1989).

7. For a discussion of the National Research Institute of Social Sciences Academia Sinica research see p. 14 of Myers (1970). For use of the data collected by students of Buck see p. 287 ff in Rawski (1989) and p. 55 in Tawney (1964). For extensive use of the South Manchurian Railway Company data see Huang (1990) and Myers (1970).

8. Tawney (1964) incorporates both views in his analysis. He emphasizes poor land management, inadequate infrastructure (in my opinion an important reason for the existence of surplus labor in rural China) and landlordism.

9. Citing data collected by Buck Riskin (1975: p. 69) estimates rural idleness at 1.7 months per able bodied man amounting to 14% of the year. For another study that cites surplus labor as a major impediment to republican era Chinese agriculture see Chao (1975) who employs a definition of surplus labor — the marginal product of labor falling below the costs of subsistence for that labor — that differs from the one that I employ in this study.

10. Huang (1985: p. 180).

11. Huang (1985: p. 195).

12. Studies conducted by the National Research Institute of Social Sciences Academia Sinica emphasize unequal distribution of land ownership, parasitic landlordism and exploitative money-lending practices. Basing his analysis on a surplus labor interpretation Huang (1985) argues that income distribution was actually worsening during the late 19th and early 20th centuries, because managerial farms operating with hired labor were more efficient than family farms. He argues that managerial farms were better able to take advantage of commercial opportunities opened up by increasing trade with the Western powers and Japan. For other estimates of income distribution in pre-1949 China, see Brandt and Sands (1992).

13. Beginning with the signing of the Anglo-Japanese treaty of commerce and navigation in London in 1894 that abolished extraterritorial rights for British citizens in Japan, the Japanese government moved to eliminate all of the special rights granted to the Western powers by the Tokugawa government. By 1900 it had achieved this goal. It also secured the right to freely set its own tariffs although the right to do so did not commence until the early 20th century.

14. For details on the development of the Manchurian economy prior to the takeover of Manchuria by the Japanese army in 1931–1932, see Chao (1982) and Sun (1969). Under Qing rule the right to reside in Manchuria was originally restricted to Manchu people, Chinese immigration being forbidden (though it did occur to a limited extent some Chinese moving there in defiance of the ban). After the Taiping Rebellion, the Qing dynasty opened up Manchuria to migration from the rest of China and population increased jumping from around 3.3 million in 1860 to 19.7 million in 1914 and 31.3 million in 1930. One of the Twenty One demands made by Japan in 1915 concerning the right of Japanese nationals to migrate freely to Manchuria enjoying the right to purchase land (the Japanese military viewed the creation of an emigration

"safety-valve" as one of its contributions to solving political tensions between landlords and tenants in those regions of Japan where the number of farm households was rapidly increasing). While the Chinese government did agree to allow Japanese to purchase land and establish farms outside the territories leased to Japan — in the South Manchurian Railway zone — it did so with reluctance, discouraging the immigration of Japanese in actual practice. This was a source of friction between Japan and China that contributed to the decision of the Kwangtung Army to engineer a phoney attack on the railway as an excuse for defeating the Chinese warlord who managed to control most of Manchuria.

15. For details on the negotiations setting up the foreign settlements in Shanghai see p. 61 ff in Murphey (1953). For all intents and purposes, administration of greater Shanghai was carried out by foreign consulates operating in the International Settlement and the French Concession. A Chinese magistrate did help the consular administration handle adjudication cases involving Chinese. But until 1925 a Shanghai Mixed Court was the only real body expressing Chinese political power in the metropolis, the vacuum of Chinese government being filled by an underworld dominated by the Green Gang that generated revenue through extortion, control of drug trafficking, and management of prostitution. On these points see pp. 177–179 in Fairbank (1986).

16. For details concerning the modern Chinese silk industry see Bell (1992) and Li (1981).

17. According to pp. 45–46 in Hunter (2003) the number of female silk reeling workers employed in filatures in Japan — over 80% of the workers in the filatures were female — increased from 172.9 thousand in 1895 to 234 thousand in 1930 (Hunter argues that these numbers are underestimates to some degree).

18. For instance account books were kept for each worker listing luster and strength of thread produced, number of reels generated, and so forth. See p. 117 in Mosk (2008) and pp. 186–187 in Hunter (2003). Local community associations all over the silk producing regions of central Honshū — mainly in Gifu, Gumma, Nagano, Saitama, and Yamanashi prefectures — created umbrella organizations aimed at ferreting out markets abroad and producing specifically for those markets.

19. Figures secured from Hunter (2003: 45–46).

20. For details on the specific provisions of the Treaty of Shimonoseki regarding Japan's access to treaty ports in China see pp. 172–173 in Peattie (1989).

21. See, for instance, Wray (1989).

22. Testimony to the fact that Chinese manufacturing outside of Manchuria was largely concentrated in the lower Yangzi provinces of Jiangsu and Zhejiang — the opportunity to generate household incomes in excess of those generated in most of rural China being largely limited to those districts — is the fact that Chinese in central China and in southern China tended to be shorter than those Chinese residing in the lower Yangzi provinces. On this point see

the study based on health examination records conducted at various Chinese government enterprises and agencies during the 1930s and 1940s carried out by Morgan (2004).

23. For an extensive discussion see Sheridan (1983).

24. See footnote 3 in this chapter for the major features of the five power model.

25. On the setting up and functions of these two agencies see Strauss (1998) and Thornton (2007).

26. For a discussion of the setting up of a state managed enterprise system see Bian (2005).

27. On Chinese banking see Cheng (2003).

28. One of the reasons for taking China off of the silver standard was the decision of the United States Treasury to purchase silver in the mid-1930s, thereby driving up the price of silver on international markets, hence forcing up the value of China's official exchange rate with respect to other currencies like the United States dollar and British pound sterling. Upward movement in the exchange rate for China's official currency tended to depress the level of Chinese exports and enhance the volume of China's imports.

7

Militarism, 1930–1945

7.1. A Changing Geopolitical Environment

Beginning in the early 1930s militarism took hold throughout the Eurasian land mass.

Given the command and control nature of military organizations the spread of militarism was linked to the spread of government agencies for the overseeing of national economics distrusting untrammelled adherence to markets. As well the growth in militarism ushered in an era of cynical alliances of convenience based roughly on the principle that "my friend is the enemy of my enemy." With alliances of convenience military elites can increase the effective resource base they are able to tap for raising arms and recruiting soldiers and/or they may be able to neutralize threats to their military actions wielded by nearby powers. Under alliances they may garner the opportunity to tap into superior technologies for making weapons enjoyed by their allies, or superior methods of military organization. In short cunning duplicitous strategy making accompanied attempts to control economic activity through centralized state planning agencies.

In China military elites had already taken hold of the political agenda after Yuan Shikai's demise in 1916 launching a full decade of internecine warfare. The success of the Northern Expedition launched by the Guomindang under Chiang Kai-shek did lead to the co-opting or defeat of many of China's warlords. Moreover Chiang himself rose to prominence as a military leader, continuing to think in military terms — obsessed with fears of Communist rebellions and Japanese aggression — after assuming the mantle of political leader of the Nationalist government ensconced in Nanjing.

Early 1930s witnessed the ushering in of totalitarian Fascist regimes in both Germany and Italy. The political organizations that launched Fascist leaders like Hitler and Mussolini on their road to power had a strong military flavor, their propaganda machines exploiting the power of radio and motion pictures in order to venerate their leaders as strong figures more than willing to resort to military measures in order to seize or revive earlier national glory. Marshalling national resources in a bid for hegemony within European and northern Africa was a natural agenda for the Fascist dictators of the 1930s in Europe.

That the Fascist model had a strong appeal to Chiang Kai-shek demonstrates how entrenched was the logic of militarism within the upper echelons of the ruling elite of the Guomindang. Creating a cult of the personality movement within the Guomindang — known popularly as the Blue Shirts — consisting of a few thousand military officers loyal to Chiang himself, Chiang worked at building up his image as a European style Fascist dictator. In point of fact while he tried to launch a New Life Movement through a carefully calibrated propaganda campaign, his ability to hold onto supreme power as the leader of the Guomindang reflected his eclecticism. Responding to the deep divisions with the political and economic elites of China, he tried to appeal to a variegated audience of elites: on the one hand he was a sincere Methodist, lobbying the Christian community in China for resources; on the other hand his ethical statements reflected classic Confucianism; and like the leaders of the Qing dynasty before he allowed rampant corruption to spread throughout his administration.[1]

The appeal of following the example of Yuan Shikai, becoming a dictator, by taking on the trappings of a Hitler went hand in glove with Chiang's anti-Communist stance. Trading on his anti-Communist credentials Chiang negotiated with the German government, securing the kind of military advisors who were playing a major role in German rearming under the aegis of Hitler and the Nazi party. Indeed, had Germany not been drawn in an proto-alliance with Japan with the signing of the anti-Comintern Pact, it is possible Fascist tendencies within the Nationalist government would have been strengthened even further. However, the cementing of a basis for a future German–Japanese military alliance precipitated the withdrawing of

German military advisors from China, American advisors taking their place. Japan's search for allies outside of the Anglo–American political arena pushed the Nationalist government in Nanjing closer to the United States.

Japan's desire to enter into an alliance system that guaranteed it some kind of protection against military action taken by the Anglo–American powers was largely dictated by the actions of the Kwantung Army in Manchuria. The interest of a faction of the military leadership of the Imperial Japanese Army in expanding its control over Manchurian territory beyond the perimeters of the South Manchurian Railway zone was evident even during the early 1920s. The Imperial Japanese Army did occupy substantial territory in Siberia during the civil war in Russia that saw the Bolsheviks eventually prevail against the White Army military forces. Reluctantly Japan's forces did withdrew from Soviet territory in 1922, a treaty of 1924 between the Soviet Union and Japan resolving any outstanding geopolitical issues. Still the Soviets retained a sphere of influence in Manchuria and so did Japan. The possibility that hostilities would resume remained real. As it turned out Japan's army decided to seize the military initiative.

Factionalism within the Kwantung Army played a role in the decision making of the military leaders of the Kwantung Army. Those officers in the Army hostile to the clique of officers from Chōshū that outranked them decided to instigate conflict, attempting to carry out provocations that would bring the Kwantung Army into conflict with the forces of the Chinese warlord controlling most of Manchurian territory. Attempts made in 1927 and 1928 failed to ignite all out warfare, but the Mukden Incident of 1931 — in which the Kwantung Army blew up a portion of the South Manchurian Railway, laying the blame on the Chinese warlord controlling Manchuria — ultimately ushered in conquest of Manchuria by Japanese forces.

By 1932 the Kwantung Army had completed its conquest of Manchuria. Diplomats in Tokyo — unable to reign in Japan's own military — now sought to regularize the facts on the ground, eventually settling on the creation of a puppet government for a new state in Manchuria that they named Manchukō. Requiring a group of collaborationist Chinese political elites to put a polite political varnish over an ugly seizure of territory by Japan, the Japanese authorities invited the former emperor of China — who had formally abdicated in 1912 — to become the regent, later the emperor, of the newly created regime in Manchuria.

Concerned with securing a buffer zone between Manchukō and northern China where warlords allied with the Nationalist government in Nanjing the Kwantung Army moved to the southeast, securing a stranglehold over the former Chinese province of Jehol. Once again Tokyo was forced to pressure the Nationalist government in Nanjing to acknowledge what boots on the ground had made a de facto reality, setting up a second puppet state in the newly conquered territory. As in China, Germany, and Italy, military elites were seizing the initiative in Japan pushing to expand the scale and scope of Japan's empire in Asia.

7.2. Nationalism and Anti-Imperialism in China

Japan's takeover of Manchuria and Jehol created both opportunities and challenges for the Nationalist government in Nanjing and the Communist party that had managed to establish enclaves, soviets, within a few districts of China. On the one hand Japanese military aggression awoke feelings of nationalism among the Chinese, feelings that could be co-opted by the Nationalists as an important component of the Guomindang's political agenda for forging a unique Chinese identity; on the other hand a Marxist–Leninist party could interpret Japanese aggression within the Leninist model of imperialism, embedding it within a theoretical framework worked out by Soviet Marxist–Leninist theoreticians.

The political response of the Nationalist government was to put pressure on Japan and on the Japanese business community managing factories, carrying on trade, and making bank loans. Even before the Kwantung Army moved to take over Manchuria there had been boycott campaigns of Japanese goods and employers — four campaigns had been launched between 1918 and 1928, the first in response to the Twenty One demands of the Japanese government but some campaigns were also directed against British interests in China during the same period — but these had not been organized systematically by a Chinese government prior to the setting up of the Nanjing regime in 1928. Now managing anti-Japanese boycotts became a political weapon that could be wielded by Chiang Kai-shek's regime.[2]

For the Chinese and Japanese business elites in Shanghai, any response to the anti-Japanese boycotts involved mixed feelings and incentives. For the Chinese business community there were some clear pluses: the campaigns strengthened the hands of Nationalist government diplomats negotiating for tariff autonomy for China (secured in 1931) and made it easier for Chinese firms to recruit motivated workers who might otherwise have worked for Japanese (or British) managed firms. At the same time the campaigns potentially closed off markets for exports in the Japanese Empire, strengthened the hands of Nationalist government administrators seeking to tax Chinese companies and made it difficult for the firms to secure funding from Japanese, mostly *zaibatsu* owned, banks. For the Japanese business community supporting the actions of the Japanese military also elicited ambiguous feelings. On the positive side of the ledger support for the Japanese military made credible requests by the Japanese community in China for show of force guaranteeing its protection (the Yangzi Patrol carried out by the Japanese Navy was an important factor inhibiting Chinese attacks on the foreign communities living in the treaty ports) and strengthened the hand of the Japanese government in its negotiations over tariffs and extra-territorial rights with Nanjing. On the negative side of the ledger was the possibility that anti-Japanese boycotts would proliferate.

Despite the ambiguous nature of incentives felt on the part of both the Japanese and Chinese business communities politics tended to trump economics on both sides. The Japanese tended to support actions of the Japanese Army, the Chinese business community actions of the Nationalists. Chinese nationalism was becoming a growing issue in Chinese–Japanese business relations. It was playing into the hands of both the Imperial Japanese Army and the Nationalist government.

The Chinese Communist party, active in recruiting party members amongst Chinese urban workers, also stood to benefit from the anti-imperialist campaign since it nicely coincided with its worldview about the overlap of capitalism and imperialism. For the pro-Moscow Bolshevik faction of the Chinese Communist party the boycott campaigns could and were co-opted by Communist organizers looking for party members amongst the working class. But the Bolshevik faction was not the only faction within the party. Also active was a rural-based faction the organized anti-landlord campaigns amongst the peasantry, drawing strength amongst the vast majority of peasants alienated from landlords by exorbitant land rents, high interest rates, and landlord cooperation with warlords. One of the leaders of the rural peasant — as opposed to urban worker — oriented wing of the Communist Party was Mao Zedong, who began his revolutionary career as a May Fourth Movement radical, returning to his native province of Hunan to organize peasant unions in 1925, eventually spearheading the establishment of a rural based Soviet Republic in south eastern Jiangxi.

Through his work organizing peasants Mao developed a set of principles that the Communists were able to effectively apply after the mid-1930s: an emphasis on concrete action, theory being only useful when it can be directly applied to formulating policy and strategy; promoting the development of a new elite — cadres — who, by learning from the peasants, could formulate a "mass line" that would appeal to the great majority of Chinese who were peasants; and the organization of military campaigns that relied heavily on guerrilla warfare.

The Maoist vision for fomenting Chinese revolution was squarely opposed to the approach of both the Nationalists and the Moscow directed Comintern that advocated organizing in metropolitan centers like Shanghai that were tainted with by the imperialistic activities of the foreign business community. Mao's chief enemies within the Chinese Communist party were 28 students — known as the twenty eight Bolsheviks — who had returned from Moscow in the company of a Comintern agent. To fight off his opponents within the party, particularly Red Army officers whose betrayal he feared, Mao carried out purges. In turn his adversaries in the party had him detained.

Mao's rise to supremacy within the Communist Party itself was the direct result of Chiang's campaigns to destroy the Chinese Soviet Republic headquartered in Ruijin on the Jiangxi–Fujian border (two other major Soviets had been established, one on the Hunan–Jiangxi border, the other in Hunan). With the aid of a German advisor who advocated the use of blockhouses to encircle bandit areas, Chiang initiated a series of encirclement campaigns aimed at shrinking the size of the territory controlled by the Ruijin Soviet government. Begun in 1932, the campaign continued on through 1933 and into 1934 at which point the Soviets operating as units of the Red Army — losing territory and concerned that they could not survive unless they established a base outside of the region of China that Chiang and his warlord allies controlled — decided to retreat.

In the famous Long March of 1934–1936 more than 100,000 partisans commenced a march of over 5000 miles — the vast majority dying from fatigue, starvation, wounds suffered in conflict with Nationalist or warlord forces who harassed the marchers as they retreated — eventually establishing a new base for the Soviet government in Yan'an in Shaanxi province. From a strict military viewpoint the fruits of the Long March were mixed, the Nationalists gaining adherents in the rural areas through which the march preceded but as propaganda the Long March was a victory for the Communists, testifying to the willingness of the Communists to suffer hardship and privation in defense of their principles. And in terms of the internal politics of the Communist party the Long March represented a tremendous victory for the Maoists, Mao himself establishing a position of pre-eminence reflected in the fact that he began sleeping apart from his compatriots as the March progressed.

By the mid-1930s three groups — all dominated by militarists or political leaders relying upon military strategy — had established territorial bases within China: the Imperial Japanese Army in Manchuria and Jehol; the Nationalists in the Yangzi River delta and in south eastern China; and the Communists in north western China. Each group offered a unique vision for a future political elite dominating China as a whole. The Japanese promoted and garnered support from an elite discredited in 1911, the old guard loyal to the defunct Qing dynasty. Perhaps this made sense to Japanese elites who came to prominence with the restoration of an emperor in Japan. The Nationalists built their base around old elites — compradors, landlords, and warlords — who had been transformed into new elites after the destruction of the Qing dynasty. In many ways this recycling of old elites into new elites was characteristic of Meiji Japan itself. Only the Communists advocated the creating of new elites, the cadre imbibing the "mass line" by living amongst and learning from the peasantry itself.

7.3. Japan's Drive to Hegemony in Asia

While the Communists and the Nationalists contended for power and territory within China they had a common enemy: Japan. Once the Communists established a relatively secure base in Shaanxi, they approached the Chiang Kai-shek regime with an offer to cooperate in fighting off the Japanese military presence in Manchuria, Jehol, and along the Yangzi River in exchange for a ceasefire allowing both groups to coexist within Chinese territory. In short the proposal was for an alliance of convenience, one that guaranteed that the Nationalists would not enter into an alliance with the Imperial Japanese Army in order to crush the Chinese Communist party altogether. Chiang himself was opposed to this idea but reconsidered after being taken captive by a warlord who had gone over to the Communist side and released on the recommendation of the Communist leadership. Under the umbrella of a Nationalist–Communist patriotic front the Soviet government in Shaanxi would function as a regional Chinese government, and the Red Army of the Communists would become part of a Nanjing controlled military force aimed at driving out, or limiting, Japanese military moves within China.

These moves were taken as a threat by the Kwangtung Army that was busy creating the blueprint for a command and control economy in Manchuria. In their famous manifesto of 1932, "Outline for Economic Construction in Manchukō," the Kwangtung Army officers stated their clear opposition to an "uncontrolled capitalist economy," advocating the use of state power to direct and control economic activity.[3] The emphasis on state planning echoed the state managed approach pioneered by the Soviet Union. To this the army planners added on the idea of developing a "bloc" economy in Manchuria linked to Japan through coordination of production throughout the Empire bloc with Japan at its center.

To achieve these goals the Manchukō government promoted rapid heavy industrialization, pouring capital into 26 new companies, one in each of the following fields: aviation, gasoline, shipping, automobiles, and military vehicles. Beginning in 1937 the government set up a five year plan establishing specific targets for a range of industries and for agriculture. To further these ends the Army invited industrial groups known as "new" *shin-zaibatsu* — Nissan in vehicle manufacturing and Nitchitsu in explosives and synthetics production and hydroelectric power are examples of industrial combines favored by the Army over the old line *zaibatsu* that they considered too capitalistic in orientation — to produce under contracts drawn up by the militarists.

In actual point of fact the Kwangtung Army was unable to completely implement its strategy of creating a command and control economy that avoided the contamination of profit-oriented market activity. The officers did compromise, cutting deals with the *zaibatsu*. But their goal was to create a bloc economy for the Japanese Empire along the lines of the flying geese model. As developed by the economist Akamatsu Kaname employed by the Imperial Japanese Army, Japan would promote economic development for all of East Asia — not only in Korea and in Manchuria but also in those areas of China and Southeast Asia seized by the Japanese military between 1937 and 1945 — under the aegis of the flying geese model, the lead goose for each industry passing across the horizon in the heartland of the empire, Japan proper first, moving out into the periphery of the empire under the pressure of rising wages in the heartland. For instance textiles, later on iron and steel would be developed within Japan first, then move out into periphery zones like Korea, and Manchuria and China later on. This was the logic of the Greater East Asia Co-Prosperity Sphere, the ideas being initially formulated in Manchukō, refined subsequently as Japan's empire grew under its military advances throughout the Asia-Pacific region.

In order to safeguard the "jewel in the crown" that was Manchuria from the threat of a Nationalist–Communist military alliance the Kwangtung Army sought to establish a buffer zone in northern China separating Manchuria and Jehol from the zone controlled by the Nanjing government. That the Communists were now allied with the Nationalists provided the Imperial

Japanese Army an ideological cover for their campaign: the defeat of Communism in Asia. Friction between Japanese and Chinese forces in the vicinity of the Marco Polo Bridge located to the southwest of Beijing in early July 1937 was the powder keg that set off actual conflict. In its aftermath the Japanese Army began a full scale invasion of northern China, establishing a provisional puppet government in Beijing that consisted mainly of former Qing dynasty military and political elites. This government attempted to control four northern provinces of China — Hebei, Shandong, Henan, and Shanxi — although its actual ability to tax and police the populations of these districts was limited at best.[4]

Between the summer of 1937 and December 1941 when Japan attacked the United States at Pearl Harbor precipitating the Pacific War, fighting between the Japanese Army and Chinese forces first revolved around fighting in the Yangzi River delta, Chinese forces eventually retreating from bloody fighting in Shanghai, abandoning Nanjing and moving south and westward along the Yangzi River to Chongqing. Between the fall of 1938 when Wuhan fell to Japanese forces and late 1941 the war basically turned into a stalemate, Chinese troops destroying dams and levees in order to flood the territory across which Japanese forces were moving. During this entire period there was no formal declaration of war on the part of either Japan or the Nationalist government. Japan treated the conflict as an "incident."

With the aim of setting up a government for China that offered an alternative to the Chiang Kai-Shek's Nationalist regime, the Japanese Central China Army pushed for an alternative to the Provisional Government sponsored by the Japanese North China Area Army in 1937. The result was the creation in 1940 of the Restoration Government of Wang Jingwei, a former colleague of Sun Yat-sen during the period Sun resided in Japan and an official in the Guomindang during the mid-1930s. Convinced that the Nationalists could not defeat the Japanese and dreading the spectre of Chinese Communism, Wang attempted to appeal to that element of the Chinese political and economic elite that loathed Maoist Communist more than the threat of Japanese militarism.

The strategy of the Japanese militarists was not just shaped by events in China. During the period when fighting within China bogged down into a stalemate the European powers and the Soviet Union went to war over Germany's bid for hegemony in the European theatre. The actual fighting was initiated by the military invasion and division of Poland by Fascist Germany and the Communist Soviet Union under a treaty signed by the two powers in 1939 that, on paper, were ideological opponents. Geopolitics had trumped ideology. With German aggression directed at surrounding countries threatening to precipitate another European conflict the Soviet Union — the pivot area of the Eurasian land mass, the only country stretching from Western Europe across to the Sea of Japan — entered into negotiations with England and France on the one hand, Germany on the other in an effort to shore up its security by entering into a powerful alliance system. Because Poland — allied with the United Kingdom and France — refused to allow Russian troops to cross its territory in the event of war, the Soviet Union turned to Germany which agreed to divide Poland, giving each country a buffer zone separating one from the other. This was a pure alliance of convenience.

The German invasion of Poland was the trigger forcing the United Kingdom to declare war of Germany. After a year of "phoney war" in 1939 when little fighting transpired, full-scale conflict broke out in mid-1940, the German blitzkrieg ripping through the Netherlands and Belgium, toppling the French government in short order. Intent on defeating the United Kingdom so that Germany could despoil the 'bankrupt real estate of the British Empire" a flotilla of German warships gathered across the English Channel set to carry out a landed invasion of England relying on German bombers to clear the way for their landing on British shores.

Rebuffed by the British Royal Air Force in the Battle of Britain, the German leadership began planning for an invasion of the Soviet Union, its nominal ally, bristling with oil fields and minerals. When Germany's blitzkrieg attack on Russian soil did commence in the summer of 1941, the United Kingdom gained a new ally, an ideological adversary the Soviet Union, in its effort to defeat Germany. The geographic pivot of Eurasia had switched sides.

The Japanese Army viewed the outbreak of war in Europe as an opportunity to seize European colonial possessions in South East Asia. In effect the outbreak of the European conflict increased the "distance" between Europe and Asia, making it far more difficult for the British, the Dutch, and the French to stave off Japanese military moves against Hong Kong, Singapore, Vietnam, and the Dutch East Indies. That Japanese diplomats had negotiated a nonaggression treaty with the Soviet Union in 1940 — the result of settling a border dispute between the two countries that raged on the Manchurian/Outer Mongolian border in 1938 and 1939 — strengthened the hand of those Japanese militarists advocating a strike southward into South East Asia. With these calculations in mind Japanese diplomats, acting at the behest of the army, signed the Tripartite Pact with Germany and Italy, thereby neutralizing German concerns about Japan's move against the European colonies in Asia, thereby cementing a relationship with a major industrial and scientifically advanced military power.

For the Japanese military the greatest remaining potential military threat limiting its aggressive designs against China and South East Asia lay with the United States that remained committed to the Open Door policy guaranteeing China's sovereignty. In a bid to limit Japanese advances in China the United States government moved to embargo the shipment of scrap iron and steel to Japan and shifted the headquarters of the Pacific Fleet from the west coast of California to Hawaii. To send an even more pointed signal to Japan the United States Congress passed a huge naval expansion bill in 1940 providing the resources to build gigantic aircraft carriers and submarines. Realizing that its navy had a short time window within which it could cripple American naval forces gathering at Pearl Harbor in the Hawaii the Japanese high command decided to gamble, ordering dive bombing raids on the American fleet stationed in Pearl Harbor in late 1941. With this attack on its territory the United States entered the global conflict — at war with Japan and its ally Germany — allied with the United Kingdom and the Soviet Union battling Germany.

Seizing upon the opportunity to ally themselves with the Anglo–American powers now at war with Japan, the Nationalists declared that a state of war existed between their regime representing China and Japan. At the close of 1941 Japan found itself at war with the United States, the United Kingdom, and China, its northern flank protected against Russian attack through its nonaggression treaty with the Soviet Union.

7.4. Surrender

In the immediate aftermath of its attack on Pearl Harbor the evolving military situation went well for the Japanese High Command. British Hong Kong fell to Japanese forces at the end of 1941 and Manila in January of 1942. Shortly thereafter all of the Philippines had fallen into Japanese hands. British Singapore was next. Then Japanese forces moved into the Dutch East Indies, acquiring access to oil, rubber, tin, and other strategic materials required by Japan's armies and naval forces.

Still the long run prognosis for Japanese military success was not good. Japan faced an alliance consisting of three mighty foes. It was vulnerable to aerial and submarine attacks that threatened its supply lines, particularly in the Indian Ocean, the South China Sea, and the Pacific Ocean. And the sheer magnitude of the American economy — five times that of Japan's — presented a major problem for Japan if the war settled into a long struggle of attrition. The American capacity to churn out air craft carriers, submarines, destroyers, jet fighters, and long range bombers far exceeded Japan's capacity. If Japan was to create a New Order in Asia it could not rely on sheer military might. It required economic diplomacy of the highest order, namely the appeal to Asian populations of the Greater East Asia Co-Prosperity Sphere hitched to a hatred of European colonialism. Since the late 18th century Europeans operating in Asia had been arrogant, racist in their attitudes, contemptuous of local peoples. The New Order might be a cover for Japanese imperialism but at least it was the imperialism of an Asian, not a European, people.

Unfortunately for Japan's militarists the ultra-nationalism of the Japanese went hand in hand with racist ideas of the Japanese. Feeling superior to other Asian peoples, their military was often brutal to other Asian peoples, cruel and vicious in the campaigns they carried out throughout China and South East Asia. This undermined the appeal of the New Order as the basis for a new regional economic structure for Asia.

After the great naval battles on the Coral Sea and Midway in 1942 — defeats for Japan's Imperial Navy — Japan's military position on the high seas deteriorated. That said, Japanese armies fared better, securing control over French Indochina, Thailand, and Burma. In China Japanese armies were able to expand the geographic extent of the zone that they occupied throughout most of western China. By 1945 this zone included Shandong, Shanxi, Hebei in the north, the Yangzi River delta (including Shanghai and Nanjing) in the center, and swaths of territory in Jiangxi, Hunan, and Guangdong in the south. But in much of the territories held within China fighting with Chinese forces continued and Japanese military control was mainly limited to key cities and to zones along transportation lines.

By early 1945 Japan's military was in retreat on most fronts, losing islands in the Pacific and territories it had acquired in South East Asia. To add to Japan's woes the warfare in Europe was coming to an end, as Russian forces advanced on Germany from the east and Anglo–American forces converged on Germany from Italy in the south and from Normandy in the west.

Under the doctrine of unconditional surrender originally put forward by Franklin D. Roosevelt of the United States and Winston Churchill Prime Minister of the United Kingdom all of the Axis Powers — Germany, Italy,

and Japan — were ordered to surrender without conditions. Heavily criticized by many who viewed this as an impediment to Japan's surrender —
what was an Allied Occupation of Japan going to do about the perpetuation
of the emperor system in Japan? — the doctrine of unconditional surrender had its own logic because it prevented any one of the allied powers
from signing a separate peace treaty with the Axis powers. It must be kept
in mind that the alliance between the United States, the United Kingdom,
and the Soviet Union was an alliance of convenience, each power having
its own separate geopolitical aims. The United Kingdom wanted to
re-establish control over the empire it had lost in part during the global
conflict. Soviet authorities wanted to create a buffer zone between itself
and Western Europe especially Germany. The United States government
was keen to become more active in global economic and political affairs,
abandoning the isolationism that had kept it from joining the League of
Nations. These goals were not necessarily consistent with one another.
By tying the hands of each of the major parties to the Allied alliance the
unconditional surrender doctrine in theory simplified the diplomacy of
bringing World War II to an end. But it did complicate the problem of
securing Japan's surrender.

Shortly after Germany's surrender in May of 1945, the leaders of the
allied alliance met in Potsdam in August. They laid out key provisions for
a Security Council that would serve as a key locus for great power nego-
tiation in a United Nations that would replace the League of Nations as a
global collective security institution. They worked out a declaration dividing Germany into four zones of occupation: American, British, French, and
Russian. They ordered the dissolving of the Nazi Party. Meeting separately
at Potsdam, President Harry Truman of the United States (who replaced
Roosevelt as President on the death of Roosevelt), Winston Churchill, and
Chiang Kai-shek laid out the conditions for Japan's surrender. They stated
their intent to occupy Japan until their objectives — stamping out the economic, political, and social bases for militarism in Japan, the strengthening of democracy and the establishment of freedom of speech, religion,
and thought — were met. This is known as the Potsdam Declaration.
Privately and separately Stalin agreed to tear up the nonaggression treaty
that had protected Japan's army from Russian invasion coming through
Manchukō.

Events now moved swiftly. The United States dropped an atomic
bomb on Hiroshima on August 6; the Soviet Union declared war on

Japan on August 8, its troops sweeping through Manchuria and taking Japanese held islands in the Kurile island chain north of Hokkaidō; on August 9 the United States dropped a second atomic bomb, this time on Nagasaki. Six days later, on August 15, the emperor of Japan delivered a radio address announcing that Japan would "endure the unendurable" by surrendering.

With Japan's defeat and the removal of Japanese forces from China the alliance of convenience between the Chinese Communists and the Nationalists broke down. Indeed even before the Japanese surrender, Chiang Kai-shek's forces had blockaded many areas of Communist power. At the same time the Communists had gone about building their political base in northern China where resentment against previous Chinese governments was strongly entrenched. Under the control over Communist Party doctrine that Mao was able to secure — emphasizing the importance of developing a brand of Marxism along Chinese national lines, rejecting the errors of Confucianism, highlighting the importance of concrete practice and empiricism as the basis for policy making, demanding constant criticism and self-criticism as a vehicle for generating a correct "mass line" — the Communists became an increasingly well-organized party operating under a strict set of principles. From a command and control point of view the Communists had a huge advantage over the Nationalists.

Though outnumbered by the military forces of Nationalists, the highly motivated and ideologically disciplined Peoples Liberation Army of the Communists was able to prevail in the civil war ushered in by Japan's surrender. In 1949 the Communists established a new government for China with Beijing as its capital and the Nationalists fled to Taiwan. The civil wars that had dominated Republican China since the collapse of the Qing dynasty came to an end.

Between 1930 and 1945 both Japan and China struggled with militarism. With Japan's surrender in 1945, and the final defeat of Nationalist forces on the mainland of China, the era when both countries remained mired in the trap of militarism came to a conclusion. With the end of the era of militarism, a new configuration of elites emerged in both nations opening up opportunities for economic growth that had been stymied by the militaristic elites who seized and held the reigns of power for over a decade and a half. A new day was about to dawn in both Japan and China.

Endnotes

1. Much of this paragraph is based on pp. 220–223 in Fairbank (1986).

2. For a discussion of the anti-Japanese campaigns see Jordan (1991) and Junji (1989). Jansen (1975) is an excellent general source for discussion of the interplay of Japanese and Chinese politics during the period between World War I and World War II.

3. See pp. 43 ff in Young (1998). For studies that focus on the economic development and industrialization of Manchukō see Myers (1982, 1989) and Nakagane (1989).

4. For details about the provisional government see Taylor (1980).

Part IV
Consequences, 1945–2005

8

Elites in Decline

8.1. Elites Disappearing and Emerging in Japan, 1945–1960

In surrendering to the allied powers and accepting the terms of the Potsdam Declaration Japan lost its empire, renounced militarism, and underwent a peaceful revolution that saw old elites vanish and new elites arise.

Between 1945 and 1952 the transformation of Japanese politics, economy, and culture took place under conditions of Allied Occupation. Three non-Japanese institutions oversaw sweeping changes in Japan's constitution and laws — the Supreme Commander of the Allied Powers, the Far Eastern Commission (consisting of all 11 countries involved in the occupation), and the Allied Council for Japan that included representatives of the Soviet Union and China. In actual point of fact the occupation authority rested largely in the hands of the Americans and Japanese. Arguably it was the Japanese who dominated the process largely because the resources that the United States and its allies could devote to guiding occupation policy were limited in scope.[1]

An additional constraint limiting the intensity of the American commitment to carrying out "root and branch" reform of Japan was the outbreak of the Cold War. After the Iron Curtain came down over Eastern Europe, the Soviet Union encouraging the toppling of

regimes in regions it liberated from German armies by Communist parties —
in Hungary, Poland, Czechoslovakia, Romania — Stalin acquired the buffer
zone he sought triggering Anglo–American fears about the ultimate security of Western Europe. Victory by the Communists in mainland China
meant that a significant portion of the Eurasian land mass was under the
rule of Communist regimes. Outbreak of the Korean War in 1950 further
intensified American concerns about Communist inspired expansionism.
The American purge of Japan's prewar elite lost some steam at the end
of the 1940s as the Americans began looking with favor on individuals in
Japan who had commanded positions of influence during the 1930s, the
Americans acknowledging that even though the prewar elite had been
contaminated with undemocratic ideals at least it could garner a modicum
of residual respect in a post-surrender environment in which new pro-
democratic elites were flexing their political muscle.

The prewar elites most profoundly impacted negatively by the changes
instituted during the occupation were military elites, political and bureaucratic architects of Japan's empire and the command and control model for
managing economies, owners and high level professional managers of the
zaibatsu and *shinzaibatsu*, and landlords.

Revamping of the Japanese constitution was the most significant
contribution made by the allied powers to the restructuring of Japan's elite.
In the draft of the revised constitution ultimately accepted by the Supreme
Commander of the Allied Powers political and civil liberties were guaranteed
for all Japanese citizens (the right to vote was extended to women and the
segregation of the sexes in the education system was abolished) and checks
and balances were written into way laws were promulgated and reviewed for
consistency with basic constitutional principles, the Supreme Court given
the right to declare laws unconstitutional. In Clause 9 of the document
Japan renounced militarism, committing itself to a "no-war" clause.

Working with a theory that Japan had lurched toward militarism by
feudalistic militarists owing their prestige to the cult of the emperor and
supported in this endeavor by economic elites — by *zaibatsu* and *shinzaibatsu*
lobbying Diet members for restraints on union organizing and by landlords
fighting off rural unions advocating land reform — the occupation authorities backed those Japanese officials who believed in promoting sweeping
land reform, the legalization of collective bargaining, the breakup of the
zaibatsu, and an wholesale expansion of the educational system.

Most of the specific legislation revamping the educational system
occurred between 1947 and 1949. Under the reforms Japan adopted an

American style 6-3-3-4 system: six years of compulsory elementary school leading to three years of compulsory middle school. Upon graduation from the compulsory segment students could elect to continue on to three years of high school preparing students willing and able to continue on to a four year university education or a two-year junior college program. As part of the effort to reduce disparities between the well educated cultural elite and the general populace of prewar Japan, the Ministry of Education committed itself to a simplification of the writing system, reducing the number of Chinese characters employed in standard Japanese and simplifying the writing of a number of the characters used by reducing the number of strokes required in their construction. The net impact of this legislation and policy reform was to reduce the social divide between cultural elites and the mass of the population, enhancing the general level of education attained by all adults in Japan male and female alike.

In the field of labor law, legislation passed during the first two years of the occupation — the Trade Union Law, the Labor Adjustment Law, and the Labor Standards Law — guaranteed workers the right to form a union, to engage in collective bargaining, and to benefit from mediation, conciliation, and arbitration. Indentured servant contracts were outlawed. All of this legislation reversed laws and police policies suppressing union organizing campaigns and breaking up meetings advocating strikes. One of the most important implications of these reforms was the extension of so-called "permanent employment" status — long-term employment contracts for employees not caught engaged in misfeasance, wages tied to age and seniority within the enterprise — to rank and file blue collar workers. Prior to the Pacific War this status was largely limited to professional white collar workers who had graduated from higher level institutions of learning. The result was a sharp reduction in the status gap between shop floor workers and professional managers and technically trained engineers, a major step towards industrial democracy.

Land reform undertaken during the occupation destroyed landlordism in Japan. Legislation passed in 1948 set a low limit for the amount of farm land that could be owned by a family, establishing prices for upland and paddy lands that were to be sold by families owning more than the stipulated limit, and providing government loans to tenant farmers that could utilize in purchasing the lands sold. In the subsequent inflation the real value of the buyout prices received by former landlords plummeted. The wealth of the landlords as a group was wiped out.

Wealth was also stripped away from the owners of the *zaibatsu*. While many of the companies that appeared in the original list of enterprises to be dissolved by the Holding Company Liquidation Commission escaped action, the most famous of the corporate groups — Mitsui, Sumitomo, Mitsubishi, Yasuda — were broken up, their assets sold, many of their high level managers purged.

The weakening or wholesale destruction of Japan's pre-Pacific War elite opened the door for new elites: liberal civilian bureaucrats; entrepreneurs; and rural-based politicians.

Indicative of the new brand of entrepreneurs are Honda Soichiro and Fujisawa Takeo of the Honda Motor Company.[2] An inventor, Honda teamed up with an equally talented entrepreneur Fujisawa to build up a major automotive enterprise from an initial base producing motorized bicycles in 1948. Moving on to manufacture full-fledged motorcycles like the Dream and the Cub, the tandem of inventor and marketing guru jumped into automobile production with the fuel-efficient Honda Civic, and slightly more upscale Accord (in 1976) and a decade later the luxurious Acura. As a self-made inventor who relied on his creative wits and his intuition, Honda wished to create a "paperweight" type structure for the product design side of the business, one in which the title chief engineer or executive engineer could be held by a number of talented individuals favored not by seniority but by pure ability and achievement. This vision flew in the face of elitism.

The emergence of politicians like Tanaka Kakuei is a similar example of how cunning and ruthless ambition rather than association with elitism could lead to highly successful careers measured not by growth in corporate sales but rather through the acquisition of power.[3] Building his power base in rural Niigata through the sponsorship of a group known as the Niigata Mountain Association whose primary function was to secure pork barrel projects for Niigata prefecture — the Tadami River hydroelectric power project, the bullet train (Shinkansen) line providing high speed train service to Niigata constituents — Tanaka promoted the careers of a select corpus of political protégés in exchange for contributions to his Association. The master of the bribe and the shady real estate deal, Tanaka built up a powerful faction, a clique, within the Liberal Democratic Party that had a monopoly on political power in Japan between 1955 (when the party was formed) and the early 1990s. Unlike pioneers of the party system in post-World War I Japan like Hara Takashi (Kei) who was a former *samurai*, Tanaka rose up through the ranks of power without benefit of an elitist background.

Factionalism, the formation of cliques centered upon powerful figures like Tanaka Kakuei, was a defining characteristic of the Liberal Democratic Party. Originally formed as an alliance of convenience, forged out of a coalition of conservative parties determined to deny a left leaning Japan Socialistic Party from dominating the Diet in 1955, the Liberal Democratic Party became an almost unbeatable vote garnering machine. From the election of 1955 in which the Liberal Democratic Party secured 58% of the popular vote until 1993 the party managed to maintain a tight lock on the cabinet, winning majority after majority. But within the party itself brutal rivalry between factions headed by power brokers like Tanaka was unending, forcing continual cabinet reshuffles designed to strike a power balance within the party itself.

Military defeat shakes up a country in profound ways. Japan's unconditional surrender in 1945 ushered in a period in which old elites went into rapid decline and new elites enjoyed careers stunning in their meteoric ascent. At the time of the Meiji Restoration the transformation of elites was also remarkable. But in the Meiji transformation many of the old elites re-emerged as key members of the new elite, *samurai* becoming high ranking officials, military leaders, engineers or key professional managers in *zaibatsu*. The first one and a half decades of post-surrender Japan witnessed even greater turbulence in the ranks of Japan's elites, setting the stage for the Miracle Growth period of Japan's economic development.

8.2. Elites Disappearing and Emerging in China, 1945–1960

In the wake of Communist victory over the Nationalists in late 1948 and 1949 a new elite committed to destroying once and for all old elites gained control over mainland China. Three old elites disappeared: the landlord gentry in rural villages; intellectuals, especially those trained in Confucian thought; and capitalist entrepreneurs mainly concentrated in the former treaty ports, particularly Shanghai and in Manchuria that had been under Russian, then Japanese influence throughout most of the late-Qing and republican eras.

Given the fact that most of China was agricultural and rural, the toppling of the landlord gentry strata was certainly the most important in terms of sheer numbers. In the aftermath of Japan's military withdrawal from China, even before the Nationalist forces went down in defeat, Communist Party cadres began waging a violent campaign against village elites with the aim of breaking up traditional social organization in the villages in anticipation of creating a wholly new architecture for rural life. As a tool in this campaign, and as a recruiting tactic designed to bring poor landless peasants into the Communist Party and its guerrilla war campaign against the Nationalist armies, the cadres wielding the weapon of land reform.[4] Between 1946 and 1949 in the regions of China falling under Communist control, these campaigns often degenerated into revolutionary terror, wealthier and more experienced village elders being violently shoved aside by cadres lacking knowledge of local agricultural techniques and conditions.

With the securing of political control over the entire mainland in 1949 the elites securing control over the government and Party center in Beijing moved to curtail the "leftist excesses" of the post-World War II civil war period. The result was a land reform law promulgated in 1950 that did away with the more radical aspects of the revolutionary terror, ushering in a regime of regular orderly procedures. By 1952 the land reform was by and large completed, dooming once and for all the landlord-gentry elite of Qing and republican China.

Less important in quantitative terms were campaigns aimed at taming intellectuals and capitalists. During the mid-1950s in a country of 600 million, there were less than 4 million intellectuals, including technicians and engineers. Simplifying the writing system, reducing the number — and complexity — of characters required to write Chinese, introducing pinyin as an alphabetical system for representing written Mandarin Chinese now promoted as a national language, were steps designed to strip away advantages enjoyed by China's traditional elite. Sending intellectuals down to villages to learn from the peasant masses and to bring schooling to villages through the Socialist Educational Movement enjoyed a similar logic, pointedly narrowing the status gap between those with formal educational and the great mass of mostly illiterate villagers. Thought reform required of those wishing to advance their careers by joining the Communist Party was another weapon employed by the new elite.

Still, especially during the First Five Year Plan period 1953–1957 during which a Soviet style industrialization drive dominated policy making, Soviet advisors playing an important role in the construction of heavy industrial plants (especially in Manchuria) and infrastructure, there was strong growth in demand for the services of expert technicians.[5] Not surprisingly this encouraged pragmatic accommodation of intellectuals. A similar pragmatic attitude governed official attitude toward market oriented entrepreneurs, most engaged in running light industrial firms, in the silk reeling and cotton spinning and weaving sectors of Shanghai for instance. State planners, realizing that they could not ignore the consumption needs of a growing population requiring consumption goods like clothing and bicycles and processed foods decided to co-opt the capitalist elite rather than oversee its total destruction.

Indeed the philosophy of Mao, developed during the 1950s as a practical set of dicta designed to guide Party thought in applying Marxist–Leninist theory to the particular problems faced by a predominantly agricultural nation like China, recognized that there were inherent contradictions — not antagonistic in the sense that they could be resolved through correct Communist Party policies and indoctrination — between cadres, expert technicians and intellectuals, and the mass of workers mostly rural based. Mirroring these contradictions, for instance between "red" cadres primarily political in their orientation and technically trained "experts," were contradictions between rural and urban, between consumer good oriented light industry and capital goods intensive heavy industry, between labor intensive sectors and capital intensive sectors.[6] For instance, the "three-unification" movement launched by the Party was aimed at reducing and resolving contradictions between "reds," "experts," and the mass of workers.

To be sure, in so far as the vast majority of the new political elite in Communist China were committed to a utopian Communist vision for their country, their agenda was to ultimately do away with the landlord gentry, capitalist, and intellectual elites of the republican period. That they could be pragmatic and cautious in doing this was more a matter of strategy than genuine commitment. The long run goal was to resolve the short run contradictions that reared their ugly head before the longed for future utopia was reached.

8.3. China in the Japanese Mirror: Similarities and Dissimilarities

A standard mantra is that post-Tokugawa period Japanese industrialization and economic development is radically different from post-World War II Chinese industrialization. After all, the former was always strongly tilted toward the market while the latter was dominated by central planning; in the former political democracy gained force; in the latter single party rule by the Communist Party strongly constrains political expression. That Japan became a staunch ally of the United States in the aftermath of World War II while China was a key player in the Eurasian Communist bloc that did not collapse until the end of the 1980s is indicative of these differences.

The thesis of this book calls this standard interpretation into question. While acknowledging the obvious differences between the modernization experiences of the two countries, it argues that there are three strong similarities between the Chinese and Japanese experiences: (1) draining substantial pools of surplus labor out of rural areas (through the augmenting of labor); (2) the emergence of elites taking over the economic and political agenda from old elites, the transition in elite orientation being a crucial concomitant of sustained industrialization coupled with infrastructure build-up; and (3) passing through a phase of virulent nationalism, later on discarded in favor of a more open less xenophobic stance towards the rest of the world.

In Japan the nationalistic agenda of *fukoku kyōhei* was crucial to the forging of an alliance between militarists and advocates of market oriented industrialization that oversaw a massive expansion of infrastructure in support of both agendas but ultimately led to Japan's surrender in 1945. In China a period of strident nationalism ushered in after the First Five Year Plan was associated with the Great Leap Forward of the late 1950s and the Cultural Revolution beginning in the mid-1960s, ending in the mid-1970s. For all of the disruption associated with these periods in Chinese history, the period of extreme nationalism in China witnessed massive infrastructure expansion, heavy industrialization, and augmentation of rural labor instrumental to the draining of surplus labor out of village China.

Lying at the heart of China's period of extreme nationalist is the cult of Mao and the break-up of the alliance with the Soviet Union. Indeed the two went hand in hand. As early as the 1930s it was apparent that Mao's concept of Chinese Communism was radically different from that espoused by ideologues and policy markers in the Soviet Union. In Russia the victorious Communists inherited a country that had a reasonably well developed urban industrial economy in which surplus labor concerns were minimal. The Russian Communist Party built a base among industrial workers, cultivating technical expertise of engineers and rank and file industrial workers alike in developing its bureaucratically conceived Five Year Plans. To be sure it did not ignore the rural sector, promoting collectivization of farming. But developing the rural economy was not part of its central vision. Following this logic the Bolshevik faction of the Chinese Communist Party during the late 1920s and 1930s focused on organizing industrial and urban workers, rejecting Mao's commitment to creating rural Communist power bases from which Communist armies could carry on guerrilla warfare.

Thus it is not surprising that the faction in the Communist Party that aligned itself with Mao's theories rejected Soviet style industrial policies,

pushing for an alternative utopian vision in which rural collectives —
cooperatives later on communes organized around production brigades —
would form the backbone for a rapid industrialization drive, one in which
rural based blast furnaces would serve as a vehicle for China's rapid industrial growth by tapping the underutilized labor potential of the rural sector. The decisive face off between the pro-Soviet planning school and the
Maoists occurred in the first half of the 1950s, the Maoists managing to side-
line the proposals of Chen Yun in the debates of the Central Committee
of the Party.[7] In their place the Maoist faction pushed for the formation
of Agricultural Producers Cooperatives as the key to Chinese development
planning. In doing so they set the stage for the "high tide" of cooperative
creation in 1956, the consolidation of cooperatives into communes dominated by production brigades a few years later.

As part of this strategy the Maoists advocated the militarization of the
peasantry and the Socialist Education Movement, the building of educational facilities in rural communes taking precedence over investing in
urban schools aimed at training future technical experts. In denigrating
the value of urbanized intellectual labor, the Maoists argued that sending
down city educated technicians to villages should be integral to mobilizing
rural labor with the aim of expanding the network of irrigation ditches,
building and improving rural roads, and shoring up the banks of rivers to
prevent flooding.

China's passing over a Soviet style Second Five Year Plan in favor of a
Maoist Great Leap Forward model put policy makers in China and in the
Soviet Union on a collision course. Indeed in asserting that China had a
better model for achieving utopian Communism, China's leadership established itself as an ideological contender to the Soviet Union, bidding for
support in Eastern Europe and the developing world. That China's sheer
size alone accorded it considerable respect in the Communist world is evident from the following estimates of population for the year 1960: China,
667 million; the Soviet Union, 214.8 million; the combined populations of
seven Iron Curtain countries (including Albania, Bulgaria, Czechoslovakia,
Hungary, Poland, Romania, and Yugoslavia), 99 million. To be sure the
1960 Russian per capita income level was over 5 times that of the Chinese.
Nevertheless China's bid for ideological supremacy was not without merit
particularly amongst those regions of the developing world that were
primarily agricultural.

Not surprising the bitter contest for leadership in the international
Communist movement ultimately led to the Sino–Soviet split of 1960. It

also set the stage for an extreme assertion of Chinese nationalism during the Cultural Revolution when the Maoist faction in the ascendancy claimed that Mao's thought took precedence over Marxist–Leninism. Rather than being a practical application of Marxist–Leninist thought that was the claim made for Mao's views during the 1950s, the ideologues of the Cultural Revolution effectively turned Communist theory on its head with Mao's vision on top. This was Chinese nationalism expressed with a vengeance.

In sum there are crucial similarities between Japanese and Chinese economic development. These are summarized in Chart 8.1. To be sure crucial differences remain and are important. These are also touched on in

Chart 8.1: Two phases: some similarities and dissimilarities, post-1950 China and Japan, 1870–1980.

A Initial Phase: Ideology Tinged Nationalism and Initial Industrialization	
China, 1950–1978	**Japan, 1870–1945**
Broad Similarities	
Competing agendas — technocratic industrialization versus utopian socialism — contending under the umbrella of Maoism	Competing agendas — militarization versus market oriented industrialization — competing under the umbrella of *fukoku kyōhei*
Cult of Mao	Cult of the emperor
Chinese model of utopian peasant based Communism versus Soviet Union model	Ultra-nationalism: mystical notions about domestic and global role of Emperor
Land reform of 1950 and increase in hours worked per worker in agriculture, surplus labor freed up for manufacturing	Land reform (ending of Tokugawa fief system) carried out with Land Tax Reform of 1873, increase in hours worked per worker in agriculture, surplus labor freed up for manufacturing
Infrastructure expansion: physical (railroads, hydroelectric power grids, ports, dams, and irrigation), human capital enhancing primary schooling, public health), and financial	Infrastructure expansion: physical (railroads, hydroelectric power grids, ports, dams, and irrigation), human capital enhancing (primary schooling, public health), and financial
Relatively early development of heavy industry (iron and steel, chemicals, and machinery)	Relatively early development of heavy industry (iron and steel, chemicals, and machinery)

(Continued)

Chart 8.1:   (*Continued*)

A Initial Phase: Ideology Tinged Nationalism and Initial Industrialization

China, 1950–1978	Japan, 1870–1945
Broad Differences	
Command and control economy	Market oriented economy
Geopolitics: alliance with the Communist bloc that stretched from the Iron Curtain in the West to the coastline of China, continental orientation, Communist Party monopoly over politics	Geopolitics: alliance with the Anglo–American powers gives away to alliance with the Axis powers, oceanic orientation, democracy of growing importance between 1880 and early 1930s
Conflict between competing political agendas largely carried out in the domestic arena	Conflict between competing political agendas largely carried out in the international not domestic arena
Technology and organizational forms largely imported from Soviet Union and Communist bloc	Technology and organization forms largely imported from England, Western European continent, and the United States
Relatively closed to trade	Relatively open to trade, flying geese pattern of trade
Heavy industry widely dispersed, not concentrated along coastline	Heavy industry concentrated in Tōkaidō industrial belt on Pacific coastline

B Second Phase: High Speed Growth

China, 1978–2005	Japan, 1955–1980
Broad Similarities	
Rapid structural change, total factor productivity growth fueled by import and adaptation of foreign technology	Rapid structural change, total factor productivity growth fueled by import and adaptation of foreign technology
Exports to high income markets important	Exports to high income markets important
Industrial democracy important	Industrial democracy important, internalization of labor in large and medium sized firms important
Factionalism and power balancing important in Communist Party	Factionalism and power balancing important in dominant Liberal Democratic Party

(*Continued*)

Chart 8.1:   (*Continued*)

B Second Phase: High Speed Growth	
China, 1978–2005	Japan, 1955–1980
Broad Differences	
Surplus labor is still abundant in rural areas	Surplus labor largely absorbed, little left in rural areas
State owned enterprises and town and village enterprises important in domestically owned production, foreign direct investment important in nondomestically owned sector	Private industry dominant throughout the economy though some state owned monopolies are important (railroads, tobacco)
Communist Party monopoly over politics, censorship, elite dominated politics remains strongly entrenched	Full fledged democracy, political competition, press freedom guaranteed, gradual erosion of elite dominated politics
Limited private property rights in farming	Private property rights in farming entrenched

the chart. The message of this chapter is that it is easy to overemphasize the significance of the two Cold War alliance systems that saw China and Japan lining up on opposite sides of the geopolitical divide. That China became increasingly nationalistic promoting a cult — the cult of Mao — during the 1950s and 1960s is as important as the fact that its elite leadership opted for a command and control model during the same period. The pre-1940 nationalism that created a big tent ideology under which Japan built up its infrastructure and industry has important echoes in Maoist China during the two decades following Communist victory and Nationalist defeat on the mainland.

Endnotes

1. For details concerning the occupation of Japan see pp. 231–238 in Mosk (2008).
2. For more details see pp. 257–259 in Mosk (2008).
3. For further details see pp. 319–320 in Mosk (2008).
4. For a detailed account of the campaign directed at China's landlord gentry see p. 431 ff in Schurmann (1968). For discussion of pre-1949 land reforms carried out by the Communist Party in the regions they controlled see Liu (2007).
5. The Soviet Union and China signed the Sino–Soviet Pact of Friendship and Alliance in 1950. This pact was primarily designed to encourage trade between

the two nations but it also contained protocols concerning Soviet cooperation in developing its industrial responsibility system in Manchuria.

6. For an excellent discussion of two key publications of Mao — *On Contradiction* and *On Practice* — see p. 53 ff in Schurmann (1968).

7. For the views of Chen Yun see Chen (1983).

9

Miracle Growth and Its Aftermath in Japan

9.1. The Main Characteristics of Miracle Growth

The destruction of old elites during the Allied Occupation ushered in an era of high speed growth in Japan. No longer was the military elite in the ascendancy promoting investment of capital and human resources in empire building, advocating the virtues of command and control for both the domestic and colonial economies under Japanese control and denigrating market oriented activities. Infrastructure construction funded by the Japanese government and private Japanese sources was now devoted to Japan alone, not to the colonies, to Taiwan, Korea, and Manchuria. No longer did the *zaibatsu* dominate the banking sector, shutting out risk-taking entrepreneurial projects from capital markets. No longer did tension between landlords and tenants poison the political atmosphere. With the simplification of the writing system and expansion in the scope of compulsory education those children growing up in poor households had a greater chance of realizing their ambitions, whether in agriculture, manufacturing or services. The search for new technologies was now concentrated on the production of civilian not military goods, for instance on lens for cameras not lens for submarines, on engines for passenger cars not engines for tanks.

Eager to take the place of the old elite was an elite committed to rebuilding Japan's war damaged economy. The new elite emerging in the aftermath of Japan's surrender consisted of three major groups: Liberal Democratic Party politicians; high level bureaucrats in key ministries involving the economy (the Ministry of International Trade and Industry, the Bank of Japan, the Economic Planning Agency, the Ministry of Construction); and the major business federations, *Nikkeiren* and *Keidanren*. This is known as the elite "iron-triangle" of the period between the mid-1950s and the late 1970s.

The high speed growth era between 1956 and 1970 is known as the Miracle Growth era in Japan. Growth over that 15 year period was considered miraculous because the growth rates for per capita income were so high and were sustained for such a long period of time. The figures in Appendix Table A.4 document this fact. But this is not the only reason why growth over the period 1956–1970 is considered miraculous. There are other important dimensions to Miracle Growth.

A comprehensive list of these characteristics should include the following: (1) high rates of augmentation of the factors of production — especially labor and capital but land as well — that promoted, and was promoted by, high rates of total factor productivity growth in key manufacturing subsectors; (2) high and rising rates of accumulation of capital especially in manufacturing, particularly in heavy industry and machinery; (3) the absorption of most if not all of the surplus labor that existed in the rural sector, farm production becoming increasingly mechanized; (4) growth with equity, income distribution being relatively equal; (5) an explosion of consumerism, particularly a massive increase in the purchase of consumer durables like electric vacuums, electric washing machines, refrigerators, television sets, air conditioners, and passenger cars; and (6) completion of the demographic transition, life expectancy rising and fertility falling to low levels.

The augmentation of labor was very important. Not only did the number of middle and senior high schools increase by leaps and bounds so did the number of colleges and universities, the private sector entering the fray in order to meet the surging demand for advanced schooling. In 1950 there were 199 universities and colleges in Japan, of which 104 were private; by 1970 there were 382 universities and colleges of which 274 were private.[1] At least initially — during the 1950s — the rate of return expected for a student securing a high school, college or university education was very high. This reflected the fact that demand growth was far outstripping supply growth due to the massive expansion of demand for technically trained professionals — accountants, electrical engineers, and shop floor managers — in iron and steel, automobiles, and consumer durable manufacturing. But as supply caught up with demand, the rate of return on investment in higher education plummeted. Consider the following evidence concerning supply and demand for males with different levels of schooling. In 1965–1969 among male fresh school graduates securing first jobs 18% were middle school graduates, 39% high school graduates, and only 5% college/university graduates. A decade later — in the five year period 1975–1979 — these percentages were 5%, 34%, and 27%, respectively.[2] The massive improvement in the augmentation of labor services occurring before and during the Miracle Growth era was partly a response to the high rate of return associated with the expansion of demand for individuals with an advanced education; and as the degree of this augmentation improved the rate of return fell.

On the capital side augmentation also took place. A classic example is capital invested in iron and steel manufacturing. During the American Army Air Force aerial bombing campaign of Japan's Tōkaidō industrial belt that took place in early 1945 most of the plant and equipment in the industry was destroyed. Japanese firms rebuilding this capacity in the aftermath of the war naturally looked to employing the capital that was most advanced from a technical point of view, namely the basic oxygen furnace installed in massive plants generating output with continuous slab or billet casting procedures. Putting a newer vintage of capital into place gave a strong push to productivity in the industry.

That both capital and labor augmentation soared during the decades following the conclusion of the Pacific War played an important role in total factor productivity growth in post-war Japan. One of the basic arguments of this book is that augmentation of the factors of production can and does accompany total factor productivity growth in certain — mainly market oriented — environments. That there can be a tight connection between the two causes of productivity advance follows from the logic of rates of return in a market oriented economy. Total factor productivity growth is rapid when workers can acquire new skills quickly. Conversely in an environment when total factor productivity growth improves markedly the demand for workers who either have a high level of skill already acquired through job experience (or who can acquire the skills rapidly) expands, thereby raising the rate of return expected from securing an advanced education. Thus rapid total factor productivity growth tends to foster augmentation of labor, and in turn is fostered by the augmentation of labor in a market oriented economy. Similar arguments apply to the augmentation of the capital stock.

These points must be kept in mind in understanding why the rate of investment soared as it did during the period 1951–1975 a fact evident from Panel A.1 in Appendix Table A.4. Capital accumulation rates rose in response to high expected rates of return on new capital formation, partly because new capital generally enjoyed higher levels of augmentation than old capital. All of this took place during a period when total factor productivity growth was fairly high in some — but not — all sub-sectors of manufacturing and services. In short high rates of capital formation were linked to high rates of total factor productivity growth. That the growth in the capital stock outside of agriculture was so high was crucial to the brisk absorbing of labor from the agricultural sector, the incidence of surplus labor diminishing rapidly during the Miracle Growth era. That labor input was being augmented rapidly in the agricultural sector also contributed to relatively seamless transfer of massive amounts of labor input from farming to manufacturing and services.

The rise in investment proportion was by and large matched by an expansion in the savings rate. Why did the savings rate rise? Among households savings rose because households were saving to purchase consumer durables and because they were putting away funds to educate their children in vocational schools, junior colleges, colleges, and universities. Household incomes were rising rapidly during the Miracle Growth era so households were benefiting from income increases that were partly unanticipated. Many companies that enjoyed record rates of profit — due to productivity growth — rewarded their employees with significant bonuses that tended to end up in bank accounts. Companies funded some of their investments out of their own corporate savings. In short both saving and investment rates tended to increase during Miracle Growth, most of the savings being channeled to investors through banks.

The fact that income distribution was relatively equal during Japan's high speed growth era was due to policy and market forces. Consider agriculture. Abandoning a quota system instituted during the Allied Occupation, a government dominated by the rural based Liberal Democratic Party moved to subsidize agricultural incomes by creating a dual price system for domestically produced rice. Under the system government purchased rice from farmers — for instance from agricultural co-operatives — at a relatively high price set so that a typical farmer would achieve an income equivalent to a typical blue collar urban dwelling worker. It sold the rice to consumers through government managed stores at much lower prices. Key to making this system viable was protectionism. Japanese style glutinous rice could and was produced at far lower prices in California. If Japan's rice market been open to unrestricted imports Japanese import-export companies would have brought in vast amounts of cheap rice from abroad, wrecking havoc on the careful management of domestic prices. Protectionism cum subsidy of another sort was achieved through a law limiting the size of department stores. The idea was to ensure that small scale "mom-and-pop" retail outlets would be able to survive. Keeping large international retailers out of the domestic market was integral to this policy.

It should be emphasized that the subsidization bolstering the incomes of farmers and miniscule retailers was achieved through regulation and protection, not through direct transfers through a welfare system. During the Miracle Growth period the government managed welfare system was in its infancy. To actually realize a certain standard of living farmers and retailers had to work hard, competing in a market environment.

The nature of collective bargaining also contributed to the equalization of incomes, in this case by pushing wage increase rates within and between sub-sectors of manufacturing toward common levels. At the heart of collective bargaining system was enterprise unionism.[3]

During the 1950s the efforts of labor union organizers to form industry wide unions largely failed. It failed largely because rank and file shop floor workers in large and medium sized firms were given guarantees of so-called "permanent employment," long-term labor contracts ensuring they could keep their jobs even during downturns in demand for the output of their employer. Given the rapid change in technologies employed in manufacturing during the Miracle Growth era the "permanent employment" condition went hand in hand with a wage system ensuring a high level of worker flexibility in task assignment. The basic wage was closely tied to age, seniority, and family needs. However the payment of bonuses was selective providing incentives for extra effort and outstanding diligence. With wages largely independent of specific job assignments and workers dependent on the economic success of their particular employers union organizers found it easiest to organize workers along company lines eschewing the establishment of job specific wage scales of the sort developed by industry specific or occupation specific unions.

Try as they might union organizers bent on creating industry wide unions ran into opposition: at the hands of management — especially in large and medium sized firms the main target of unionization drives — and at the hands of employees loyal to their employers. During the 1950s — a relatively turbulent era in Japanese labor-management relations — most strikes failed, most employers got what they wanted wielding the bludgeon of the lockout to beat back union militancy when they reckoned harsh tactics were required. By the late 1950s the world of large and medium sized firms was heavily internalized: workers tended to stay with their companies from recruitment until mandatory retirement; wages were largely determined on the basis of age, seniority, and overall performance evaluation independent of specific occupation or work group assignment; and unions were organized along enterprise lines. Workers within an sub-sector of manufacturing were divided, segmented, along enterprise lines.

To counter the "divide-and-rule" reality of this labor market, union federations attempted to organize general strikes, taking on all employers at one time. The result of this effort was the development of the "Spring Offensive" collective bargaining system, unions making demands for a certain "base-up" increase in the overall level of wages — in effect a percentage increase in the overall wage bill within the enterprise — around the same time, threatening to slow down production through coordinated "work-to-rule" campaigns as a bargaining ploy. In effect under the logic of these labor market institutions the "base-up" increase rate could not be excessive lest the least competitive firms in an industry were forced into bankruptcy. The upshot was the development of a national consensus for the "base-up," variance in wage hikes between firms and between sub-sectors of manufacturing plummeting, the more technologically dynamic companies within an industry granting wage increases that were decidedly more modest than the labor productivity gains they were garnering.[3]

In short, a combination of policy initiatives and market forces promoted equality of economic outcomes during the Miracle Growth era. By the early 1970s most Japanese considered themselves members of the middle class. The elitism of the pre-war era was a thing of the past.

Contributing to the sense of most households joining the middle class was the diffusion of consumer durables. In 1976–1980 most Japanese families had electric vacuum cleaners (98.5% did); most had a refrigerator (98.8% did); most had an electric washing machine (98.8% did); most had a television set (96.6% had a color television); and a majority owned a passenger car (51.2% did).[4] The consumer revolution of the Miracle Growth era transformed Japan economically and socially.

During the Miracle Growth era health improved dramatically. This is evident from Panels A.4, A.5, and B of Appendix Table A.6. Life expectancy

soared as did the biological standard of living of the population as calibrated by the anthropometric measures. Contributing to an improvement
in health for children was a dramatic drop in reproduction. Panel A.6
of Appendix Table A.6, employing the Hutterite index of fertility as an
index of reproduction — the index basically calibrates the overall fertility of women by comparing it as a percentage of a "maximal level," that
obtaining if the women reproduced at the rate achieved by an interwar
cohort of highly fertile Hutterite women — demonstrates that by 1960
fertility had fallen throughout Japan, in urban districts, in rural districts,
in agricultural prefectures, and in industrial prefectures.[5] A process com-
mencing during the interwar period — mainly restricted to industrialized prefectures — was by and large completed by the end of the Miracle
Growth period. Change in family dynamics — dependence of children
on parents for their marriages and their careers eroding — was occurring
throughout Japan. Infant mortality had reached low levels everywhere.
The opportunity cost of having children — measured in terms of earning
power forgone in raising children — had risen everywhere. In particular
the demand for the labor input of women soared in rural areas, legions
of males in farm households holding down factory jobs, coming home to
work their farms on the weekends, mainly relying on their wives to till the
fields and attend to the crops.

9.2. Productivity Gain in Agriculture

During Miracle Growth surplus labor vanished from Japanese farming.
Attributable to a surge in demand for workers in manufacturing, the rapid
mechanization of agricultural production is a clear indicator of this historic
turning point in the Japanese economy.

The key to the elimination of surplus labor in Japan is augmentation.
Labor was augmented because the health and educational attainment of
the rural population improved. Labor was augmented because workers in
agriculture substituted use of fixed capital — power tillers, tractors — for
labor input.

The substitution of fixed capital for labor is evident in the figures
given in Panels B.3 and B.4 of Appendix Table A.8. Growth in the input
of machinery and implements — slow in the decade immediately following Japan's surrender — picked up dramatically during the first decade of
Miracle Growth. By contrast the rate of growth in variable capital input —
fertilizer — was relatively fast in the period 1945–1955 and relatively slow

during the period 1955–1965 when fixed capital was being substituted for labor input.

The market was largely dictating the transformation of Japanese agriculture. With the disappearance of surplus labor in rural Japan as farm workers abandoned their villages to take up jobs in manufacturing, wages paid to workers in agriculture rose — relative to the prices received for the sale of agriculture products — dramatically. This is apparent from Panel B.5 in Appendix Table A.8. At the same time as is evident from Panel B.5 the relative price of fixed capital equipment purchased by farm households dropped, mass production and technological progress in the machinery sector driving down the prices for tractors and power tillers. The substitution of machines for workers in farming — a hallmark of the elimination of surplus labor from village Japan — was the result of market forces. But it was also the indirect consequence of the dual price system for rice designed to equalize incomes enjoyed by rural and urban Japanese households. By bolstering the price of agricultural output government policy rendered the terms of trade — the price of goods sold relative to goods purchased — more favorable to Japanese farmers than they would have been otherwise. Market forces — relative price changes — drove the restructuring of Japanese village life but the relative prices reflected policy to an important degree.

That augmentation of the factors of production was the dominant factor in the productivity improvements enjoyed by post-1955 Japanese farming is evident from the estimates of sector specific total factor productivity growth assembled in Panel A.3 of Appendix Table A.10. The negative estimate for total factor productivity growth over the period 1961–1973 suggests that output was growing slower than the growth of combined input for the augmented factors of production, labor, capital, and land. Factor augmentation in the sector was so overwhelming that it outstripped the growth of output by a considerable margin.

9.3. Productivity Gain in Manufacturing

Unlike agriculture, manufacturing — or more accurately certain sub-sectors of manufacturing — enjoyed total factor growth coupled with substantial augmentation of labor and capital. The main sources of total factor productivity growth in manufacturing were innovation and the import and adaptation of foreign technology. By and large market forces did dictate the nature of the processes involved — but as with agriculture — policy did play some role. For manufacturing the main contribution made by policy was industrial policy largely implemented by the Ministry of International Trade and Industry (M.I.T.I.).

During Miracle Growth the heavy industry sub-sectors of manufacturing expanded rapidly. Consider the indices for value added generated appearing in Panel B.7 in Appendix Table A.9. In comparison with relatively lethargic growth for light industries like textiles that dominated pre-World War II manufacturing production and exports, iron and steel, non-ferrous metals and chemicals grew by leaps and bounds. To be sure this statement is about relative growth, not absolute growth. In both textiles and food and tobacco total value added generated did increase between the late 1950s and the early 1970s. But relative to the 1930s the expansion of output was less impressive.

The classic heavy industries like metal working and chemicals grew extremely rapidly between 1956 and 1975. Lagging slightly behind these sub-sectors in terms of growth prior to the mid-1970s were machinery — both nonelectric machinery and electric machinery — transport equipment (including shipbuilding) and precision machinery. As the growth in the heavy industries began to slow and falter in the early 1970s, growth in all three sub-sectors of machinery production took off. In short a pattern of growth acceleration followed by de-acceleration is evident in the data on sub-sector growth. The first sectors to experience substantial growth, for instance labor intensive textiles in the Meiji period, eventually experience decline in growth, the impetus now shifting towards other industries requiring greater inputs of technically trained and skilled workers like iron and steel. Eventually the drive towards expansion shifts away from the heavy industries toward technology intensive industries like electrical machinery and precision machinery. The shift in the domestic composition of manufacturing mimics, parallels, the flying geese pattern of trade.

That the existence of a trade related component to the compositional shifts in manufacturing likely raises the issue of the geographic shift in Japan's trade pattern due to Japan's loss of empire at the close of the Pacific War. In the aftermath of the war, Japan's export markets shifted decisively away from low per capita income Asia towards high income per capita markets in North America, especially in the United States, and Western Europe. This shift made sense in terms of the geopolitical realities of the post-World War II period. Japan had alienated many of the Asian countries during the period of militarism: in particular China, Korea, and a number of South East Asian lands occupied by the Japanese Army. Resuming trade with these nations was either problematic or impossible. But in the aftermath of the Pacific War Japan became an ally of the United States, therefore a friend of those Western European nations aligned with the United States in the new Cold War environment. It was natural for Japanese trading companies and export oriented manufacturers to shift their marketing focus towards Japan's new allies. At the same time it was natural for Japanese companies to look to firms based in North America and Western Europe for technology transfer, seeking out licensing agreements that would grant them access to engineering improvements being made in those regions of the world. Japan's trade in commodities became inextricably linked to its trade in technology.

The opportunity to secure technologic improvements made in the United States and Western Europe was important for total factor productivity growth within the sub-sectors of manufacturing that commenced rapid expansion in the second half of the Miracle Growth period. That total factor productivity growth was unusually rapid in electric machinery, precision machinery, and air transportation is the message of Panel A.3 in Appendix Table A.10. The fact that the pace of total factor productivity growth slowed down during the period after 1973 suggests that Japanese firms were catching up with their rivals in North America and Western Europe during the Miracle Growth era by securing technology licensing agreements, closing in on the technological frontier. Subsequent total factor productivity growth was more desultory, the advances in knowledge increasingly coming from domestic research and development not through the securing of blueprints and methods pioneered by foreign engineers and laboratories situated abroad. Brutal competition within the domestic market, major contenders in particular sub-sectors — for instance Hitachi, Fujitsu, Matsushita, Sony, Sharp, Mitsubishi Electric in the field of consumer electronics all attempting to steal a march on competitors by cutting deals with American, British, French, and German manufacturers — was a driving force in the foreign technology importation process.

So was policy. Industrial policy largely formulated in M.I.T.I. facilitated the process by which foreign technology flowed into the new high speed growth sub-sectors of manufacturing: by driving down price for technology license agreements; and by encouraging brisk diffusion. Intervening in most technology licensing agreements during the Miracle Growth period, government bureaucrats were able to assume the role of the ultimate and sole purchaser of the licensing arrangement — thereby staving off the upward pressure on licensing price due to competition between Japanese companies all fighting to secure a deal in order to get a competitive edge on their domestic rivals — simultaneously exploiting competition within the ranks of foreign companies willing to sell the licenses at a price. By guaranteeing that patents within the domestic market were short-lived, the bureaucracy was also able to promote rapid diffusion among rival domestic companies. Catch-up growth was unusually rapid because M.I.T.I. perfected a market conforming coordination approach to stimulating technological progress within manufacturing, bureaucrats assigned to specific sub-sector bureaus working together with representatives of associations formed within the sub-sectors themselves.

The M.I.T.I. bureaucracy eschewed the top–down approach of the command and control model in which bureaucrats, politicians or military figures — lacking the detailed knowledge of how to apply technological advances that factory managers and shop floor engineers enjoy — made decisions regarding production volumes and methods of operation without serious regard to cost. Rather policies, including targeting — the Ministry sending signals out to manufacturing concerning the sub-sectors that it viewed as key, using subsidies, tax breaks, and other incentives — were developed jointly by firms vigorously engaged in competing for market share through price and product development and a corps of bureaucrats that was positioned to take a global approach above the competitive battle for market share taking place within particular sub-sectors. An important advantage that the M.I.T.I. bureaucracy enjoyed was that it worked with planning models based on matrices of sub-sector interaction linking sub-sectors supplying components and materials to sub-sectors purchasing these products as inputs.

An excellent example of how M.I.T.I. intervened in the field of electronics is its promotion of the domestic mainframe computer sub-sector through its interaction with International Business Machines (I.B.M.). During the 1950s and early 1960s the American company I.B.M. enjoyed a huge "first mover" advantage in manufacturing the massive mainframe computers that were the principal devices for carrying on large scale computation: it could rent the computers rather than selling them, providing service contracts for business users and developing new operating systems far in advance of rivals. It could afford to lease machine on service contracts rather than sell the machines outright since the revenue streams it secured on its base of service contracts were so vast. Lacking this advantage, potential rivals faced substantial barriers to entry within the industry. In particular this was a deterrent for electronics manufacturers like Hitachi and Fujitsu. Hence in Miracle Growth Japan where the demand for computers within industry was growing rapidly — in automobiles, ship-building, and iron and steel — there was a strong and growing appetite for I.B.M.'s services. Recognizing this, and bent on promoting the development of domestic rivals to I.B.M., M.I.T.I. agreed to allow I.B.M. to establish a Japanese based subsidiary (Japan I.B.M.) on the condition that I.B.M. divest itself of techniques and methods from its vast storehouse of knowledge useful to potential rivals like Hitachi and Fujitsu. This action sped up the pace of both mainframe software and hardware total factor productivity growth within Japan. To overcome I.B.M.'s market advantage in being able to lease rather than sell very expensive mainframe computers to business enterprises, M.I.T.I. created a partly private/partly public subsidiary, the Japan Electronics Equipment Corporation (J.E.E.C.) that purchased mainframes from Japanese rivals to I.B.M., leasing the machines out to businesses seeking computation power.

As important as diffusion of foreign technology was to the pace of total factor productivity growth, domestic innovation was also important. A prime example is the *kanban* ("flag") system developed at Toyota Motor Corporation.[6] This system — in place at Toyota Motor Corporation vehicle assembly plants prior to the widespread introduction of robots in place of assembly workers in Toyota's plants — rested on doing away with production targets for each division within the plant, relying instead on the "pull" of the assembly process to determine what each division produced on a given day. Alongside each division was a pallet designed to accommodate boxes each flagged with a *kanban* indicating the number of components in the box and the exact specification for each component, for instance diameter and threading for bolts. A small vehicle picked up empty boxes at each division, the components having been used up by that division, delivering it to the division that produced the particular component involved. For instance when the door division exhausted the bolts generated by the bolt division it placed an empty box on its pallets flagged to communicate the type and number of newly fabricated bolts required. The division in receipt of the empty box was expected to respond as soon as possible, setting up its machines in order to turn out the desired number of components requested as soon as it possibly can muster the effort. Components were not warehoused; rather they were produced just-in-time.

The just-in-time system was an innovation, one that went hand in hand with the drive to improve product quality through the relentless search for "zero-defects" in each stage of manufacturing. That a high rate of defect was a problem in this system of production followed from the fact that under a "just-in-time" regime, the existence of defects would slow the flow of assembly to an unacceptably lethargic pace. Moreover producing defective components was immediately apparent. If the door division received a box of incorrectly threaded bolts the group of workers committing the errors was obvious. The drive to overcome Japan's reputation of producing low quality products — earned during the period between the world wars by companies orienting their exports towards low per capita income markets in Asia — was closely associated with the drive to build quality into consumer durables through the "zero defect" and "just-in-time" principles that became hallmarks of assembly industries in Miracle Growth Japan.

From a human resource management point of view the advantages of this innovation for organizing shop floor work flow are quite apparent: workers monitor each others' output. A worker unwilling to work flexibly in teams that maintain high standards in manufacturing was easily identified, denied bonuses, put on the slow track for promotion to more responsible positions in the hierarchy of the firm's internalized labor market.[7] Indeed flexibility in accepting job assignments was a key aspect of the system. In the event of unavoidable absences within a division — say due to illnesses suffered by workers — colleagues who normally worked in other divisions might have to take their places. That wages were determined independently of work assignment or de facto job classification, largely shaped by age and seniority, facilitated introduction of "just-in-time" and "zero-defect" throughout the world of large and medium sized manufacturing firms during Miracle Growth. An additional factor contributing to the spread of these practices throughout Japanese manufacturing was the augmentation of labor quality due to enhanced education and improved health amongst rank and file shop floor workers. Education was definitely a potent factor. For example in search of "zero-defects" shop floor worker teams participated in quality control circles, using basic principles of statistics and engineering to devise methods for eliminating, or at least cutting down, on product defects.

In sum, total factor productivity growth in Miracle Growth Japan was closely associated with augmentation of labor and the reduction of elite/nonelite distinctions in the workplace. All employees — blue collar and white collar — wore company uniforms. Engineers worked closely with quality control circles formed by assembly line workers. Wages were not independent of educational attainment to be sure — starting college graduate worker wages exceeded those earned by starting high school workers within a cohort of freshly hired employees — but over the long-term promotion for a worker was closely tied by work effort, diligence, and willingness to take on job assignments flexibly. The spread of compulsory middle school education and the spread of industrial democracy were integral to total factor productivity growth.

Overall, for those thinkers attempting to conceptualize the Miracle Growth Japanese economy as a total system the various components are not difficult to pinpoint: augmentation of labor and capital; high rates of capital formation; import and adaptation of foreign technology assisted by coordination style industrial policy involving the cooperation of government and private industry in the formulation of market friendly polices; innovation linked to the diffusion of institutions for managing and motivating workers exemplifying principles of industrial democracy that explicitly rejected elitism; and the spread of mass consumerism yielding huge increases in demand for the output of the manufacturing sector.

9.4. Struggling with the Legacy of Miracle Growth, 1975–2005

Miracle Growth ended in the early 1970s, the growth rate of the Japanese economy slowing down dramatically. Gone where the days when income per capita was growing at rates of over 5% per annum.

Diminishing returns had set in.

Diminishing returns set in to total factor productivity growth because Japanese firms had managed to reduce the gap in technology between themselves and the most advanced firms abroad, exhausting to an important extent the cornucopia of foreign techniques and engineering advances that they drew from during Miracle Growth. Once a country's firms are on the cutting edge of new technology development they face tremendous uncertainties about which research and development projects will pan out in the marketplace. The pace of total factor productivity change is slow for a nation near the technological frontier.

Diminishing returns set in for labor augmentation. As income per capita rose during the Miracle Growth era more and more families found themselves able to finance the higher education of their offspring. As advancement rates from junior high school to high school and from high school to college or university increased, the quality of the marginal student, the one just on the cusp of deciding to advance or not advance, dropped. Early on in the Miracle Growth period only the very talented children of poorer households advanced on to university. By the early 1970s this had changed.

As more and more children competed for entry into college and university departments the competition for slots in the most prestigious school intensified. To be successful one had to memorize historical facts more accurately, master the logic of mathematics and the theories and experiments integral to modern scientific research even more intently. Private cram schools proliferated to prepare students for the grueling competition. To get into a highly ranked university one had to pass the entrance tests for a highly ranked high school; to enter a highly ranked high school one had to enter a highly ranked middle school; and so forth. As cram schools proliferated the costs of gaining entry to the best schools soared. The result was a drift back towards elitism, in this case educational elitism.

Diminishing returns set in for capital. As the ratio of capital to output increased — by the early 1980s Japan's ratio exceeded that of the United States due to the high savings and investment rates in Japan — the return on putting a new machine in place fell. With the number of workers increasing fairly slowly — population growth rates in Japan mainly reflecting the difference between fertility and mortality (both rates reaching low levels during the early 1960s) — increase in the number of lathes, computer screens, and trucks above and beyond the modest population expansion did little to improve the level or quality of output per worker. With technological progress slowing down, the opportunity to embody the latest techniques in a newly minted machine diminishes as well. The benefits of incremental capital augmentation declined.

This was not only true for private corporate capital. It was also true for infrastructure: for roads, container port harbors, for hydroelectric grids, for airports, for bridges. There are economic limits on how much of this infrastructure can be built up. At some point, say in the 1980s, roads and harbors under construction were not truly facilitating output increases.

Diminishing returns set in for structural change. As is apparent from Panel A.2 in Appendix Table A.10 between 1955 and 1973, moving workers out of agricultural employment and out of self employment into employment elsewhere — mainly in manufacturing — contributed to total factor productivity growth. By the close of the Miracle Growth period there was much less potential for securing this type of structural change because the labor force left in farming and in self employment had been substantially reduced. The same holds for shifting workers within sub-sectors of manufacturing say from labor intensive textiles to electronics. Of course it was possible to move workers from manufacturing to services, but Japanese firms in the service sector — in mom and pop store retail, in department stores, in banking — were generally incapable of seizing upon the institutional innovations in labor markets that yielded innovations like *kanban*, nor were they able to exploit a wealth of foreign corporate techniques, to raise their total factor productivity. In short structural change ran into diminishing returns.

To say that returns diminished does not mean that total factor productivity growth ceased in all sectors of the Japanese economy. From Panel A.3 of Appendix Table A.10 it is apparent that it did not. But the pace of growth fell off. Japan's slowdown was apparent by the end of the 1970s. As can be seen from the long-run estimates of total factor productivity growth for the Japanese economy as a whole, total factor productivity gradually increased from the late 19th century through the end of the Miracle Growth period, then fell off. This is the long-run arc of total factor productivity growth for Japan. That there was acceleration in total factor productivity growth can be attributed to augmentation of the factors of production; to institutional and policy responses to the opportunities for importing and adapting foreign technology; to domestic innovation; and to infrastructure construction. But eventually this augmentation ran into diminishing returns.

Also running into constraints on expansion was trade. Throughout the period between the late 1880s and 1950 Japan's net trade balance was generally negative: imports exceeding exports. This state of affairs changed during the Miracle Growth era, Japan's net export demand moving into the black after the mid-1960s, remaining positive through 2000.[8] A mix of market forces and policy explain these movements.

On the domestic policy side restrictions on imports played an important role. These consisted of tariffs and nontariff barriers like quotas, government regulations for product quality, and the distribution system. Tariffs protected infant industries from international competition. As Japanese firms moved down their cost curves, tariffs and quotas (the most egregious and visible protectionist measures) were dismantled. More problematic were regulation and the domestic distribution system. The latter involved so-called vertical organized business groups, vertical keiretsu marketing chains linking producers to wholesalers to retailers being closed off to all companies other than those admitted to the group. Regulation was another issue since it involved policy. Government ministries set product standards for domestic products — for automobiles, pharmaceuticals, fruit, and meat — holding up entry of imports from abroad under the guise of requiring adequate guarantees about the imported product quality. Studying the components of imported automobiles could require months of testing.

Market forces were crucial as well. One involved the exchange rate, the other total factor productivity growth in export oriented firms. From the early 1950s until the early 1970s when the Bretton Woods system (a revived gold standard centered around exchange rates fixed to the United States dollar) collapsed, the Japanese yen was set at an exchange rate of 360 yen to a United States dollar. This arrangement was made during the American Occupation period. The rate was set to eliminate Japan's chronic balance of payments problem, imports exceeded exports. For successful Japanese companies that enjoyed substantial total factor productivity growth — Toyota, Honda, Sony, Fujitsu, Hitachi, Mitsubishi Electronics, Sharp — unit costs of production fell dramatically over the Miracle Growth period. The result was a massive expansion of exports under the fixed exchange rate system, in particular a massive growth in Japan's exports of iron and steel, consumer electronics, and automobiles to the United States.

After the early 1970s this changed, mainly because policy makers in the United States were becoming increasingly concerned about the American component of Japan's exports profile, the fact that American exports to Japan fell far short of Japanese exports to the United States, a growing source of political friction between the two nations. One approach adopted by the American and Japanese negotiators was to realign the relative values of the two national currencies, driving up the yen, driving down the dollar in a bid to discourage American import of products and encourage Japanese imports of American products. The best example of this is the Plaza Accord of 1985. Partly as a result of the Accord the yen climbed relative to the United States dollar at a rate of 8.7% per annum between 1986 and 1990; at a rate of 9.1% between 1991 and 1995.[9]

The era between the mid-1980s and the mid-1990s is known as the *endaka* (the "high yen" era) period. One feature of this era is that despite Japanese export volumes to the United States — units shipped — declining, the trade imbalance between the two countries computed in American dollars remained substantial simply because each Japanese product became more expensive when calibrated in American dollars. One reason why Japanese products remained relatively competitive in the American market despite their soaring price tag is product quality. For instance most Japanese automobiles were still considered a good buy because their repair records were excellent.

Because exchange rate realignment did not prove to be the panacea United States negotiators hoped it would be, the American side was not content to restrict its pressure on Japanese political leaders to central bank action. As well the United States secured Japanese government commitment to a program of voluntary export restraints designed to limit through set quotas the volumes of certain Japanese products exported to the United States. In addition the two countries opened up talks regarding structural impediments to trade, the Americans pushing for deregulation in Japan and the abolition of the department store law limiting the size of distributors. In short friction between the United States and Japan over time did put limits on Japan's trade growth. Similar friction between Japan and some of its trade partners in Western Europe also contributed to foreign countries placing restrictions on the Japan's growing penetration of markets abroad.

One of the most important consequences of the upward movement of the Japanese yen after the early 1970s followed by the remarkable surge in the yen's value during the *endaka* period was the growing export of capital out of Japan, especially into other nearby Asian countries — South Korea, Taiwan, later China — where labor costs were lower. More and more Japanese companies established subsidiaries throughout Asia. A side benefit of this search for lower production costs was the fact that exports from these companies coming out of countries like Taiwan or Thailand were not treated as Japanese imports by the United States and Western European countries. From a domestic viewpoint, however, this meant loss of jobs at home, the hollowing out of some venerated sectors of manufacturing like cotton textiles and iron and steel. This was the flying geese pattern with a vengeance.

Industrial policy also ran into limits, into diminishing returns. An excellent example is the TRON project. Emerging out of embarrassment over the revelation of a technology stealing operation carried out by Mitsubishi and Hitachi designed to secure secrets from I.B.M., the Japanese government sponsored a research effort in the Japanese computer industry contrived to lead it away from its almost obsessive focus on I.B.M., encouraging the development of a Japan-specific operating system for Japanese computers. While this project did yield some benefits within Japan itself — it created nontariff barriers to import of American and European designed software — it damaged the capacity of the Japanese business software industry to generate exports abroad. In the international arena, I.B.M.'s mainframe and personal computer remained unassailable. From that perspective TRON was a failure.

Testifying to the growing importance of popular culture, however, was the success of Japanese software developers who focused not on business clients but on video game users. Companies like Nintendo — which eschewed participation in government sponsored industrial policy — enjoyed robust growth in sales both inside and outside of Japan.

A combination of *endaka*, weak domestic banking, the success of a small group of Japanese companies in holding onto customer bases in the high income per capita companies, the overall decline in total factor productivity growth and the fall in rates of return on new capital formation in manufacturing (that discouraged investment), the misguided protectionism of industrial policy, all came together to generate a massive twin asset market bubble in Japan. Two markets were profoundly impacted: the real estate market and the stock market. From the mid-1980s until December 1989 when the bubble began to burst the upward movement in asset prices was remarkable. Indicative of this upward pressure on prices is that fact that residential prices roared up almost 70% during 1988 alone.

After the bubble burst Japan entered a period of anaemic growth in output. For instance as shown in Panel A.1 of Appendix Table A.4 income per capita barely increased at all between 1991 and 2000. A hallmark of this period was the failure of Japanese banks that were heavily involved in lending on the real estate market. Caught in the downward slide of asset prices several went under, most propped up a government determined to avert financial bankruptcy, a government attempting to introduce a measure program of structural reforms and bailouts.

After the collapse of the bubble economy and several decades of flagging aggregate economic performance, there was a growing cacophony of public criticism chastising the elites of the Miracle Growth period. Within Japan's domestic political arena and popular press made cynical over scandals in the bureaucracy and in political circles alike there was more and more grumbling about Japan's elite. Once venerated as the architects of Japanese Miracle Growth, the iron triangle found itself increasingly vilified by a body politic angered by bursting bubbles, bank failures, bailout packages designed to prop up uncompetitive financial institutions, and stagnation. At the beginning of the 21st century Japan found itself rejecting the very elite that had led, or at least claimed to have led, Japan out of the abyss and shambles of unconditional surrender. Once again Japanese elites were in decline.

Endnotes

1. See p.146 in Mosk (1995). For the increase in average number of years of schooling completed in Japan see Panel C.1 in Appendix Table A.6.
2. For the figures on which these calculations are based see p. 125 in Mosk (1995).

3. For an extended discussion of these issues see Chaps. 5 and 6 in Mosk (1995).

4. The percentages are based on household expenditure surveys conducted by agencies of the Japanese government. See p. 288 of Mosk (2008).

5. For details see pp. 294–300 in Mosk (2008).

6. For a more detailed account of the *kanban* system see pp. 253–256 in Mosk (2008).

7. See p. 255 in Mosk (2008).

8. See Table A.6 on p. 364 of Mosk (2008).

9. For movement in the United States dollar/Japanese exchange rate over the period 1961–2000 see Table A.4 on p. 361 of Mosk (2008).

10

Command and Control and Its Aftermath in China

10.1. The Main Characteristics of Command and Control in China

In principle when the Communist Party assumed control over the government and economic policy making agencies of mainland China it was committed to a command and control model for Chinese economic development. While not untrue, the statement is incomplete.

Command and control systems come in a variety of flavors. The variant that guided policy making in the People's Republic of China over the three decades between 1949 and 1978 was inextricably linked to and shaped by three basic policy goals of the Chinese Communist Party: (1) guaranteeing national security against all disruptive forces threatening it both foreign and domestic through a program of militarization and nationalism; (2) managing transition to a utopian Communist future characterized by egalitarianism and political mobilization for continuing national revolution and purification of individual behavior through the creation of a "mass line" flowing from the bottom up from local level cadres to Party organs that refine the line, broadcasting it back down to the masses as propaganda; and (3) raising the average standard of living by combining a state controlled sector — consisting of state owned enterprises operating under a nexus of mandated quotas and prices shaping selfish incentives — with a private sector adhering to both mandated and market prices.

These goals overlapped to some extent, conflicted to some extent. Not surprisingly factions developed within the Party, some emphasizing national security goals above all else, some concerned with maximizing the growth rate of income per capita through a calibrated program of incentives, some emphasizing purification and political mobilization.

The priorities of the factions conflicting to a degree, the outbreak of infighting between Party factions was almost inevitable. Perhaps implying that the priorities only differed to a modest degree is an understatement. Appealing to individualistic greed and naked ambition undercuts romantic revolutionary utopianism advocating egalitarianism and selfless conformity to a "mass line" channeled out of the political center. In order to build military force respectable economic growth was essential, especially in the weapons producing heavy industrial sector. Could this be achieved without sacrificing consumer goods like clothing, food, and adequate housing hence the standard of living of the masses? Could it be achieved without making use of selfish incentives designed to discourage waste, to direct manufacturers to take into account the ever present tradeoff between quota driven production volume and price driven product quality? What use are shoddily fabricated guns that misfire? Could purification campaigns and ongoing Party purges contain the natural tendency toward corruption that exists in hierarchically organized bureaucracies and political parties, powerful figures enjoying the capacity to extract economic rents from subordinates and supplicants, thereby abusing their privileged positions?

That the new elites of post-1949 China fought with one another over principles and priorities through factional infighting is only part of the story however. They also competed with one another in a naked search for power, jockeying for positions of influence in the Central Committee and the Politburo of the Communist Party. Exactly what dynamics characterized this competition for power within the upper echelons of the Party remains a mystery. Based on empirical analysis of leadership changes at least two models have been suggested: one based on the principle of balance of power and the other based on the idea of winner-takes-all in a well defined hierarchy.[1] Most analysts favor a winner-takes-all model for the period leading up to the Cultural Revolution, arguing the Maoist faction managed to dominate most of the policy making agenda until the acknowledged failures of the Great Leap Forward and the outbreak of the massive famine of the 1959–1961 period ushered in a period of political instability.

The key concepts of the Maoist program of development owe their origins to the Yan'an period of the 1930s, refined during the 1950s.[2] They mixed utopian Communist ideals based on the promotion of a "mass line" sensitive to the practical needs of rural China — for education and health care — with militarism and a strong emphasis on public as opposed to private ownership of the means of production, favoring state managed factories in the manufacturing sector and collectivized farms in the agricultural sector. Given the emphasis on military needs Maoist policy put a priority on accelerating the growth of output of the heavy industrial sector — iron and steel, chemicals, machine making — through investment in large urban factories and rural based blast furnaces and chemical plants attached to communes.

While it was rooted in a utopian vision, the Maoist program was not insensitive to practical economic considerations. For instance the collectivization of agriculture was designed to extract surplus labor out of village China, bolstering the health and educational levels of farm populations in order to free up the labor of farm populations for work in rural manufacturing but it was basically hostile to private market incentives. For strategic purposes the Maoists did tolerate private farm plots but they viewed this as a temporary expedient to be jettisoned with collectivization wedded to campaign glorifying the selfless commitment of workers to Communist egalitarian goals. A similar hostility towards private sector activity informed the Maoist strategy regarding the geographic focus of urbanization. In general the Maoist faction shunned the old treaty ports like Shanghai in which capitalist enterprise and interchange with foreign commercial interests — British, German, French, Americans, and Japanese — had become entrenched by the mid-1930s. They favored rural over urban; they favored cities in the interior over those on the coastline. This became the basis for the Third Front strategy of urbanization designed to construct factory towns and cities within the hinterland, in some instances in green field sites, far from the coast, less vulnerable to bombing or takeover by an invading enemy power.

Opposed to the Maoist vision were key political actors like Chen Yun who emphasized incentives over propaganda, political mobilization and utopianism.[3] Chen's program did not reject the command and control planning model. Indeed it was strongly in favor of technologically sophisticated bureaucrats — intellectuals — setting production quotas and state mandated prices for some branches of industry and agriculture through a State Planning Commission working with Five Year Plans. But the Chen faction believed that private markets responding to the forces of supply and demand should co-exist with state managed markets. They did not believe that collectivizing agriculture would solve China's agricultural problems, arguing that cadre directed communal management was inferior to the wisdom of market oriented family farmers responding to price signals. The Chen faction favored balanced growth — agriculture, light industry producing consumer goods, and heavy industry all growing in tandem with one another — not unbalanced growth in which heavy industry investment outstripped by a large margin investment in the other two sectors. They believed that investment rates should be modest, at least in the early period of industrial development, so that the average household could experience a rise in its consumption, an improvement in its standard of living. They emphasized that a set of mandated prices should be designed in such as way as to induce suppliers to meet both quality and quantity targets, being sufficiently differentiated along quality lines to ensure a proper mix.

It would be fair to crudely summarize the contrast between the two factions by saying that the Maoist model put utopian politics and militarism in command, the Chen model put economics, elite bureaucrats, and mundane market incentives in command.

As a sweeping generalization drawn from the statistical record it would appear that the Maoist program prevailed over the Chen program prior to the late 1970s. Or rather it would be more accurate to say the Chen faction managed to tone down the Maoist program on the margins but was unable to dominate overall.

Consider the issues of balanced versus unbalanced growth and the degree of state ownership in manufacturing plant and equipment during the 1952–1978 era. In 1949 state managed factories generated 26% of manufacturing, the corporate private sector 49%, and plants owned by individuals 23%.[4] By 1957, these percentages were 54% for the proportion of state managed manufacturing output, around zero for the corporate private sector, and about 1% for individually owned enterprises. Again consider the sector by sector composition of capital construction investment: in 1957, 1962, 1965, 1975, and 1979 over 50% went into heavy industry.[5] In those same years the percentage allocated to light industry never exceeded 10% and the percentage accruing to the agricultural sector never exceeded 22% (in most of the above mentioned years agriculture's share was below

15%). Again consider output growth by sector: Panels A.3, A.6, and A.8 in Appendix Table A.3 make clear the dominance of industry in overall output expansion — construction and transport and communications growing somewhat slower — these sectors far outstripping farming, services, and commerce. Again as Panel C.7 of Appendix Table A.9 demonstrates employment growth in light industry lagged behind employment growth in heavy industry despite having a capital/labor ratio far below that of the typical heavy industrial sector plant.

That not taking into account the importance of incentives mimicking those operative in a market oriented economy posed a problem for the Maoist policy making agenda — a major reason for the rejection of the agenda by the advocates of Chen's approach — is apparent from the total factor productivity growth figures given in Panel C.1 of Appendix Table A.10. The estimates in that table suggest that total factor productivity growth was actually negative during the period 1957–1978. This was the case despite the fact that the pace of labor augmentation was also modest during this era.

The relative slow pace of urbanization — particularly in the coastal zone — is another characteristic of the period when command and control policies of a Maoist cast were shaping economic development. To be sure China's urban population grew faster than its total population during this period, but in comparison to the 1980s the rate of rural to urban transfer was modest.[6] There are a number of reasons for this: difficulties encountered in transferring ones family registration to a metropolitan center, and informal and formal pressure by the authorities to keep rural dwellers in their communes.[7] Had the authorities not restricted rural to urban migration it is likely the pressure on city resources would have been far greater. That there was excess demand for slots in the urban sector stemmed from a combination of policy and the relatively rapid pace of industrial expansion. The policy involved tilting the terms of trade against agriculture by setting relatively low prices for foodstuffs secured by government agencies from the farming sector. The poor terms of trade for agriculture acted as an implicit subsidy for urban dwellers. One of the side effects of the policy was to slow the pace at which the farming sector could acquire outputs from the manufacturing sector.

In short, the particular version of the command and control model adopted by the Chinese political elite during the three decades following Communist takeover of the mainland was more Maoist than Chen inspired. No where was this more evident than in the agricultural sector.

10.2. Productivity Gain in Agriculture

The Maoist inspired program for reducing the burden of surplus labor in rural China was simultaneously utopian and pragmatic.

The logic of collectivization of agriculture was designed to promote the diffusion of Party ideology and militarization in the countryside. This was the political side of the agenda.

At the same time the underlying logic of much of the Maoist strategy was designed to raise hours worked and enhance the productivity of each hour worked, thereby freeing up labor for industrial work. For instance placing midwives and clinics on communes improved health and dramatically reduced infant mortality rates. Raising the educational attainment of the average rural dweller through the Socialist Education Movement saw rural illiteracy rates plummet. Marshalling scale economies through the management of large production units by trained cadres was designed to improve efficiency and bring accountability into the system, reducing the incidence of corruption. Mobilizing teams of farm labor to build roads, dig tube wells, and fashion irrigation ditches augmented land. Paying workers on the basis of work points (a policy temporarily abandoned in favor of paying according to need rather than according to contributions to productivity during the heyday of utopianism) gave workers incentives to work longer hours. Assigning technically trained experts to communes who were familiar with high yielding Green Revolution seed varieties fostered the diffusion of technology and promoted land augmentation.

Testimony to the marrying of political utopianism to hardboiled pragmatic considerations is the fact that the collectivization of Chinese agriculture took place through a set of carefully calibrated stages.[8]

In the first phase between 1952 and 1955 Party cadres encouraged farm households enjoying private property rights in land to pool their labor in Mutual Aid Teams. From mid 1955 to 1956, cadres began the push to create Agricultural Producers Cooperatives (A.P.C.'s). In the first stage of the A.P.C. movement agricultural work and capital investment in farming was managed by the cooperative. From the yield of the co-operative the state took a certain quota of foodstuffs plus taxes, the remainder to be divided up among members of the cooperative on the basis of work points. The cooperative rented the land from the households that were still clinging to their private property rights. Through the Spring of 1956 the focus of the rural reform program was on securing scale economies in the management of agriculture and on motivating farmers to increase labor input by remunerating effort on the basis of hours worked. But private property rights in the land — secured by poor peasant households in the contentious years of land reform — still prevailed.

The next stage of reform was designed to deal a blow to nascent capitalism in the countryside by doing away with private property rights in land. To some extent the drive to collectivize land and the other means of production in farming was a response to the emergence of groups of middle income farmers — so-called "rich" peasants — in some regions of the country. For those utopian Communists within the Maoist faction this was anathema. As a lead-up to a crucial component of the Great Leap Forward strategy designed to promote the building of blast furnaces in rural China spewing out vast quantities of pig iron — the complete collectivization of agriculture in communes operating in an increasingly egalitarian manner, households being allocated food on a so-called "free" basis, that is in part on the basis of needs not contributions to commune labor supply — cadres restructured the A.P.C.'s. Hallmarks of the restructuring were the creation of three tiers for commune management — collectives, production brigades, and production teams — and the complete collectivization of land without compensation. Commenced in the Spring of 1956 the early version of this drive to create Advanced Stage Agricultural Producers' Cooperatives private plots continued to allow the holding of some farmland in private plots but subsequent campaigns, begun in 1957 and intensified in the Spring of 1958 were designed to further erode the existence of rural private property.

The utopian Communist vision for rural China was almost completely realized between the late summer of 1958, and spring, 1958. Village China was completed integrated into People's Communes. The Communes coordinated all activities, political, military, and economic. All land and assets with the exception of a miniscule number of animals were collectivized. A percentage of all food distributed in commune mess halls was provided to households on the basis of consumption needs, the remainder being allocated as before on the basis of work points. This is as close as village China came to realizing the utopian Maoist vision, retrenchment setting in 1959 and 1960 with the decentralization of commune management and the reduction in the percentage of food allocated on a "free" basis.

Why did retrenchment set in? The answer is the Great Famine of 1959–1961. The exact loss of life due to starvation will never be known for sure: estimates range widely, for instance from 16.5 million excess deaths to 29.5 million excess deaths.[9] What is clear is that the Great Leap Forward was a failure in the sense that it led to the worst famine in the history of the 20th century. Why did the famine occur? Debate continues: Kueh (1995) implicates the weather; others argue that commune egalitarianism was at fault, households consuming too much food since some of it was provided on a "free" basis. Other arguments include the overly ambitious reallocation of labor from farming to iron production and resistance to collectivization on the part of richer peasants who destroyed draft animals in anticipation of the capital levy.

The political consequences were far reaching. The Maoists were attacked, perhaps unfairly because the Central Committee of the Party that represented the voices of all major factions including the Chen faction had signed off on the Great Leap Forward program. The resulting faction fighting served as a prelude to the Cultural Revolution that began in 1966 and resulted in chaotic political fighting, harsh purges, attacks on key factional leaders, and massive waves of violence that were not completely suppressed until the early 1970s.[10] Was the call to action of massive numbers of Red Guards dedicated to the cult of Mao an attempt on the part of the Maoists to gain an upper hand over other factions in the Party? Was it designed to slow the slide away from utopian Communism or was it the result of a bid by a key military leader of the People's Liberation Army, Lin Biao, to secure a position of hegemony within the party by venerating the thoughts of Mao Zedong vigorous promotion of the little Red Book culling from Mao's writings the key concepts of the Maoist vision used to indoctrinate soldiers in the army?

What is clear is that many rural cadres assigned to communes became disenchanted with the Great Leap Forward philosophy, realizing creating a system of incentives are crucial to raising agricultural productivity in China. In effect the middle peasants co-opted cadres, particularly in districts of China where the influence of central government policy making was muted. Indeed Yang (1996) argues that cadres disillusioned with Maoist utopianism took the lead in promoted market friendly reforms in Chinese agriculture in the late 1970s and early 1980s.

How did Chinese agriculture fare under Maoist inspired command and control policies? To evaluate this question it is useful to employ Japan's experience as a benchmark against which to judge China's experience.

In setting the stage for comparison it is important to keep in mind that the dynamics of population growth were remarkably different in Japan and China over the period of command and control in China. Japan was completing the demographic transition, fertility falling dramatically in urban and rural areas alike. As a result population growth was relatively slow in Japan during the period. According to Panel A.5 of Appendix Table A.6 Japan's population increased about 40% between the mid-1950s and the late 1970s. By contrast as can be seen from Panel A.1 in Appendix Table A.6 China's population increased by almost 80% over the corresponding period. To an important degree China's population increase was fueled by Maoist policies in the countryside. Introducing "barefoot doctors," midwives and clinics into cooperatives and communes reduced mortality rates for all persons, especially babies and infants. This is apparent from Panels A.2 and A.3 in Appendix Table A.6. The surge in human numbers — broken only by the upward thrust in mortality during the Great Famine — was tolerated by policy makers at first; eventually the Party introduced the One Child policy, designed to set a quotas of one birth per household that could be exceeded but only at considerable cost. In short population growth in China was far more vigorous than it was in Japan, growth in human numbers putting greater pressure on Chinese farming than was the case in Japan.

Comparing the two farming sectors statistically boils down to looking at three variables: labor augmentation, land augmentation, and the substitution of physical capital for labor. The relevant statistics appear in Appendix Tables A.6, A.8, and A.10. As Panels C.1–C.3 in Table A.6 make clear, Chinese educational attainment made massive improvements during the Maoist command and control period, particularly in rural China. In the case of the village this was largely an outgrowth of the Socialist Education Movement. To be sure much of the teaching carried out in the Socialist Education Movement campaigns of the late 1950s and 1960s was designed to promote Party ideology, Mao Zedong thought in particular after the early 1960s. Still, rural illiteracy rates dropped, promoting an increase in the efficiency of an hours work in communes. Panel C.1 of Appendix Table A.10 confirms the importance of educational improvements for labor augmentation, albeit for all sectors of the economy.

Labor augmentation was also important in China. Irrigation, fertilizer, and new seed varieties all played a role. This is apparent from Panels C.3, C.4, and C.6 of Appendix Table A.8. In so far as land and labor augmentation preceded substitution of machinery — tractors, power tillers — there is a close correspondence between Japan's market driven experience and China's command and control experience. Did Chinese planners reach conclusions about the appropriate way to develop Chinese farming that mimicked market shaped outcomes in Japan? That this was not completely the case in the message of Panel C.7 in Appendix A.8. Chinese planners were influenced by the collectivization campaign in the Soviet Union for which — reflecting a very different ratio of human labor input to land it should be said — mechanization played a very important role from the outset.[11] So it is apparent that using the criterion of quantitative structural change as a guide the Chinese command and control model was not a perfect replica of the Japanese model.

10.3. Productivity Gain in Manufacturing

Putting the development of the Chinese agricultural sector in the Japanese mirror revealed significant similarities. From a structural point of view — as revealed in the statistics on land and labor augmentation — a cogent case can be made out for the proposition that Chinese cadres and central planners responded to similar constraints, adopting similar approaches. True differences existed. But despite the existence of a huge divide in terms of the institutional and political setting under which surplus labor was removed from the Japanese and Chinese villages, the similarities are quite striking. However a similar proposition does not hold for manufacturing.

At first glance this assertion might appear to be wrongheaded. After all in both post-1950 Japan and post-1950 China heavy industry grew rapidly during the three decades following Japan's surrender. But this very fact testifies to an important difference. The post-1950 heavy industrial drive of Japan built on extensive pre-1940 growth of manufacturing, both heavy and light. In the Japanese case light industry expanded first paving the way for heavy manufacturing and consumer durables through decades and decades of accelerating total factor productivity growth. After all this is the essence of the flying geese model.

To see this, compare total factor productivity growth in Japan and in China over the two decades after 1950 (see Panels A.1, A.2, and C.1 of Appendix Table A.10). In Japan growth was unusually rapid; in China growth was basically negative. China's heavy industrial sector was not building on a successful light industrial base. Japan's was. In Japan firms in industry after industry were harnessing foreign technology and innovation. China, isolated from most major industrial powers after the Sino–Soviet split of 1960 was mired on a path of stagnation. Quotas and state imposed prices encouraged waste, and low quality. The lack of domestic competition in China discouraged innovation and cost cutting. Unlike Japanese firms intent on gaining access to market niches in high income per capita countries like the United States through a combination of price competitiveness and reputation for quality, Chinese firms wallowed in inefficiency but survived. That few foreign firms from countries producing high quality products had open entry to the Chinese market guaranteed the survival of gigantic state owned albatrosses in iron and steel, chemicals, and machine making.

The geographic dispersal of Chinese manufacturing was an additional barrier to total factor productivity growth. In Japan heavy manufacturing tended to concentrate in the Tōkaidō industrial belt at first, then spread out into remoter rural zones. This concentration generated tremendous scale externalities, external to firms: economies realized in marketing and product distribution, in raw material and energy acquisition, and in terms of diffusion of technology. By and large these were absent from China during the period of command and control, partly due to the Maoist inspired Third Front policy.

In the aftermath of Mao's death and the crushing of his chief supporters, the door was open to embracing Chen Yun's approach. In moving in this direction China's political elite was operating under political and economic constraints and opportunities that were absent in the early 1950s. For instance from a security point of view the environment was totally different than it was a quarter century earlier. Japan was a staunch ally of the United States, committed to rejecting the path of militarism. The United States under President Richard Nixon had abandoned its policy of promoting the Nationalist Chinese government on Taiwan at the expense of expanding diplomatic relations with the People's Republic of China: even before Mao died Nixon visited China opening the door to a new geopolitical configuration in East Asia. Indeed, from a security point of view it was internal dissent, not external threats, that was the biggest potential problem threatening the careers of elite Chinese political figures. The chaos visited on China by the Cultural Revolution was on the minds of all Chinese — especially its political elite many of whom had suffered grievously under the vicious attacks of Red Guard factions — in the aftermath of Mao's demise.

That nearby Hong Kong, South Korea, and Nationalist Taiwan followed Japan in achieving high rates of income per capita growth that rested on substantial gains in total factor productivity was galling to China's elite. This is apparent from Appendix Table A.5 and Panel B in Appendix Table A.10. Would the Chinese masses be content to accept indefinitely per capita income differentials on the order of four to one (South Korea); five to one (Taiwan); nine to one (Hong Kong); and thirteen to one (Japan)?

At the same time that existence of these differentials threatened China's political elite they also provided an opportunity: entice companies in Japan, Taiwan, Hong Kong, and South Korea, eager to employ China's vast supply of cheap labor, eager to market products in the massive domestic Chinese market, to invest in China. By opening this door the Chinese leadership could accomplish three economic goals: absorb surplus labor; secure foreign technology; create competition for lethargic state managed enterprises. If anything opening up would foster security, not endanger it. In the aftermath of World War II foreign direct investment did not tend to carry with it the imperialist connotations that it did before the war. Encouraging investment by a foreign country raised the costs to that foreign power of intervening in China's domestic political affairs — governments no longer wanted to see the success of the investments undertaken by their corporations damaged by politics as Japanese investment in Shanghai had been threatened by the actions of Japan's army — rather than diminishing these costs.

10.4. Struggling with the Legacy of the Command and Control Period

While it would be simplistic to argue that China's reform program undertaken in earnest in the late 1970s and the 1980s was an embrace of the direction advocated by Chen Yun's faction in the 1950s, there is much merit to this proposition. Through a succession of policy reforms that involved adopting many of Chen's recommendations, China's political elite guided China from a regime of Communism tainted by Maoist utopianism to Market Socialism. Agriculture collectivization was reversed in the early 1980s, land being turned over households under long term leases. Special enterprise zones were created on China's coastline, inviting in American, Japanese, Hong Kong, Taiwanese, and South Korean investment. The nexus of state mandated relative prices was revamped in a bid to gradually introduce market prices and phase out state mandated prices. By the late 1980s prices had been completely liberalized. State owned firms shed workers. A stock market was introduced. Private firms were allowed to operate. Town and village enterprises, emerging out of the manufacturing divisions of communes, blossomed.

The fruits of this reform are clear enough. Per capita income growth picked. Light industry growth, suppressed under command and control, expanded dramatically reversing the emphasis on heavy industry first.

This is clear from Panels C.7 and C.9 of Appendix Table A.9. A good example is textiles. As can be seen from Panel C.8 of Appendix Table A.8 farms responded to the opportunity to sell cotton to a rapidly expanding cotton textiles sector. In effect China was now following Japan's path to developing manufacturing.

By the late 1990s China had reduced the per capita income gap between itself and its Asian neighbors. It had fallen below seven to one with respect to Hong Kong; to around seven to one with respect to Japan; to under five to one with respect to Taiwan; to around four to one with respect to South Korea. Moreover, China's income per capita was pulling away from the level achieved by India, a country that had enjoyed a per capita income approximately equal to that of China's through the years of command and control.

Despite these successes the legacy of command and control lingers in the China of the early 2000s. The specter of rural surplus labor has not yet been dispelled. This is clear enough in the figures appearing in Panels B.2 and B.3 of Appendix Table A.7. To be sure on the coastline, particularly in the regions near the special enterprise zones and the former treaty port cities, surplus labor has been largely absorbed. Labor flowed into these booming areas from the immediate hinterland; town and village enterprises near these growth poles found the demand for their products soaring, also absorbing labor from the surrounding villages. As China's coastline has become a huge industrial belt, infrastructure — roads, harbors, power grids, banks, universities, and vocational schools proliferating — the incidence of surplus labor has sharply declined in that region. But in Western China and the hinterland away from the growth poles this has not been the case.[12] In the West and the hinterland the existence of surplus labor and poverty remains stubbornly entrenched. Indeed with the breakup of the communes welfare may have actually worsened in these areas. The communes provided medical services. With de-collectivization public health and medical infrastructure has deteriorated in many sections of the hinterland.[13] In reforming agriculture to engender market incentives China's government has also dismantled important facets of Maoist command and control rural infrastructure, thereby fostering growing inequality of income and opportunity. From extreme Maoist inspired egalitarianism has sprung extreme inequality, a sure threat to China's future political stability.

More important China's Communist Party elite clings to power, reluctant to encourage national banks to shower funds on private enterprise (see Panel C.11 of Appendix Table A.9). To be sure entrepreneurs are encouraged to join the Communist Party. But can the Party continue to capture a nascent and — in terms of sheer numbers — rapidly expanding middle class? If a large bourgeoisie emerges in China that is not somehow brought into or under the thumb of the Communist Party is the monopoly over power held by key Chinese political elites safe? Without the whip of a free and vigorous press and political competition can China's political elite avoid wallowing in a morass of corruption?[14] In the post-Cultural Revolution era China's has steadfastly moved in the direction of diminishing the impact of traps, political, and economic, but it has not completely escaped them. The ghosts of command and control continue to haunt Asia's new economic giant.

Endnotes

1. See Bo (2007).
2. See Schran (1975).
3. For a summary of Chen's position see the introduction to Chen (1983).
4. These figures are reported on p. 90 of Bramall (2009).
5. These figures are reported on p. 14 of Perkins and Yusuf (1984). In their text Perkins and Yusuf do not decompose the "other" sector but it is likely that the main sub-component of "other" is infrastructure construction.
6. See Chen (1991).
7. For instance see p. 140 in Perkins (1966).
8. For details on the collectivization of agriculture see Kueh (1995), Perkins and Yusuf (1984), Walker (1965), and Yang (1996).
9. Figures taken from p. 37 of Yang (1996). For a detailed account of the Great Famine loss of life see Chap. 4 in Bramall (2009). It would be fair to say that Bramall's account deemphasizes the impact of egalitarianism in supplying food to households. I am grateful to Richard King of the Pacific and Asian Studies Department at the University of Victoria for his observations on the relationship between Maoist Communist utopianism during the Great Leap Forward and the Great Famine.
10. Different accounts of the Great Proletarian Cultural Revolution date provide different dates for its conclusion. Some argue that it basically ended in 1969; others argue that it continued on until Mao's demise in 1976 and the arrest of some of the key players who organized the campaign.
11. On p. 80 of Perkins (1966) there is an interesting discussion of the push to use the double-bladed plough in collectivized agriculture. The plows had performed well in some districts in 1954 and 1955 but were not appropriate for other parts of the country as it turned out. However with the push to collectivize farming the authorities ordered a massive increase in the production of the

plows, forcing cadres throughout the countryside to purchase them regardless of their utility or lack of utility in a particular setting. While this is an extreme example it does illustrate why command and control policies can foster inefficiencies. This said, market oriented production can and does foster inefficiencies as well.

12. The Chinese government is attempting to foster regional development in China's interior as a vehicle for absorbing surplus labor in the interior and Western regions. For the development planning for Western China see Lu and Neilson (2004).

13. For data on height and weight of children and adults that bears on this issue see, for instance: Shen *et al.* (1996) and Shimokawa (2007).

14. For corruption amongst Chinese Communist Party cadres see Lü (2000).

11

Conclusions

Navigating the transition from an organic to an inorganic economy is not easy. Countries can and do fall into traps that impede the process, completely stopping it in some cases. Broadly speaking the traps involved fall into four categories: economic, political/military, cultural, and demographic. A key argument of this book is that the behavior of elites — economic, political, and/or cultural — is crucial to embracing or escaping traps.

In the mid-19th century Japan and China both struggled with a common trap: the existence of surplus labor in densely populated rice producing regions. As the Western powers flexed their growing political and military muscle — fueled by the transition to an inorganic economy — in the East Asian region Japan and China contended with the problem of how to break out of the surplus labor trap.

The key to mobilizing surplus labor in densely populated rice producing areas is clear enough. Augment labor through health improvements, education, and opening up opportunities to escape the surplus labor stemming from infrastructure construction and nascent industrialization. Augment land through the systematic expansion of irrigation, widespread application of fertilizer, and the development of new high yield seed varieties. But actually accomplishing these tasks requires the active involvement of elites. Elites may or may not be enthusiastic in redirecting their focus from the activities that had sustained their elite status in the organic economy to the activities that foster labor and land augmentation among the great bulk of the rural populace.

In Tokugawa Japan a political and military elite — the *samurai* — had little to lose in embracing the necessary changes required to mobilize surplus labor and augment land. Since their status was based on heredity not intense investment in education, since most were largely poor and landless, their resistance to making the requisite political and economic changes was minimal. Responding to the forcible opening of their country by the Western powers, the *samurai* moved quickly to destroy the Tokugawa regime, in the process doing away with the *samurai* status itself as well as the entire class system of Tokugawa society. Joining former *samurai* in building steam power using factories, steam railroads, harbors accommodating deep hulled steam ships, universities teaching Western science and engineering, modernized armies and navies were the other two important elite groups of Tokugawa society: powerful merchants and wealthy rural landlords. Operating under the umbrella ideology of *fukoku kyōhei* that promoted military buildup and industrialization many members of Japan's old elite emerged as key players in the new elite of Meiji Japan. As a result Japan's economy escaped the surplus labor trap, the growth process accelerating in the period between World War I and 1930s.

By contrast the Confucian elite in Qing China — the powerful landlord/ gentry of rural China — resisted embracing the changes that Japan's *samurai* embraced with such abandon. Having invested years and years in diligent study of the Confucian classics in order to compete for a small number of positions of wealth and political power that were offered to that handful of successful competitors in China's brutal civil and military examination competition, they naturally resisted abandoning the Qing system. Unlike Japan, China's response to the Western challenge was inadequate, both in military and economic terms.

While Meiji era political and military elites in Japan were successful in building up Japan's military prowess — thereby neutralizing military threats emanating from the Western powers — and at the same time accomplishing the transition to an inorganic economy increasingly centered around a burgeoning manufacturing sector that was able to absorb copious surplus labor from village Japan, China's elite failed to mount a determined military response to the West, failed to promote industrialization outside of a few enclaves. Symbolic of the anemic Chinese response was the fact that the Qing dynasty that acquiesced to on-going

Western — later Japanese — pressure to turn over territory on the coast and along the Yangzi River, granting foreigners special privileges denied Chinese themselves, staggered on, surviving for over seven decades before its final collapse in the early 20th century. Moreover once the Qing dynasty passed from the scene, the elites that emerged in post-1911 China were too deeply divided to coalesce around a Meiji style umbrella ideology. After all the great majority of those who had enjoyed status as the Confucian elite of the Qing period was too bitter over the loss of its investment in endless years of study of the Confucian classics to enthusiastically embrace a new economic and political order.

The tragic consequence of the diverging experiences of early 20th century Japan and China was Japan's growing military, economic, and political aggrandizement in China exemplified by Japan's takeover of Manchuria. Increasingly military elites assumed control in both Japan and China as Japan's pressure on China intensified. By the late 1930s the ongoing friction between Japan's army bent on making Japan hegemonic in Asia and China's Republican government established in Nanjing in the late 1920s led to full scale Japanese invasion of China. An uneasy alliance of convenience between the Chinese Communist Party and the Nationalists yielded a combined military resistance to the Japanese onslaught. Both Japan and China had fallen deeply in the trap of militarism, military elites taking charge in both countries.

With Japan's unconditional surrender to the allied powers in 1945, the stage was set for the destruction of elites in both countries. In Japan the military was discredited and sweeping land reform did away with the landlord elite. In China the victory of the People's Liberation Army in the civil war that broke out between the Communists and the Nationalists after Japan's military had departed China ushered in control of the mainland by a Communist regime committed to doing away with the old Confucian landlord/gentry once and for all.

With old elites crumbling in both countries, both countries embraced heavy industrialization under remarkably different political regimes. In Japan command and control experiments carried out by militarists during the 1930s were jettisoned in favor of market oriented economic development conditioned by industrial policy. By contrast, in China a new political elite committed to command and control took over.

Given the advantages of ruthless competition and selfish incentives built into the market oriented development that Japanese industry enjoyed over its Chinese rival, the result was a growing gap in achieved income per capita between the two countries. Japan experienced high speed growth nicknamed Miracle Growth, surplus labor basically eradicated from village Japan during the late 1950s and early 1960s. In China growth was slower. That said, under Maoist inspired command and control land and labor were augmented in rural China, much surplus labor being drained off. This was the result of infrastructure buildup and steadfast improvements in rural health and education that augmented both land and labor.

As Japan's Miracle Growth experience came to a conclusion in the 1970s, China came to the end of a period dominated by Maoist inspired command and control. Responding to the growing gap between China and its East Asian neighbors who had embraced Japanese style (in Taiwan and South Korea) or British style (in Hong Kong) market oriented economic development, China's political elite embraced reform, opening up the country to foreign direct investment, adopting a gradualist program of economic advance in which a state controlled sector co-existed with a market oriented sector. The result was rapid industrial expansion in China and the draining of much surplus labor from rural China, especially on China's coastline.

Despite the striking differences between the economic development of modern Japan and modern China there are remarkable similarities. By the end of the 20th century both countries escaped political, economic, and cultural traps that stood in the way of the embrace of the infrastructure buildup and industrialization. Both countries struggled with surplus labor, augmenting land and labor in response to the challenge of absorbing workers from rural districts. In short, both countries ultimately managed to break free of most of the trammels of the surplus labor trap, Japan more so than China. In this sense both Japan and China share a common economic destiny in the modern world, a common fate. This is the most important lesson to draw from this study of the role of elites in the economic development of Japan and China.

Statistical Appendix

Calibrating economic development involves more than compiling data and constructing variables from the assembled figures. Interpretation is as important as estimation. Statistics are only meaningful when they contribute to an argument, a story, advanced by their user. It is essential to keep this point in mind in studying the text and tables assembled in this appendix.

There are three major approaches to calibrate economic development for a country or region: (1) estimating the flow of goods and services generated by the economy, then putting the resulting numbers on a per capita basis by dividing by estimates of population (the income per capita or output per capita approach arrived at through national income accounting); (2) estimating a mix of the capabilities and abilities for the average individual in the population by combining figures on per capita income, life expectancy and educational attainment into a summary measure (the human development approach); and (3) estimating a set of demographic and anthropometric characteristics of the population, particularly concentrating on young persons still growing (e.g., life expectancy, the infant mortality rate, height, weight, chest girth, muscular capacity; the term "biological standard of living" is often used to describe the standard of living as measured through the agency of the anthropometric measures). Most economists and the World Bank in particular favor the income per capita approach; the United Nations Development Programme favors the human development approach; and the World Health Organization recommends using anthropometric measures like height and weight for growing children.

From an economist's perspective the income per capita approach has much to recommend it.[1] Summary measures of total marketed output (in principle equal to total income received by the factors of production) are useful in and of themselves. In addition they can be decomposed: into sector estimates on the supply side (agriculture, fishing, and forestry adding up to primary production; mining and manufacturing constituting secondary or industrial production; and services the tertiary sector); into the components of aggregate demand — consumption, investment, government spending, imports, and exports — on the demand side.

Moreover, growth rates for overall income or income per capita can be generated by computing income levels in different years in so-called constant prices (known as "real income" as opposed to "nominal income"). Finally comparisons between different regions or countries in terms of income or income per capita can be generated by coming up with a common set of prices for the various regions or countries involved, deflating the nominal figures for income generated in the various regions or countries by the purchasing power parity — the actual buying power in terms of securing a specific bundle of goods and services — of the currencies for the various jurisdictions involved. In theory the income approach is compelling because it allows for the calibration of levels of income and income per capita as well as growth rates for income and income per capita.

In practice finding a common set of prices for evaluating the growth of income within a country is difficult. No perfect solution exists. Consider a time series of nominal income figures, prices and volumes being known. Whether one uses prices for the base period in the series or the final period in the series matters in making the actual calculation. This is known as the index number problem. Even more challenging is estimating purchasing power parity of currencies, official exchange rates being a poor proxy as exchange rates tend to reflect the prices of traded goods — most goods and services are not traded — and central bank policies of countries.[2]

Problems encountered in estimation aside, income and income per capita estimates are ubiquitous in the empirical economic development literature. Most of the tables in this Appendix — Tables A.2–A.5 and A.10 — make use of them. Estimates of the human development index, life expectancy, infant mortality, and the biological standard of living appear in Table A.6. From the point of view of this study the human development index and the biological standard of living are useful supplements to the income per capita measures — and do capture important aspects of human capabilities important to understanding the determinants of the efficiency of an hour worked — but are best used to supplement the income per capita estimates.[3]

Table A.1 provides a basic growth accounting framework used throughout this study. It is discussed in the Appendix to Chap. 2, Sec. 2.6. Please note that the notation, the symbols used for variable names, employed in this table differs somewhat from that utilized in Chaps. 2 and 3. A key feature of the table is the analysis of augmentation in the three factors of production. Note the list of factors that contribute to total factor productivity growth: scale economies, structural change (particularly important is transferring workers from agriculture to industry), and technological and organizational change. This list is important because it points toward the interaction of augmentation and capital accumulation with total factor productivity growth, supporting the argument that the dichotomy between total factor productivity growth and accumulation either of capital and/or accumulation of labor, when combined to make total factor accumulation, is false. Examples supporting the interaction of augmentation of labor and technological progress appear in Chap. 5 (the example of the reverse engineering project of the Japan National Railroads (where the existence of a supply of well trained engineers was crucial) and in Chap. 9 where it is pointed out that the upgrading of educational attainment for blue collar workers imparted a major push to the effective application of "zero defect" and quality control circle principles in the Japanese automobile industry. Another illustration of this principle is the buildup of physical infrastructure — paved road networks, hydro-electrical systems, railroads, container ports and dredged harbors — generating geographic scale economies especially in metropolises. Again consider the following proposition: without physical investment in plant and equipment in manufacturing can structural change, namely the transfer of workers from farming to industry, take place?

Historical estimates of levels of income per capita and population and growth rates for income per capita and population appear in Table A.2. Noteworthy points established by the table are: (1) the existence of Malthusian constraints on growth in per capita income and population prior to the industrial revolution of the 18th century that set the stage for the refinement and diffusion of the inorganic economy; (2) the existence of the great divergence; and (3) the existence of a fundamental shift in the

Table A.1: Growth accounting equation and the aggregate production function.

From the basic multiplicative aggregate Cobb–Douglas Production Function that assumes constant returns to scale (or rather captures them in the A variable):

$$Q = A(K^*)^\alpha (L^*)^\beta (LA^*)^{[1-(\alpha+\beta)]}$$

where:

> Q = flow of output (GDP); K^* = flow of services from augmented capital; L^* = flow of services from augmented labor; and LA* = flow of services from augmented labor; and A = index of total factor productivity.

We can derive the basic growth accounting equation:

$$G(Q) = G(A) + \alpha\, G(K^*) + \beta\, G(L^*) + [1 - (\alpha + \beta)]\, G(LA^*).$$

In the table we discuss issues involving the measurement and interpretation of each of the five major variables, Q, A, K^*, L^*, and LA*.

Variable	How is the variable augmented or adjusted?	Comments on interpretation of augmentation
$G(Q)$ Aggregate output growth	Adjust the flows of commodity and service output for quality	Adjustment involves index number problems and assumptions about the values of components of products and services
$G(A)$ Total factor productivity growth		Underlying growth in total factor productivity are (1) scale economies (stemming from geographic externalities and those internalized by firms); (2) structural change in the composition of output; and (3) technological and organizational change. It is possible that all three factors are correlated with $G(K^*)$.
$G(K^*)$	Through changes in the quality of capital, for instance due to the changing vintage (age) of capital	Controversy surrounds the question of whether changes in technology are embodied in K^*.

(Continued)

Table A.1: (*Continued*)

$G(L^*)$	Raw labor input is augmented by changes in the efficiency of labor $e(L)$. Underlying changes in the efficiency of labor are (1) changes in the demographic, educational composition of the labor force; (2) changes in the health of the labor force; (3) changes in hours worked (h) per worker; and (4) changes in incentives that impact work intensity per hour worked	The four factors underlying efficiency of labor may be shaped by (1) the organization and management of production units; (2) the quality of managers; and (3) the range of opportunities open to workers (shaped by geographic barriers and barriers to achieving socioeconomic mobility, for instance through acquiring education, hence by public policy)
$G(LA^*)$	Land — for instance agricultural land — is augmented through the application of fertilizers and irrigation. Land is also augmented by converting it from one use to another, for instance from wasteland or forest to arable land	Technological progress in agriculture may have a land augmenting bias due to the relative price of land services relative to labor services or due to the elasticities of supply of labor and land (e.g.: inelastically supplied land tends to promote augmentation of land.)

In principle in analyzing the sources of growth it is important to decompose the growth of each of the three factors of production into their components, namely:

$G(K^*) = G(q_K) + G(K)$ where q_K captures the average quality of capital services and K is the flow of raw unadjusted capital services.

$G(L^*) = G[e(L)] + G(L)$, where the average efficiency of labor $e(L)$ depends upon hours worked h; intensity of work effort per hour worked; the demographic structure of the labor force (shaped by age and gender composition); the level of education and health of the population, especially those employed in the labor force; and barriers to exploiting potential opportunities (e.g., geographic isolation from markets may be a barrier); and incentives provided by the way production units are managed. L is raw labor input.

$G(LA^*) = G(q_L) + G(LA)$ where q_K is the average quality of land that depends upon land use practice.

Table A.2: Estimates of levels and growth rates for income, population, and income per capita for regions of the world and for china and Japan, 1500–1998.

A. Long-run estimates of growth in GDP per capita and population

Region/ Country	1500– 1820	1820– 1870	1870– 1913	1913– 1950	1950– 1973	1973– 1998
A.1. GDP per Capita(%)						
World	0.05	0.53	1.3	0.91	2.93	1.33
Western Europe	0.15	0.95	1.32	0.76	4.08	1.78
Western Offshoots [a]	0.34	1.42	1.81	1.55	2.44	1.94
Asia (except Japan)	0.00	0.15	0.38	−0.02	2.92	3.54
Latin America	0.15	0.1	1.81	1.42	2.52	0.99
Eastern Europe/ former USSR	0.1	0.64	1.15	1.5	3.49	−1.1
Africa	0.01	0.12	0.64	1.02	2.07	0.01
Japan	0.09	0.19	1.48	0.89	8.05	2.34
China	n.e.	−0.25	0.1	−0.62	2.86	5.39
Difference, Japan–China	n.e.	0.44	1.38	1.51	5.19	−3.05
A.2. Population						
World	0.27	0.4	0.8	0.93	1.92	1.66
Western Europe	0.26	0.69	0.77	0.42	0.7	0.32
Western Offshoots [a]	0.43	2.87	2.07	1.25	1.55	1.02
Asia (except Japan)	0.29	015	0.55	0.92	2.19	1.86
Latin America	0.06	1.27	1.64	1.97	2.73	2.01
Eastern Europe/ former USSR	0.34	0.87	1.21	0.34	1.31	0.54
Africa	0.15	0.4	0.75	1.65	2.33	2.73
Japan	0.22	0.21	0.95	1.31	1.15	0.61
China	n.e.	−0.12	0.47	0.61	2.1	2.74
Difference, Japan–China	n.e.	0.33	0.48	0.7	−0.95	−0.77

(*Continued*)

Table A.2: (*Continued*)

B. Levels of GDP per capita, long-term estimates (1990 Geary–Khamis Dollars)

Region/Country	1500	1820	1870	1913	1950	1973	1990
World	565	667	867	1510	2114	4104	n.e.
Western Europe	774	1232	1974	3473	4594	11,534	n.e.
Western Offshoots [a]	400	1201	2431	5257	9288	16,172	n.e.
Asia (except Japan)	572	575	543	640	635	1231	n.e.
Latin America	416	665	698	1511	2554	4531	n.e.
Eastern Europe/ former USSR	483	667	917	1501	2601	5729	n.e.
Africa	400	418	444	585	852	1365	n.e.
Japan	500	669	737	1387	1926	11,439	18,789
China	n.e.	600	530	552	439	839	1858
Ratio (Japan/China) multiple	n.e.	1.12	1.39	2.51	4.39	13.63	10.11

C. Levels of population (in 1000s) for Japan and China, 1820–1998

Date	Japan	China	Japan/China (%)
1820	31,000	381,000	8.14
1870	34,437	358,000	9.62
1913	51,672	437,140	11.82
1950	83,563	546,815	15.28
1973	108,660	881,940	12.32
1990	123,540	1,135,185	10.88
1998	126,486	1,242,700	10.18

D. Levels of GDP (Millions of 1990 Geary–Khamis international dollars), Japan and China, 1820–1998

Date	Japan	China	Japan/China (%)
1820	20,739	228,600	9.07
1870	25,393	189,740	13.38
1913	71,653	241,344	29.69
1950	160,966	239,903	67.10
1973	1,242,932	740,048	167.95
1990	2,321,153	2,109,400	110.04
1998	2,581,576	3,873,352	66.65

(*Continued*)

Table A.2:   (*Continued*)

E. Share of world GDP, regions, and Japan and China, 1500–1990 (%)

Region/Country	1500	1820	1870	1913	1950	1973	1990
World	100	100	100	100	100	100	100
Western Europe	17.9	23.6	33.6	33.5	26.3	25.7	20.6
Western Offshoots [a]	0.5	1.9	10.2	21.7	30.6	25.3	25.1
Asia (except Japan)	62.1	56.2	36	21.9	15.5	16.4	29.5
Latin America	2.9	2.0	2.5	4.5	7.9	8.7	8.7
Eastern Europe/ former USSR	5.9	8.8	11.7	13.1	13.1	12.9	5.3
Africa	7.4	4.5	3.7	2.7	3.6	3.3	3.1
Japan	3.1	3.0	2.3	2.6	3.0	7.7	7.7
China	34.17	22.42	7.75	3.9	1.8	7.0	11.6

F. Growth rates for GDP per capita, Japan, China, Hong Kong, South Korea, and Taiwan, 1913–1999 (%)

Country	1913–1950	1950–1999	1950–1973	1973–1990	1990–1999
Japan	0.9	4.9	8.1	3.0	0.9
China	−0.6	4.2	2.9	4.8	6.4
Hong Kong	n.e.	4.6	5.2	5.4	1.7
South Korea	1.5	4.9	4.4	6.8	4.8
Taiwan	0.6	5.9	6.7	5.3	5.3
Difference China–Hong Kong	n.e.	−0.4	−2.3	−0.6	4.7
Difference China–Taiwan	−1.2	−1.7	−3.8	−0.5	1.1

[a]Western Offshoots = United States, Canada, Australia, New Zealand.
n.e. = not estimated.
Sources: Pages 126–127, 143, 146, 214–218 in Maddison (2006).

global distribution of output. Regarding the last point it is noteworthy that Asia accounted for over 60% of global output in 1500, its percentage dropping thereafter bottoming out with a low of 15.5% in 1950 then climbing back somewhat. With the recent dramatic expansion of China's economy Asia's share is expected to grow to much higher levels than it enjoyed in the immediate aftermath of World War II.

Structural change in the national output of China is the theme of Table A.3. Noteworthy are the following points: (1) between 1890 and 1933 there was a slight — but only slight — fall in the share of primary production in Chinese national income; (2) between 1950 and 1978, the drop in primary production as a share of Chinese output was dramatic, outstripping the decline between 1978 and 1995. Paralleling this decline was a massive expansion of the industrial sector; and (3) Shifting labor out of primary production into industry and construction played an important role in the growth of national income in post-1952 China, particularly in the period 1978–1995 after the reform period commenced.

Decomposition of growth in income per capita in terms of aggregate demand components for Japan over the period 1886–2000 is the focus of Panel A.1 of Table A.4. Noteworthy conclusions emanating from the table are: (1) a rise in the investment proportion over the periods 1886–1900, 1906–1925, 1931–1940, and especially 1956–1975; (2) a shift in the regime of net exports, pre-1951 net exports negative (imports exceeding imports) followed by a period in which net exports tended to be positive (and growing until the early 1990s). Panel A.2 documents the sharp decline in the proportion of Japan's national output generated by the primary sector.

Putting post-1950 Japanese and Chinese economic growth into a broader Asian context is the message of Table A.5. Two points are worth mentioning in the context of this table: (1) the gap in income per capita between most of China's East Asian neighbors and China — Japan, Taiwan, Hong Kong, and South Korea — widened between 1950 and 1979, shrinking thereafter; and (2) per capita income in China and India were quite similar through the period 1950-1979, after which China grew much faster than India.

Population size and the dynamics of population growth are the themes of Table A.6. Interesting findings culled from the data are: (1) over the period from the 17th century to 2000 the populations of both Japan and China expanded tenfold suggesting population growth *per se* is not a barrier to launching industrialization in the long-run nor is it a major determinant of the timing of the spread of the inorganic economy within a country; (2) population decline was significant in China in the wake of major rebellions — especially the Taiping Rebellion — that took place during the 1850s and 1960s; (3) between 1720 and 1950 Japan's population growth was virtually zero, growth being quite rapid in the century prior to 1720 and resuming after 1850; (4) Japan commenced the demographic transition during the period prior to 1940 while China did not; (5) average life expectancy

Table A.3:   Structural change in the Gross Domestic Product (GDP) of China, 1890–2004.

A.1. The composition of China's GDP in 1890, 1913, 1933 (% in each sector) and changes between 1890 and 1933 in the share of the sectors

Sector	1890	1913	1933	Change in % 1890–1933
Farming, fishery, forestry	68.5	67.0	64.0	−4.5
Handicrafts	7.7	7.7	7.4	−0.3
Modern manufacturing	0.1	0.6	2.5	+2.4
Mining	0.2	0.3	0.8	+0.6
Electricity	0.0	0.0	0.5	+0.5
Construction	1.7	1.7	1.6	−0.1
Traditional transport and communications	5.1	4.6	4.0	−1.1
Modern transport and communications	0.4	0.8	1.5	+1.1
Trade	8.2	9.0	9.4	+1.2
Government	2.8	2.8	2.8	0.0
Finance	0.3	0.5	0.7	+0.4
Personal services	1.1	1.2	1.2	+0.1
Residential services	3.9	3.8	3.6	−0.3
Total	100.0	100.0	100.0	n.e.

A.2. Index of GDP and sector outputs for 1933 (1914 = 100) and growth rates (%) for GDP and the sectors for the period 1914/1933

Item	Index	Growth rate (%)
Agriculture	117.0	1.0
Modern industry and transport	419.2	8.8
Other industry and transport	100.4	0.0
Services	125.2	1.3
GDP	126.4	1.4

A.3. Shares of broad sectors in GDP (%) and changes in the shares, 1890–1995

Sector	Shares of sectors (%)			
	1890	1952	1978	1995
Farming, fishery, forestry	68.5	58.6	33.7	23.2
Industry	8.1	9.9	34.7	41.1

(*Continued*)

Table A.3: (*Continued*)

Construction	1.7	1.7	3.3	5.8
Transport and communications	5.5	2.4	3.5	5.2
Commerce and restaurants	8.2	6.5	5.0	7.3
Other services (including government)	8.0	20.9	19.7	17.4
GDP	100.0	100.0	100.0	100.0

Change in shares of sectors

Sector	1890/1995	1890/1952	1952/1978	1978/1995
Farming, fishery, forestry	−45.3	−9.9	−24.9	−10.5
Industry	+33.0	+1.8	+24.8	+6.4
Construction	+4.1	0.0	+1.6	+2.5
Transport and communications	−0.3	−3.1	1.1	+1.7
Commerce and restaurants	−0.9	−1.7	−1.5	+2.3
Other services (including government)	+9.4	+12.9	−1.2	−2.3

A.4. Composition of government revenue sources in 1753 and 1908 (%)

Item	1753	1908
Land Tax	81.5%	43.5%
Salt Tax	9.4	12.7
Native Customs	7.3	1.7
Maritime Customs	—	14.0
Likin	—	9.1
Miscellaneous	1.8	19.1
Total	100.0	100.0

A.5. Composition of government revenue and expenditures (%) and percent of GDP for government revenue and expenditures, 1936

Share of revenue				Revenue/GDP
Customs	Salt tax	Consolidated taxes	Other (not borrowing)	
33.3%	22.5%	16.5%	27.7%	2.8%

(*Continued*)

Table A.3:   (*Continued*)

Share of expenditure			Expenditure/GDP
Military	**Indemnity/Debt service**	**Other**	
33.0%	24.9%	42.1%	4.0%

A.6. Growth rates for GDP by sector, 1890–1995

Sector	1890–1952	1952–1995	1952–1978	1978–1995
Farming, fishery, forestry	0.3	3.4	2.2	5.1
Industry	1.7	9.2	9.6	8.5
Construction	1.6	8.7	7.2	11.1
Transport and communications	0.9	7.6	6.0	10.0
Commerce and restaurants	0.8	5.9	3.3	9.9
Other services (including government)	1.1	5.2	4.2	6.7
GDP	0.6	5.6	4.4	7.5
GDP per capita	0.0	3.8	2.3	6.0
GDP per worker	0.0	2.9	1.8	4.7
Export volume	1.6	9.2	6.4	13.5

A.7. Growth rates for GDP, various components of GDP, population (*P*), and GDP per Capita (GDP/*P*), 1979–2000

Item	1979–1984	1985–1995	1996–2000
GDP	8.8	9.7	8.2
Agriculture	7.1	4.0	3.4
Industry	8.2	12.8	9.6
Services	11.6	9.7	8.2
Foreign trade	14.3	15.2	9.8
Imports	12.7	13.4	9.5
Exports	15.9	17.2	10.0
P	1.4	1.4	0.9
GDP/*P*	7.1	8.3	7.1

(*Continued*)

Table A.3: (*Continued*)

A.8. Growth rates for GDP(%), employment(%), and labor productivity for total GDP and for its major sectors (%), 1952–1995

Sector	1952–1978	1978–1995	Change between two periods (2) − (1)
	Agriculture		
GDP	2.20	5.15	+2.95
Employment	2.02	0.84	−1.18
Labor productivity	0.17	4.27	+4.10
	Industry and construction		
GDP	9.29	8.82	−0.47
Employment	5.84	4.83	−1.01
Labor productivity	3.25	3.81	+0.56
	Tertiary		
GDP	4.18	7.86	+3.09
Employment	3.20	6.73	+3.53
Labor productivity	0.96	1.05	+0.09
	Whole economy		
GDP	4.40	7.49	+3.09
Employment	2.57	2.62	+0.05
Labor productivity	1.78	4.74	+2.96
Impact of shift in sectoral Reallocation of labor on GDP growth	0.92	1.44	+0.52

A.9. Growth rate of output per worker by broad sector(%), 1978–2004

Sector	1978–2004	1978–1988	1988–2004
Total	6.96	6.74	7.09
Agriculture	6.76	5.70	7.43
Nonagriculture	4.65	2.47	6.02
Nonagriculture: state owned	4.87	3.30	5.86
Nonagriculture: nonstate owned	5.59	3.89	6.67

Sources: For Panels A.1, A.3, A.6, and A.8 various tables in Maddison (1998). For Panels A.2 and A.5 p. 15 and p. 272 in Rawski (1989). For Panel A.4 p. 176 in Perkins (1969). For Panel A.7 p. 482 in Huang *et al.* (2008). For Panel A.9 p. 696 in Brandt *et al.* (2008).

Table A.4: Growth of GDP per capita and the structure of Gross Domestic Expenditure and aggregate output in Japan, 1886–2000

A.1. Growth of Income per Capita [G(y)], Percentage of Gross Domestic Expenditure from Consumption (C), Investment (I), Government Spending (G), Exports (EX), Imports (IM) and Net Exports (NX = EX – IM)

		Structure of Gross Domestic Expenditure (%)					
Period	G(y)	C	I	G	EX	IM	NX
1886–1890	0.97%	85.2%	9.0%	6.9%	3.2%	4.2%	−0.9%
1891–1895	2.08	84.0	9.4	7.9	3.7	5.1	−1.4
1896–1900	3.13	85.4	12.1	7.5	4.9	9.9	−5.0
1901–1905	1.66	80.2	10.6	14.3	6.5	11.7	−5.2
1906–1910	0.90	79.6	13.5	11.3	8.0	12.4	−4.4
1911–1915	3.95	79.0	15.6	9.1	10.7	14.4	−3.7
1916–1920	2.87	74.9	17.9	8.1	13.8	14.6	−0.8
1921–1925	0.15	82.3	18.8	9.0	10.4	20.4	−10.1
1926–1930	−0.25	79.8	17.8	10.3	14.5	22.3	−7.8
1931–1935	4.14	74.0	16.5	12.7	19.3	22.5	−3.2
1936–1940	5.19	63.8	25.7	12.9	21.2	23.4	−2.3
1941–1945	−9.93	n.e.	n.e.	n.e.	n.e.	n.e.	n.e.
1946–1950	8.36	62.2	21.1	9.9	4.1	6.8	−2.6
1951–1955	6.74	61.9	17.8	14.8	8.3	6.9	+1.4
1956–1960	8.51	61.6	22.8	11.9	8.8	8.0	+0.8
1961–1965	8.01	56.8	30.5	9.6	9.5	9.7	−0.2
1966–1970	9.03	55.5	34.3	7.8	12.1	11.1	+1.0
1971–1975	3.11	53.8	36.3	8.6	n.e.	n.e.	+0.9
1976–1980	3.58	57.3	31.7	10.5	n.e.	n.e.	+0.5
1981–1985	2.89	55.1	29.3	13.8	n.e.	n.e.	+1.9
1986–1990	4.36	53.8	30.6	13.3	n.e.	n.e.	+2.3
1991–1995	1.15	54.5	29.8	13.8	n.e.	n.e.	+1.9
1996–2000	0.66	55.9	27.4	15.5	n.e.	n.e.	+1.3

A.2. Percentage of GDP in Broad Sectors, Primary (P), Secondary (S) and Tertiary (T)

Period	P	S	T
1951–1955	18.4%	34.6%	46.9%
1956–1960	14.9	37.9	47.3
1961–1965	10.6	41.0	48.4
1966–1970	7.8	41.1	51.1

(*Continued*)

Table A.4: (*Continued*)

1971–1975	5.4	41.5	53.2
1976–1980	4.5	38.0	57.6
1981–1985	3.2	36.8	60.0
1986–1990	2.6	35.9	61.5
1991–1995	2.0	32.6	65.3
1996–2000	1.5	29.1	69.3

Notes: n.e. = not estimated.
Source: Pages 355 and 359 in Mosk (2008).

Table A.5: Income per capita in selected Asian countries (figures in 1990 International Geary–Khamis Dollars) and income per capita relative to that for China.

A. Income per Capita (1990 International Geary–Khamis Dollars)

Period	China	Japan	Taiwan	Hong Kong	South Korea	India
1950–1954	513	2292	1066	2379	842	640
1955–1959	644	3141	1339	2828	1082	698
1960–1964	605	4799	1700	3688	1158	774
1965–1969	714	7287	2386	4948	1533	799
1970–1974	812	10615	3640	6466	2579	851
1975–1979	928	12166	5022	8535	3754	917
1980–1984	1205	14069	6749	11536	4671	1001
1985–1989	1694	16478	9319	15216	6899	1158
1900–1994	2130	19411	11144	19119	9853	1356
1995–1999	2964	20913	14374	20979	12583	1681

B. Income per capita relative to China's income per capita

Period	Japan	Taiwan	Hong Kong	South Korea	India
1950–1954	4.46	2.08	4.66	1.64	1.26
1955–1959	4.87	2.08	4.40	1.69	1.09
1960–1964	7.99	2.83	6.13	1.93	1.29
1965–1969	10.23	3.35	6.93	2.15	1.12
1970–1974	13.07	4.47	7.95	3.17	1.05
1975–1979	13.13	5.40	9.18	4.04	0.99
1980–1984	11.75	5.60	9.61	3.88	0.84
1985–1989	9.74	5.51	8.96	4.06	0.69
1900–1994	9.20	5.25	9.02	4.64	0.64
1995–1999	7.07	4.85	7.12	4.26	0.57

Source: Maddison (2006): pp. 304–305 (Table C3-c).

Table A.6: Population, education, and human development in China and Japan, 1640–2004.

A. Population size and dynamics

A.1. Estimates of China's population size by Maddison, various indices, and alternative official estimates (for the period 1750–1850), 1640–2000

Year	Maddison estimates				Alterna-tive official estimate
	Number (1000s)	Index (1950 = 100)	Index (1760 = 100)	Index (1640 = 100)	
1650	123,000	22.5	44.8	94.6	—
1700	138,000	25.2	50.3	106.2	—
1750	260,000	47.6	94.7	200.0	179,539
1800	341,600	62.5	124.4	262.8	295,273
1850	412,000	75.4	150.0	316.9	429,931
1860	377,000	69.0	137.3	290.0	—
1870	358,000	65.5	130.4	275.4	—
1880	368,000	67.3	134.0	283.1	—
1890	380,000	69.5	138.4	292.3	—
1900	400,000	73.2	145.7	307.7	—
1910	423,000	77.4	154.0	325.4	—
1920	472,000	86.3	171.9	363.1	—
1930	489,000	89.4	178.1	376.2	—
1940	518,770	94.9	188.9	399.1	—
1950	546,815	100.0	199.1	420.6	—
1960	667,070	122.0	242.9	513.1	—
1970	818,315	149.7	298.0	629.5	—
1980	981,235	179.5	357.3	754.8	—
1990	1,135,185	207.6	413.4	873.2	—
2000	1,275,392	233.2	464.5	981.1	—

A.2. Population totals (P), birth (b) and death rates (d) per thousand population, the natural rate of increase (nri = $b - d$), and urbanization ($u\%$), China, 1950–1984

Period	P (1000s)	b	d	nri	$u\%$
1950–1954	570,328	37.3	16.7	20.6	12.1 %
1955–1959	644,294	30.5	12.2	18.3	15.6
1960–1964	677,974	31.7	14.3	17.4	18.3
1965–1969	765,306	35.2	8.6	26.7	17.7
1970–1974	870,816	29.3	7.4	21.9	17.2

(Continued)

Table A.6:   (*Continued*)

1975–1979	949,824	19.6	6.8	12.8	17.8
1980–1984	1,012,576	19.1	6.6	12.5	20.8
2000	n.e.	n.e.	n.e.	n.e.	36.2

A.3. Life expectancy for males (LFM) and females (LFF), infant mortality rate for males (imrm) and females (imrf), total fertility rate (TFR), and mean household size (MHS), China, 1929/1931–2000

Date(s)	LEM	LFF	imrm	imrf	TFR	MHS
1929–1931	25.0	24.0	n.e.	n.e.	n.e.	n.e.
1950	42.2	45.6	145.9	130.2	n.e.	n.e.
1955	n.e.	n.e.	n.e.	n.e.	6.3	n.e.
1960	n.e.	n.e.	n.e.	n.e.	4.0	n.e.
1982	66.5	69.4	36.5	34.5	2.9	4.41
1990	66.9	71.0	32.2	36.8	2.3	3.96
2000	71.0	74.8	20.8	29.2	1.6	3.44

A.4. Infant mortality rate (imr), life expectancy for males (LEM), and for females (LEF), gross reproduction rate (grr), and net reproduction rate (nrr), Japan, 1891/1895–1996/2000

Period	imr	LEM	LEF	grr	nrr
1891–1895	—	42.8	44.3	—	—
1901–1905	152.0	43.9	44.9	—	—
1911–1915	156.7	44.3	44.7	—	—
1921–1925	159.3	42.3	43.2	n.e.	n.e.
1926–1930	136.6	44.8	46.5	n.e.	n.e.
1931–1935	120.4	46.9	49.9	n.e.	n.e.
1946–1950	65.3	54.8	58.4	2.06	1.69
1951–1955	48.0	63.6	67.8	1.34	1.20
1956–1960	35.9	65.3	70.2	1.01	0.95
1961–1965	23.4	67.7	72.9	0.98	0.95
1966–1970	15.4	69.3	74.7	0.99	0.96
1971–1975	11.2	71.7	76.9	1.01	0.98
1976–1980	8.4	73.4	78.7	0.87	0.86
1981–1985	6.3	74.8	80.5	0.87	0.85
1986–1990	4.8	75.9	81.9	0.80	0.79
1991–1995	4.3	76.4	82.9	0.72	0.71
1996–2000	3.5	77.7	84.6	0.67	0.67

(*Continued*)

Table A.6: (*Continued*)

A.5. Population (*P*) and an index for population with 1950 = 100 (INDP), birth (*b*) and death rates (*d*), the natural rate of increase (nri), urbanization (*u*%), proportion of population in the six big cities (b6c%), Japan, 1600–2000

Period/Year	*P* (1000s)	INDP	*b*	*d*	nri	*u*%	b6c%
1600	12,000	14.3	—	—	—	—	—
1650	17,180	20.4	—	—	—	—	—
1700	27,690	32.9	—	—	—	—	—
1720	31,280	37.2	—	—	—	—	—
1730	32,080	38.1	—	—	—	—	—
1750	31,100	37.0	—	—	—	—	—
1800	30,650	36.4	—	—	—	—	—
1850	32,280	38.4	—	—	—	—	—
1872	33,110	39.4	—	—	—	—	—
1886–1890	39,130	46.5	28.8	20.8	8.0	—	—
1891–1895	40,864	48.6	29.0	21.4	7.6	—	—
1896–1900	42,906	51.0	31.7	21.1	10.5	12.4	n.e.
1901–1905	45,525	54.1	32.5	21.0	11.5	15.0	n.e.
1906–1910	48,031	57.1	33.6	21.5	12.1	17.3	n.e.
1911–1915	51,305	61.0	34.5	20.7	13.9	17.5	n.e.
1916–1920	54,673	65.0	33.7	24.1	9.6	18.9	9.8
1921–1925	58,158	69.1	34.7	21.9	12.8	21.6	11.1
1926–1930	62,581	74.4	33.4	19.3	14.1	24.0	11.8
1931–1935	67,377	80.1	31.6	17.9	13.7	33.0	18.3
1936–1940	71,014	84.4	28.8	17.3	11.5	38.3	20.0
1941–1945	73,116	86.9	31.2	16.3	14.9	n.e.	n.e.
1946–1950	79,948	95.1	32.2	12.3	20.0	35.3	11.9
1951–1955	80,065	95.2	21.9	8.7	13.2	56.3	15.9
1956–1960	91,962	109.3	17.7	7.7	9.9	63.5	16.5
1961–1965	96,403	114.6	17.5	7.2	10.3	68.1	17.3
1966–1970	101,553	120.7	17.8	6.8	11.0	72.2	18.1
1971–1975	109,062	129.7	18.7	6.5	12.2	75.9	16.9
1976–1980	115,133	136.9	14.9	6.1	8.7	76.2	16.0
1981–1985	119,342	141.9	12.6	6.2	6.4	76.7	15.7
1986–1990	122,692	145.9	10.7	6.4	4.3	77.4	15.5
1991–1995	124,888	148.5	9.8	7.0	2.7	77.4	15.0
1996–2000	126,216	150.0	9.5	7.5	2.0	78.7	15.2

Table A.6: (*Continued*)

A.6. The pace of the demographic transition in Japan, 1930–1960: Values of age standardized death rates (asdr), infant mortality rates (imr), and the Hutterite index of marital fertility (I_g) for the prefectures of Japan classified by percentage of male labor force engaged in primary industry in 1930 (pmlpi)

	Mortality					
	Age standardized death rate (asdr)				Infant mortality (imr)	
Pmlpi	1908	1930	1950	1960	1920	1960
Under 30%	2572	1897	1075	712	184	24
30%–49%	2213	1921	1131	848	161	32
50%–54%	2404	1969	1184	765	169	35
55%–59%	2119	1825	1145	755	158	34
60% and over	2065	1985	1277	815	163	38

	Fertility (I_g)					
	Rural			Urban		
Pmlpi	1930	1950	1960	1930	1950	1960
Under 30%	0.52	0.50	0.30	0.43	0.44	0.28
30%–49%	0.54	0.50	0.29	0.43	0.45	0.28
50%–54%	0.57	0.50	0.28	0.46	0.44	0.28
55%–59%	0.58	0.53	0.30	0.48	0.45	0.28
60% and over	0.60	0.56	0.42	0.50	0.49	0.29

B. The biological standard of living and the human development index

B.1. Male standing height (msh) at ages 6, 12, and 18 and estimates of the human development index (HDI), Japan, 1901–2000

Male Standing Height (msh) at Ages:				Human Development Index	
Period	6	12	18	Year	HDI
1901–1910	106.7	133.6	159.2	1910	0.61
1911–1920	106.9	134.4	160.8	1920	0.64
1921–1930	107.7	136.2	161.6	1930	0.65
1931–1940	108.8	138.2	162.9	1940	0.70
1941–1950	108.5	138.2	162.9	1950	0.69
1951–1960	110.3	139.3	165.0	1960	0.75
1961–1970	113.4	144.9	157.7	1970	0.83
1971–1980	115.3	148.6	169.0	1980	0.89
1981–1990	116.4	150.4	170.6	1990	0.90
1990–2000	116.8	152.2	171.1	2000	0.92

(*Continued*)

Table A.6:   (*Continued*)

C. Education

C.1. Average years of schooling in China and Japan (years of education per person aged 15–64) and the ratio (Japan/China), 1950—1992

Year	China	Japan	Japan/China
1950	1.60	9.11	5.69
1973	4.09	12.09	2.96
1992	8.50	14.86	1.75

C.2. Indices (1960 = 100) for the number of senior and junior middle schools in cities, towns, and rural districts, China, 1964–1978

Period	Senior middle schools			Junior middle schools		
	Cities	Towns	Rural	Cities	Towns	Rural
1964–1965	99.3	100.0	100.0	105.2	94.5	94.4
1971–1975	328.7	175.1	3369.7	91.3	104.6	701.9
1976–1978	540.6	277.3	7483.9	77.9	133.1	1250.9

C.3. Years of schooling completed (SCY) and estimated rates of return on schooling: High school to college (COLR), high school to technical school (TECR), junior high to high school (HSR), and primary to junior high (JHR): Urban China, 1988–2001

Period	SCY	Estimated rates of return			
		COLR (%)	TECR (%)	HSR (%)	JHR (%)
1988–1989	4.3	13.3	4.5	11.3	15.6
1990–1994	5.2	20.3	9.9	11.4	14.2
1995–1999	7.6	28.4	13.6	17.1	14.3
2000–2001	10.2	38.0	17.0	21.0	15.1

C.4. Estimated rates of return to schooling by ownership sector, China, 1988–2001

Period	State sector (%)	Urban collective enterprises (%)	Nonpublic enterprises (%)
1988–1989	3.4	4.6	8.4
1990–1994	4.3	4.1	9.4
1995–1999	6.6	6.4	10.6
2000–2001	8.8	8.0	11.6

(*Continued*)

Table A.6: (*Continued*)

C.5. Advancement rates from one level to the next higher, China, 1980–1999

| | | From higher secondary schooling to institutions of higher education | | |
| | | | | |
Period	From primary to junior secondary (%)	From general secondary (%) [1]	From technical secondary, teaching training secondary, and vocational training secondary (%) [2]	Total (%) [1] + [2]
1980–1984	68.3	12.4	9.9	22.3
1985–1989	68.9	26.6	17.6	44.3
1990–1994	78.3	34.0	19.3	53.3
1995–1999	89.6	48.4	22.5	70.9

From junior secondary to higher secondary

| | | To other higher secondary | | |
| | | | | |
Period	To general secondary (%)	Technical secondary (%)	Teaching training secondary (%)	Vocational training secondary (%)	Total (%)
1980–1984	30.0	2.7	1.9	5.5	40.1
1985–1989	23.1	4.5	2.1	10.6	40.2
1990–1994	21.5	6.2	2.3	13.4	43.4
1995–1999	22.9	8.8	2.2	14.2	48.1

C.6. School enrollment rates for children aged 12–18 in China, 1989 and 2000

| Age (group) | 1989 | | 2000 | |
	Male (%)	Female (%)	Male (%)	Female (%)
12–13	93.1	92.7	96.8	92.2
14–15	77.4	68.9	84.9	82.9
16–17	38.3	31.2	64.7	57.9
18	17.2	16.1	34.5	40.0

(*Continued*)

Table A.6:　(*Continued*)

C.7. Growth in the number of teachers and the number of students in various types of schools, Japan, 1886–1940

	Teachers (%)			Students (%)		
Type of school	1886–1900	1901–1920	1921–1940	1886–1900	1901–1920	1921–1940
Elementary	0.1	4.0	2.4	2.4	3.6	2.0
Middle (male)	12.7	6.0	19.4	17.5	5.8	5.3
Middle (female)	19.4	20.2	7.3	40.7	21.1	8.9
High school (male)	28.7	1.3	8.7	18.1	2.2	6.2
University	2.9	9.9	13.5	6.9	9.0	15.0
Vocational (regular)	23.3	13.4	8.0	31.0	15.0	9.2
Vocational (continuance)	n.e.	24.5	24.5	n.e.	59.9	6.3

C.8. Estimates of the demand and supply of engineers in Japan, 1891–1940

	Supply: Students of higher education in science and engineering			Estimated demand growth minus supply growth (%)
Period	Percentage of all higher education students (%)	Estimated growth rate of graduates in science and engineering (%)	Estimated growth in demand [a] (%)	
1891–1895	15.8	-13.7	20.5	+43.2
1896–1900	10.9	3.1	4.3	+1.3
1900–1905	7.7	12.1	14.4	+2.4
1906–1910	7.8	17.6	16.9	−0.7
1911–1915	10.2	11.5	13.3	+1.7
1916–1920	13.1	10.1	16.1	−6.0
1921–1925	14.2	17.3	11.4	−5.9
1926–1930	15.7	2.1	7.1	+5.0
1931–1935	11.8	8.3	6.1	+2.2
1936–1940	14.3	3.7	13.9	+10.3

(*Continued*)

Table A.6: (*Continued*)

C.9. Enrollment rate for compulsory schooling (COENR), and advancement rates: from upper secondary schools to high schools (HSAD); from high schools to universities (UNAD); from high schools to junior colleges (JCAD); and from high schools to universities or junior colleges (UNJCAD), Japan, 1950–2004

Period	COENR (%)	Advancement rates (%)			
		HSAD	UNAD	JCAD	UNJCAD
1950–1954	99.7	47.0	7.9	2.1	10.0
1955–1959	99.8	52.7	8.3	2.1	10.4
1960–1964	99.8	64.0	11.0	3.1	14.1
1965–1969	99.8	74.7	13.3	5.0	18.3
1970–1974	99.9	86.9	21.3	8.3	29.6
1975–1979	99.9	93.0	26.8	11.3	38.1
1980–1984	100.0	94.1	25.3	11.0	36.2
1985–1989	100.0	93.9	24.9	11.4	36.3
1990–1994	100.0	95.0	26.9	12.5	39.4
1995–1999	100.0	95.9	35.0	12.2	47.2
2000–1904	100.0	96.0	40.8	8.3	49.0

[a] Growth in demand for engineers is based on combining growth in the number of employees in railroads and public utilities with the growth in prime mover horsepower installed in manufacturing.
n.e. = not estimated.

Sources: Panel A.1 from p. 169 of Maddison (1998) and from pp. 281–282 of Ho (1959). Panel A.1 from p. 15 of Poston and Yaukey (1992) and from p. 138 of Wang and Mason (2008). Panel A.3 from p. 295 of Bramall (2009), from p. 228 of Poston and Yaukey (1992) and from p. 138 of Wang and Mason (2008). Panel A.4 from pp. 357–358 in Mosk (2008). Panel A.5 from p. 38 of Miyamoto (2004) and p. 357 in Mosk (2008). Panel A.6 from p. 296 in Mosk (2008). Panel B.1 from p. 366 in Mosk (2008). Panel C.1 from p. 63 in Maddison (1998). Panel C.2 from p. 188 in Bramell (2009). Panel C.3 from p. 186 in Cai *et al.* (2008). Panel C.4 from p. 207 in Cai *et al.* (2008). Panel C.5 from p. 231 in Hannum *et al.* (2008). Panel C.6 from p. 236 in Hannum *et al.* (2008). Panel C.7 from p. 46–47 in Mosk (1995). Panel C.8 from p. 83 in Mosk (1995). Panel C.9 from Japan. Ministry of Internal Affairs and Communications and Statistical Research and Training Institute (2009).

was higher in pre-1940 Japan than it was in pre-1940 China, Japan's advantage in life expectancy stimulating an earlier expansion in the demand for higher education than was experienced in China; (6) reflecting Japan's earlier industrialization and Japan's earlier rise in per capita income — compared to China — the biological standard of living and the human development index improved significantly in Japan, giving Japan a distinct advantage in withdrawing surplus labor from the agricultural sector; (7) in early 20th century Japan the spread of infectious diseases in densely packed urban environments drove up mortality levels in urbanized industrialized districts of Japan above those prevailing in agricultural communities but the diffusion of the germ theory of disease and associated public health and medical interventions reversed the relationship between urbanization and mortality risks by 1930; (8) in 1950 Japanese educational attainment far exceeded that prevailing in China but by 1992 the gap between the two countries had closed to a remarkable degree; and (9) the demand for engineers grew rapidly in pre-1940 Japan as the inorganic economy diffused throughout the land, supply growth tending to fall short of the surge in demand over most of the pre-1940 period.

   Documenting labor supply and demand is the focus of Table A.7. Panels A.1 and A.2 speak to the rise in work days and hours worked in Japanese agriculture during the pre-1940 period. Panels A.3, A.4, and A.5 document the fact that surplus labor in pre-1940 Japan depressed wages in light manufacturing, particularly for females and specifically in the rapidly expanding textile sector, bolstering profits in that sector (while female agricultural wages exceeded those earned in manufacturing agricultural workers were not hired year around while manufacturing workers were so that it is likely actual earnings generated in the two sectors were approximately equal). Panel B.1 of the table speaks to the existence of redundant unutilized or underutilized labor in early 1930s China. Notable are the relatively high rates for unemployed or idle population in both agricultural and nonagricultural communities. Finally Panels A.6 and B.2 document the fact that labor productivity was relatively low in both Japan and China relative to labor productivity in other sectors — especially in manufacturing — substantiating the thesis advanced in this book about the crucial importance of withdrawing labor from farming, moving it into an industrial sector where it can contribute far more to national income. This last point speaks to the importance of structural shift in generating improvements in the index of total factor productivity appearing in Table A.1 and discussed in the Appendix to Chap. 2, Sec. 2.6.

   The agricultural sector is analyzed in Table A.8. Panel A makes a crucial point: while the existence of surplus labor may not have posed a problem for the economic development of many countries — like the countries of settlement where population densities were low or even in India where the ratio of arable to total land area is high — it was a very pressing issue for Japan and China where population densities were and are high and the proportion of arable to total land area is low. Panels B.1–B.6 substantiate

Table A.7: Labor force supply and demand in China and Japan, 1880–2004.

A. Japan

A.1. Workdays per worker (wdpw) and per male equivalent worker (wdpmew) in Japanese agriculture, 1880–1940

Item	1880	1900	1920	1930	1940
wdpw	113	131	163	151	163
wdpmew	131	150	187	173	192

A.2. Means and standard deviations for hours worked per worker unit (HPW) and for consumption per consumer unit (CPC) in Yen for farm households in Japan Surveyed in 1929: Classified by the ratio of consumer units to worker units (C/W) and by the number of worker units per cultivated land area (W/CL)

	HPW		CPC	
Group	Mean	Standard deviation	Mean	Standard deviation
	Classified by the C/W ratio			
C/W < 1.1	3020	988	267	107
1.1 ≤ C/W < 1.2	3092	1127	230	69
1.2 ≤ C/W < 1.3	2947	642	230	69
1.3 ≤ C/W < 1.4	3177	977	204	57
1.4 ≤ C/W < 1.6	3369	922	212	94
1.6 ≤ C/W	3650	1043	187	61
All families	3170	959	219	81
	Classified by W/CL ratio			
W/CL ≤ 0.015	3329	1094	264	110
0.015 ≤ W/CL ≤ 0.02	3296	905	213	68
0.02 ≤ W/CL ≤ 0.025	3243	970	233	94
0.025 ≤ W/CL ≤ 0.03	3203	983	215	67
0.03 ≤ W/CL ≤ 0.035	2896	796	214	74
0.035 ≤ W/CL ≤ 0.04	3299	1460	201	69
0.04 ≤ W/CL	2779	767	177	54

(*Continued*)

Table A.7:   (Continued)

A.3. Real daily wages: Nominal wages deflated by the consumer price index (CPI), 1934–1936 = 1, and wage differentials, Japan, 1885–1914

| | Real daily wages | | | | Wage differential: manu-facturing/agriculture | |
| | Agriculture | | Manufacturing | | | |
Period	Males	Females	Males	Females	Males	Females
1885–1889	0.73	0.48	0.86	0.39	1.18	0.81
1890–1894	0.87	0.59	0.80	0.40	0.92	0.68
1895–1899	0.96	0.71	0.82	0.40	0.85	0.56
1900–1904	0.91	0.70	0.91	0.42	1.00	0.60
1905–1909	0.82	0.66	0.89	0.41	1.09	0.62
1910–1914	0.88	0.67	0.90	0.44	1.02	0.66

A.4. Nominal daily wages (Yen) deflated by price index for the sector (1934–36 = 1), Japan, 1885–1914

| | Agriculture | | Manufacturing | |
Period	Males	Females	Males	Females
1885–1889	0.65	0.42	0.51	0.23
1890–1894	0.67	0.45	0.50	0.25
1895–1899	0.75	0.55	0.54	0.26
1900–1904	0.77	0.59	0.62	0.28
1905–1909	0.72	0.58	0.60	0.33
1910–1914	0.77	0.59	0.67	0.32

A.5. Nominal daily wages (w), nominal labor productivity (q), and labor's share in value added ($S\%$), Japan, 1895–1914: Cotton spinning and cotton weaving

| | Cotton spinning | | | | Cotton weaving | | | |
| | Wages (w) | | | | Wages (w) | | | |
Period	Male	Female	q	$S\%$	Male	Female	q	$S\%$
1895–1899	0.22	0.14	0.63	25.7	0.24	0.13	1.53	9.8
1900–1904	0.34	0.21	0.51	46.6	0.37	0.22	1.32	18.2
1905–1909	0.43	0.26	0.92	32.1	0.44	0.27	1.06	27.6
1910–1914	0.49	0.31	0.88	39.8	0.53	0.34	1.90	19.2

(Continued)

Table A.7: (*Continued*)

A.6. Percentage shares of the labor force in three broad sectors of the economy (P = primary, S = secondary, and T = tertiary) and relative labor productivity in the sector (calculated as percentage of GDP in the sector divided by percentage of labor force in the sector, times 100), Japan, 1951–2000

	Percentage of the labor force in:			Relative labor productivity in:		
Period	P	S	T	P	S	T
1951–1955	38.5	24.5	37.0	47.9	141.3	126.8
1956–1960	32.9	26.7	40.4	45.2	142.0	117.0
1961–1965	26.2	30.9	42.9	40.5	132.6	112.9
1966–1970	19.8	33.8	46.3	39.1	121.4	110.5
1971–1975	13.9	35.9	50.0	38.9	115.6	106.4
1976–1980	11.5	34.7	53.6	38.7	109.5	107.4
1981–1985	9.3	34.3	56.1	34.8	107.1	107.0
1986–1990	7.9	33.6	58.0	33.2	106.6	106.0
1991–1995	6.1	33.6	59.9	32.8	97.1	109.1
1996–2000	5.3	31.7	62.5	28.4	91.7	111.0

B. China

B.1. Percentage of population of China in agriculture and non-agriculture, 1933: Working, students, elderly or unemployed and idle

Category	Percentage of total population (or percentage of category if noted)
	Agricultural
Agricultural	73.00
Working in agriculture	42.46
Working only in agriculture	23.76
Children under age 7	14.24
Students	1.02
Persons over age 65	2.20
Unemployed or idle	13.07 (17.90% of agricultural population)
	Non-agricultural
Working ages 7–64	27.0
Working in factories	0.2
Working in handicrafts	2.4
Children under age 7	5.3
Students age 7 and over	1.15
Unemployed or idle	10.39 (38.48% of non-agricultural population)

(*Continued*)

Table A.7: (*Continued*)

B.2. Percentage of China's labor force in three broad sectors of the economy (A = agriculture or primary, I = industry or secondary, and S = services or tertiary) and relative labor productivity in the sector, 1952–2000[a]

Year	Percentage of the Labor Force in: A	I	S	Relative Labor Productivity in: A	I	S
1952	84.0	7.0	9.0	59.5	300.0	322.2
1970	81.0	10.0	9.0	49.4	460.0	144.4
1980	69.0	18.0	13.0	43.5	272.2	161.5
1985	62.0	21.0	17.0	45.2	204.8	170.6
1990	60.0	21.0	19.0	45.0	200.0	163.2
1995	52.0	23.0	25.0	38.5	213.0	124.0
2000	50.0	51.0	27.5	32.0	226.7	120.0

B.3. Percentage of employed labor force in china in primary (P), secondary (S) and tertiary (T) sectors of the economy; percentage of the employed labor force that is urban (U) or rural (R); and percentage of the employed urban labor force in state owned enterprises (USOE), 1978–2004

Period	Percentage of the employed labor force in: P	S	T	U	R	SOE % of urban labor
1978–1989	70.2	17.5	12.4	—	—	—
1980–1984	67.2	18.5	14.3	—	—	—
1985–1989	60.5	21.8	17.7	—	—	—
1990–1994	57.8	21.9	20.3	27.0	73.0	60.5
1995–1999	50.5	23.3	26.2	29.7	70.3	49.7
2000–2004	49.2	22.1	28.7	33.6	66.4	29.6

Notes: See the heading in Panel A.6 above for the method of computing labor productivity in the sectors. Basically the A sector in Panel B.2 corresponds to the P sector in Panel A.6; the I sector in Panel B.2 corresponds to the S sector in Panel A.6; and the S sector in Panel B.2 corresponds to the T sector in Panel A.6. However these correspondences may not be exact.

Sources: Panel A.1 from p. 61 of Mosk (1995). Panel A.2 from various tables in Mosk (1983). Panels A.3 — A.5 from p. 113 in Mosk (2008). Panel A.6 from p. 359 in Mosk (2008). Panel B.1 from pp. 10–11 in Feuerwerker (1977). Panel B.2 from p. 272 in Bramall (2009) and p. 482 of Huang *et al.* (2008). Panel B.3 from p. 168 in Cai *et al.* (2008).

Table A.8: Agriculture in China and Japan, 1400–2006.

A. Land use patterns, circa 1993

Country	Land area (000 ha)	Arable land & permanent crop area	Proportion arable (%)	Population (000s)	Arable land per head of population
A.1. Eurasian regions with long-standing settled agriculture					
China	959,696	95,975	10.0	1,178,440	0.08
Europe	487,696	135,705	27.8	506,910	0.26
India	328,759	169,650	51.6	899,000	0.19
Japan	37,780	4463	11.8	124,753	0.04
A.2. Countries of settlement					
United States	980,943	187,776	19.1	293,172	0.73
Canada	997,614	45,500	4.6	28,386	1.58
Australia	771,336	46,486	6.0	17,769	2.62
Brazil	851,197	48,955	5.8	158,913	0.31

B. Agriculture in Japan, 1910–2004

B.1. Indices (1960–1964 = 100)

Period	Arable land area (IALA)	Paddy fields actually planted (IPP)	Farm households (IFH)	Adult farm household members fully engaged in farming (IFW) [a]	Rice output (IRO)
1910–1919	95.9	91.8	93.1	n.e.	63.6
1920–1929	98.5	95.3	93.3	n.e.	69.5
1930–1939	98.6	97.0	94.0	n.e.	74.3
1940–1944	95.8	94.3	n.e.	n.e.	71.7
1955–1959	96.7	98.9	n.e.	n.e.	93.0
1960–1964	100.0	100.0	100.0	100.0	100.0

(Continued)

Table A.8: (*Continued*)

1965–1969	97.8	99.4	93.4	79.2	106.9
1970–1974	93.9	82.8	89.1	66.3	94.1
1975–1979	90.9	81.2	82.9	55.5	98.3
1980–1984	89.4	70.0	78.2	51.6	82.5
1985–1989	87.9	67.0	73.4	49.9	85.1
1990–1994	85.1	64.4	49.4	38.2	79.3
1995–1999	81.6	58.7	43.9	32.6	77.3
2000–2004	78.6	51.9	38.5	31.3	69.0

B.2. Relative indices, percentage of arable land in paddy (ALP%) and adult farm household members fully engaged in farming per farm household (FWPFH)

Relative indices (in rice production)

Period	Land productivity (IRO/IPP)	Farm household productivity (IRO/IFH)	Adult farm worker productivity (IRO/IFW)	ALP%	FWPH
1910–1919	69.3	68.0	n.e.	50.5	n.e.
1920–1929	72.8	73.0	n.e.	51.1	n.e.
1930–1939	76.6	77.7	n.e.	53.8	n.e.
1940–1944	n.e.	n.e.	n.e.	53.9	n.e.
1955–1959	n.e.	n.e.	n.e.	55.3	n.e.
1960–1964	100.0	100.0	100.8	55.9	1.9
1965–1969	107.5	114.6	135.6	57.5	1.6
1970–1974	113.7	105.7	143.1	58.2	1.4
1975–1979	121.1	118.6	177.3	56.7	1.3
1980–1984	117.9	105.6	160.1	55.5	1.3
1985–1989	127.1	116.0	170.5	54.6	1.3
1990–1994	123.0	160.8	209.3	54.3	1.5
1995–1999	131.8	176.0	237.1	54.6	1.4
2000–2004	132.8	179.3	220.5	54.7	1.6

(*Continued*)

Table A.8: (*Continued*)

B.3. Percentage growth rate for inputs (labor)

Period	Number of workers		Workdays	
	Male	Female	Total	Per worker
1935–1945	−1.7	2.0	−0.9	−1.0
1945–1955	1.5	0.3	1.3	0.4
1955–1965	−3.5	−2.5	−2.7	0.3

B.4. Percentage growth for inputs (variable and fixed capital)

Period	Fixed capital		Variable capital (current inputs)	
	Machinery and implements	Total	Fertilizers	Total
1935–1945	−0.2	−1.4	−5.0	−6.6
1945–1955	3.1	2.0	13.5	15.0
1955–1965	11.5	7.8	3.6	8.5

B.5. Percentage growth rates of relative prices for inputs relative to agricultural output price

Period	Labor and land		Fixed capital		Variable capital (current inputs)	
	Labor wages	Cultivated land prices	Machinery and implements	Total	Fertilizer	Total
1920–1930	1.9	2.9	0.3	1.3	−1.7	−1.2
1955–1965	6.1	4.3	−3.2	−0.9	−5.0	−4.5
1960–1970	7.2	−1.1	−7.1	−1.1	−5.4	−5.0

(*Continued*)

Table A.8: (*Continued*)

B.6. Percentage growth rates of productivities of labor and land

Period	Labor productivity		Land productivity		Relative contribution to labor productivity growth of land productivity growth (%)	
	Per male equivalent (1)	Per workday (2)	Per paddy-field equivalent (3)	Per hectare of crop area (4)	(3)/(1)	(4)/(2)
1935–1945	−1.7	−0.9	−1.5	−0.7	88	78
1945–1955	2.2	1.9	2.9	2.1	132	111
1955–1965	6.9	6.5	3.4	4.3	49	66

C. Agriculture in China, 1400–2006

C.1. Growth accounting for growth in china's grain output, 1400–1957 (assuming a constant level of per capita grain consumption)

Period	Annual compound growth rates (%)					Share of total factor productivity
	Output	Labor	Land	Capital	Total factor productivity	
1400–1770	0.32	0.19	0.05	0.06	0.01	4
1700–1850	0.59	0.35	0.06	0.05	0.12	21
1850–1957	0.45	0.27	0.06	0.07	0.04	10

C.2. Indices (1950–1954 = 100) for agricultural output and grain consumption, 1950–1978

Item	1950–1956	1957–1963	1964–1978
	Sown area		
Grain	102.5	100.8	98.2
Cotton	105.1	94.8	97.0

(*Continued*)

Table A.8: (*Continued*)

Yield per hectare			
Grain	103.5	106.3	160.7
Cotton	105.6	125.6	217.1

Grain output, population, and per capita output			
Grain output	106.4	107.3	157.8
Population[b]	102.3	116.1	146.5
Per capita output	103.8	92.6	107.3

C.3. Value added (in 1987 Yuan)

Item	1933	1952	1957	1978	1995
Per head	277	225	241	235	439
Per worker	789	748	812	781	1591
Per hectare cultivated	1353	1185	1374	2265	5563

C.4 Indices (1955 = 100) for fertilizer output, fertilizer consumption, and fertilizer imports (Tons)

Item	1955–1959	1960–1964	1965–1966
Output	286.9	690.1	1345.6
Consumption	172.4	306.8	617.5
Imports	127.5	156.8	332.6

C.5. Growth rates for value added and tons of grain produced

Period	Value added (1980 prices)		Value added (comparable prices) (%)	Tons of grain (%)
	Farming(%)	Agriculture(%)		
	Collective farming			
1955–1981	2.8	3.2	2.6	2.8
1963–1981	3.3	3.6	2.9	3.5
	Family farming			
1981–2006	4.5	5.6	4.2	1.3
1984–2006	4.3	5.5	3.9	1.0

(*Continued*)

Table A.8: (*Continued*)

C.6. Growth rates of farm output, input, and total factor productivity

Item	1952–1957	1957–1978	1978–1987	1987–1994
Gross farm output	3.70	2.32	5.77	4.28
Farm gross value added	3.05	1.72	5.52	3.62
Farm inputs	6.36	2.54	4.35	4.83
Non-farm inputs	12.12	8.98	8.43	6.67
Farm employment	1.35	1.92	0.49	0.58
Farm labor productivity	1.66	−0.19	4.99	3.05
Irrigated area cultivated	6.46	2.41	−0.16	1.32
Non-irrigated land cultivated	−0.79	−2.08	−0.6	−1.49
Augmented land	1.79	0.18	−0.32	0.34
Other capital	7.81	4.43	5.00	3.48
Total factor productivity	0.63	0.57	4.56	2.67

C.7. Indices for industrial inputs into China's rural economy (1965 = 100)

Item	1962–1964	1970–1974	1975–1978
Kilowatts of power	64.6	300.0	646.9
Millions of tons of chemical fertilizer	54.8	264.0	399.6
Cement (millions of tons)	37.7	311.1	575.9
Irrigation/drainage equipment	69.2	270.0	572.1
tractors	75.8	328.2	704.6
Power tillers	n.e	273.3	1222.2
Total horsepower per cultivated hectare	76.7	310.0	692.5

C.8. Growth rates for agricultural GDP and value added produced in various sub-sectors of agriculture, 1970–2000

Item	1970–1978	Reform period		
		1978–1984	1985–1995	1996–2000
GDP	4.9	8.8	3.8	4.2
Grain	2.8	4.7	1.7	0.03
Rice	2.5	4.5	0.6	0.3
Wheat	7.0	8.3	1.9	−0.4

(*Continued*)

Table A.8: (*Continued*)

Total cash crop area sown	2.4	5.1	2.1	−0.4
Cotton	−0.4	19.3	−0.3	−1.9
Meat (pork, beef, poultry)	4.4	9.1	8.8	6.5
Fishery	5.0	7.9	13.7	10.2

[a] Farm household members aged 15 and over who work full time in farm production.
[b] The population estimates used here are those appearing in Maddison (2006: p. 292).
n.e. = not estimated.
Sources: Panel A data from p. 28 of Maddison (1998). Panels B.1 and B.2 data from various tables in Japan. Ministry of Internal Affairs and Communications and Statistical Research and Training Institute (2009). Panels B.3–B.6 data from p. 248–249 in Mosk (2008). Panels C.1 and C.4 from p. 74 and p. 82 in Perkins (1969). Panels C.2 and C.8 from p. 472 and p. 479 in Huang *et al.*(2008). Panels C.3 and C.6 from p. 71 and p. 75 in Maddison (1998). Panel C.5 from p. 228 in Bramall (2009). Panel C.7 from pp. 80–81 in Rawski (1979).

points made in Chap. 2 concerning the role of relative factor scarcities in shaping the nature of technological progress in Japanese agriculture, land augmentation achieved through use of fertilizer (coupled with the diffusion of enhanced seed varieties and better management of irrigation) preceding mechanization of agricultural tasks. In particular Panel B.5 points to the importance of relative prices in a basically market oriented economy for this process. Panels C.1 and C.3 provide estimates of pre-1950 Chinese agriculture. The pre-1950 estimates suggest that total factor productivity growth was on-going in Chinese farming throughout the period 1400–1957 but was proceeding at a relatively slow pace. This coupled with growth in land and capital permitted population to grow albeit with fits and starts, decline occurring in some periods (for instance in the two decades after 1850). Panel C.2 suggests that this pattern continued through 1963, being slightly mitigated between 1964 and 1978 when output per capita actually improved somewhat. Panels C.4 and C.6 speak to the importance of land augmentation in Chinese agriculture during the period 1952–1978, especially to the importance of fertilizer and irrigation for expanding output. Panel C.5 suggests that collective farming failed to generate growth rates for farm value added achieved by family farming in the aftermath of the reforms dismantling collectivization begun in the late 1970s. Panel C.7 documents the growing use of machinery in Chinese farming, especially in the three years leading up to the onset of the reform program commenced in 1978. And Panel C.8 speaks to the importance of the breaking up of the

Table A.9: Expansion of infrastructure and industry in China and Japan, 1880–2000.

A. The penetration of infrastructure, China and Japan compared, circa 1920 and 2000[a]

	Road length (km)		Railroads				
Item	Total	Paved	Track (km)	Oper- ation- (km)	Freight volume (ton- km)	Pas- senger traffic (passen- ger-km)	Electric- ity gener- ated (kw h)
	Per person						
China, 1920	n.e.	0.00006	0.00002	n.e.	15.5	8.6	n.e.
China, 2000	n.e.	0.02	0.00004	n.e.	11,822	355.4	971.7
Japan, 1920	15.8	n.e.	0.24	0.28	177.5	32.1	913.3
Japan, 2000	9.2	7.0	0.19	0.22	174,401	170.6	8599.5
	Per land area (Per hectare)						
China, 1920	n.e.	0.00003	0.00001	n.e.	7.7	4.3	n.e.
China, 2000	n.e.	0.02	0.00006	n.e.	15,711	472.3	1291.4
Japan, 1920	23.4	n.e.	0.36	0.42	262.9	47.5	1352.9
Japan, 2000	30.9	23.6	0.65	0.73	585,919	573.0	28891.0

B. Infrastructure and industry in Japan, 1880–1985

B.1. The expansion of railroads and the disappearance of traditional transportation in Japan (Rikusha and Small Boats, Kobune), indices with 1920–1921 = 100[b]

	Railroads (operation-km)				Traditional transport	
Period	National	Regional	Street	Total	*Rikusha*	*Kobune*
1900–1909	35.6	104.4	n.e.	45.1	162.6	266.6
1910–1919	85.1	66.7	92.5	78.6	111.9	168.2
1920–1929	115.9	141.8	113.2	120.9	70.5	86.8
1930–1941	159.4	207.4	109.1	162.6	23.3	77.5

(Continued)

Table A.9: (*Continued*)

B.2. Electricity generated (GEN), electric lights (LIGHT), wattage in lights (WATT), and electrified cars on railroads (CAR): Indices with 1920–1921 = 100

Period	GEN	LIGHT	WATT	CAR
1910–1914	30.4	30.0	47.8	46.1
1925–1929	143.4	232.0	247.2	179.9
1935–1939	724.2	555.0	732.2	190.4

B.3. Number of electric lights (LIGHT) and electricity supplied (ELEC): Indices with 1920–1921 = 100 for Japan and the Tōkaidō industrial belt (INB) and the percentage for the Tōkaidō industrial belt (INB%) [c]

	LIGHT			ELEC		
Period	Japan	INB	INB%	Japan	INB	INB%
1910–1919	41.7	51.4	65.2	70.4	74.7	45.3
1930–1937	163.1	160.4	40.2	339.6	386.7	48.9

B.4. Powered factories as a percentage classified by number of workers in factories (POW%) and composition of inanimate power sources for manufacturing: STEAM (steam engines and turbines), (INCOM) internal combustion engines, and electric motors (ELEC)

POW% classified by number of workers				Composition of power sources			
Year	5–29	30–99	100 and over	Year	STEAM	INCOM	ELEC
1909	20.5	69.7	88.4	1910	80.6	6.6	21.8
1919	54.3	88.6	99.3	1920	31.3	3.4	58.9
1930	80.1	95.3	99.6	1930	15.6	1.2	81.8

B.5. The expansion of transportation, 1955–1970: Indices for transportation flows with 1965 = 100

	Cargo				Passenger			
Year	Total	Rail	Motor vehicle	Sea	Total	Rail	Motor vehicle	Bus
1955	31.5	73.1	19.8	35.7	31.0	54.7	16.6	30.9
1970	262.1	109.4	286.4	179.6	313.7	122.1	396.3	113.1

(*Continued*)

Table A.9: (*Continued*)

B.6. Index for the price of transport (TRANSPI) relative to the consumer price index (CPI): 1880–1939 and 1955–1985

Period	CPI (1)	TRANSPI (2)	Relative cost of transport: (2)/(1)
	Pre-1940: Indices with 1934–1936 = 100		
1880–1899	16.7	25.4	154.0
1920–1939	111.7	112.5	101.4
	Post-1950: Indices with 1980 = 100		
1955–1959	22.9	26.7	116.7
1980–1989	108.1	106.6	98.7

B.7. Expansion of manufacturing: Indices of industrial production, value added weights, 1980 = 100: sub-sectors other than machinery

Period	Total	Heavy industry sub-sectors			Light industry sub-sectors	
		Iron and steel	Nonferrous metals	Chemicals	Textiles	Food and tobacco
1931–1935	4.3	2.5	3.7	2.6	26.2	18.9
1956–1960	13.4	12.4	13.4	12.1	36.5	31.6
1966–1970	51.0	56.5	52.2	45.1	83.1	70.9
1971–1975	75.8	84.0	77.6	71.4	100.5	86.1

B.8. Expansion of production of machinery: Indices of industrial production, value added weights, 1980 = 100: Machinery sub-sector as a whole and for important sub-sectors of machinery production

Period	Total	Nonelectric machinery	Electric machinery	Transport equipment	Precision machinery
1931–1935	0.8	2.1	0.2	0.6	0.8
1956–1960	6.7	9.1	4.0	7.6	5.7
1966–1970	37.5	29.1	29.1	42.9	22.0
1971–1975	62.7	52.2	52.2	73.7	34.6

(*Continued*)

Table A.9:　(*Continued*)

C. Infrastructure and industry in China, 1895–2005

C.1. Expansion of traditional and modern freight transport, 1895–1936

Year	Volumes (million tons-km) transported by: Rail	Steam ship	Junk	Share carried by modern equipment (steam ship and rail)	Index of total volume (1895 = 100)
1895	0.2	5.2	24.1	16.8	100
1915	7.3	16.3	35.8	36.2	189.8
1933	12.8	25.9	51.2	41.2	291.3
1936	14.6	26.6	54.3	41.4	309.0

C.2. Expansion of railroad track and services and length of motor roads, 1895–1983: Indices with 1949 = 100

Year	Railroads Track (km)	Freight (ton-km)	Passenger-km	Length of motor roads
1895	1.9	0.8	0.8	n.e.
1915	48.2	31.8	25.7	n.e.
1933	72.5	69.6	54.7	88.9
1949	100.0	100.0	100.0	100.0
1957	122.5	731.5	277.9	314.8
1979	n.e.	n.e.	n.e.	1,081.5
1983	236.7	3,612.0	2,380.8	n.e.

C.3. Output of chinese industry in 1933 prices (in billion Yuan)

Sector	1933	1952	1957
Factories	0.74	1.35	3.12
Handicrafts	2.22	2.33	2.66
Mining	0.23	0.68	1.40
Utilities	0.16	0.39	0.89
Total	3.35	4.75	8.07
Share of handicrafts (%)	66.3	49.05	32.96

(*Continued*)

C.4. Growth rates for major sectors of GDP (%) as estimated by Yeh and
By Rawski ("preferred estimates" given by Rawski), 1914/1936

Item	Yeh	Rawski
Agriculture	0.8	1.4–1.7
Modern industry	7.7	8.1
Handicrafts	0.7	1.4
Construction	3.5	4.6
Modern transportation/ communications	4.0	3.0
Traditional transportation/ communications	0.3	1.9
Trade	1.1	2.5
Finance	2.9	5.0
GDP	1.1	1.8–2.0

C.5. Share of regions in china's manufacturing output in 1933 and percentage
of firms in each region that are Chinese

Region	Share of region (%)	Share of Chinese firms (%)
China Proper (excluding manchuria)	85.8	78.1
Shanghai	39.7	69.2
Kiangsu	8.7	97.8
Other	37.3	82.9
Manchuria	14.2	41.1

C.6. Cost (Yuan) for a bale of 20-count yarn in Chinese and Japanese mills in China,
1930s

Item	Chinese mills (1)	Japanese mills (2)	Difference (1) − (2)	Contribution to total difference (%)
Wages	10.5	5.8	4.7	20.2
Power	5.5	4.8	0.7	3.0
Machine repairs	1.8	0.6	1.2	5.2
Materials	1.7	0.5	1.2	5.2
Salaries	1.2	0.6	0.6	2.6
Sanitation	0.2	0.5	−0.3	−1.3
Management	2.5	2.0	0.5	2.2
Taxes and interest	15.0	2.7	12.3	52.8
Total	43.7	20.4	23.3	100.0

(*Continued*)

Table A.9: (*Continued*)

C.7. Growth rates for employment in light and heavy industry, 1952–1999

Period	Light (%)	Heavy (%)
1952–1978	8.7	11.9
1978–1989	15.4	12.9
1989–1999	15.1	16.6

C.8. Relative labor productivity (Yuan per worker) of labor in commune and village enterprises, 1978–1983

Period	Percentage of employment in industry (1)	Labor productivity in agriculture (2)	Labor productivity in industry (3)	Ratio (%) (2)/(3)
1978–1989	75.8	658.5	2278.5	28.9
1980–1981	82.5	845.0	2773.5	34.0
1982–1983	86.7	1290.0	3304.0	39.0

C.9 Indices for employment in textiles and apparel (INDEM), 1980 = 100, employment per firm (SIZE), share of sector in total exports (EXPS), and share of china's textiles exports in world exports (WEXPS), 1980–2005

Year	INDEM	SIZE	EXPS (%)	WEXPS (%)
1980	100.0	132.5	19.8	4.6
1990	247.6	148.3	20.1	7.5
2000	161.6	387.6	19.8	14.7
2005	194.8	271.8	15.4	24.1

C.10. Indices for output (INDO), employment (INDEM) and output per man year (INDLP) and ratio of the difference between exports and imports relative to output (EX–IM/O), steel industry, 1980–2005

Year	INDO	INDEM	INDLP	EX–IM/O (%)
1980	100.0	100.0	100.0	−12.1
1990	179.0	129.1	138.8	−2.4
2000	346.4	103.3	335.5	−7.9
2005	952.0	115.2	827.0	−1.5

(*Continued*)

Table A.9: (*Continued*)

C.11. Share of Chinese bank loans by type

Period	Industrial (%)	Infrastruc- ture (%)	Agricul- tural (%)	Town and village en- terprises (%)	Privately owned firms (%)	Joint ventures (%)
1995– 1999	21.7	1.8	4.2	5.9	0.5	2.6
2000– 2005	15.4	1.8	5.2	5.3	0.9	2.2

[a] In the case of Japan circa 2000 the figures for railway track are for 1984. The figures for Japan's road length and electricity generated are for 1921, not 1920. Figures on paved road length are not available for Japan until 1936. In order to estimate China's paved road length for 2000 I relied on an estimate of 11 vehicles per km of roads, multiplying by the number 11 the number of reported vehicles.
[b] In the case of traditional transport the indices for 1930–1941 are actually for 1930–1938.
[c] In the case of electricity supplied, the figures for 1910–1919 are actually for 1915–1919.
n.e.: not estimated.

Sources: For Panel A the sources for Japan are various tables in Japan Ministry of Internal Affairs and Communications and Statistical Research and Training Institute (2009); for China the sources are various tables in the following: China National Bureau of Statistics (2004), Maddison (1998, 2006), Mitchell (2003), Rawski (1989), United Nations (2004), and World Bank (2002). For Panels B.1–B.4 various tables in Mosk (2001). For Panels B.5 and B.6 various tables in Mosk (2005). For Panels B.7 and B.8 p. 251 of Mosk (2008). For Panels C.1, C.2, C.4, C.5, and C.6 various tables in Rawski (1989). For Panel C.3 p. 146 in Maddison (1998). For Panels C.7 and C.8 various tables in Bramall (2009). For Panels C.9 and C.10 various tables in Brandt *et al.* (2008). For Panel C.11 p. 521 in Allen *et al.* (2008).

collective farming system for the diversity of agricultural output: under the regime of family farming and relatively unconstrained market conditions, relative prices largely determining production decisions, greater flexibility in responding to demand taking hold.

Table A.9 documents assertions made about infrastructure and industry. Panel A substantiates one of my key assertions: that infrastructure expansion was far more advanced in the Japan of 1920 than it was in the China of 1920. This is clear, Japan's superiority showing up both in terms of population and in terms of geography. Panel B.1 speaks to the importance of railroads in modernizing transport in pre-1941 Japan. Noteworthy is the sharp drop in traditional means of transport (using human pulled *rikusha* on the land and small boats, *kobune,* on the water). Panels B.2–B.4 document the crucial importance of electrification for the modernization of railroads and mechanization in factories in pre-1940 Japan. Panels B.5 and B.6 testify to the dramatic expansion of transport and communications in post-1955 Japan, the relative price of transport declining between the late 1950s and the late 1980s (a similar tendency is at work in the period between the late 1980s and two decades prior to 1940). Panel B.7 documents the massive expansion of heavy industry (chemicals, iron and steel) that took place in Japan after 1955, growth in the heavy industries outstripping growth in textiles and food and tobacco. Panel B.8 demonstrates the importance of machinery production for the surge in Japanese manufacturing in the post-1955 period.

Panels C.1–C.11 of Table A.9 offer parallel figures for China. Panel C.1 shows that traditional transport declined much more slowly in pre-1940 China than it did in pre-1940 Japan. Panel C.3 suggests that handicrafts as opposed to factory production remained strongly entrenched in China, dominating industrial output during the 1930s, continuing to play a substantial role as late as 1957. Panel C.4 provides two sets of estimates for national output growth in China between 1914 and 1936 the more cautious figures of Yeh contrasted with the more optimistic estimates arrived at by Rawski. It is important to note that the main difference between the two estimates lies in the estimates for the agricultural sector, not the industrial sector. Panel C.5 speaks to the strong regional concentration of China's manufacturing during the pre-1940 period, Shanghai and Manchuria dominating. Panel C.6 decomposes the advantage enjoyed by Japanese managed mills operating in China over their Chinese mill rivals: the main differences being wages and taxes plus interest paid. Panels C.7–C.11 explores the massive expansion of industry in post-1952 China. Panel C.7 contrasts the period 1952–1978 when heavy industrial growth outstripped light industry growth with the period after reforms were introduced, light industry growing more briskly than heavy industry between 1978 and 1987. Along these lines, Panel C.9 shows the crucial importance of textiles in the surge of China's exports after 1980, especially prior to 2000 (mimicking the importance of textiles in Japan's exports prior to the early 1960s). Finally Panel C.11 indicates that private Chinese firms have been largely shut out of the loan profiles of official Chinese banks.

The final table in this Appendix, Table A.10, presents growth accounting estimates for both Japan and China — and for Hong Kong, South Korea, and Taiwan — going back to 1888 in the case of Japan. Key points to be culled from this table include: (1) the pace of total factor productivity growth accelerated in Japan, peaking in the 1958–1970 period, declining thereafter; (2) during the period 1953–1971 when total factor productivity growth was unusually rapid in Japan economies of scale and structural change played a crucial role in the expansion of total factor productivity; (3) within the Japanese manufacturing economy some sectors — notably machinery and trade — experienced relatively high rates of total factor productivity growth while other sectors like water supply, agriculture, and medical services experienced low even negative total factor productivity growth (when total factor productivity growth is negative augmentation of land, labor, and capital outstrip the negative impact of total factor productivity growth, resources gaining in inherent efficiency being thrown into sectors that are not finding more efficient ways to utilize them); (4) total factor productivity growth was also rapid in Hong Kong, South Korea, and Taiwan over much of the

Table A.10: Growth accounting for Japan, Hong Kong, South Korea, Taiwan, and China, mainly post-1950.

A. Japan				
A.1. Long-run estimates, 1888–1990 for the growth in labor productivity				
Period	**[1] Capital–income share**	**[2] Labor productivity**	**[3] Capital–labor ratio**	**[4] Total factor productivity (TFP) growth**	**[5] Contribution of TFP growth [4]/[2] (%)**
A.1.1. Pre-World War II					
1888–1900	0.33	2.08	5.74	0.19	9
1900–1920	0.39	2.68	6.07	0.31	12
1920–1937	0.43	2.29	2.75	1.11	48
1928–1937	0.47	3.04	2.23	1.99	65
A.1.2. Post-World War II					
1958–1970	0.33	8.19	11.60	4.36	53
1970–1990	0.28	3.78	7.44	1.70	45

(Continued)

Table A.10: (*Continued*)

A.2. Estimates of sources of growth of national income, 1953–1971

A.2.1. Growth in income, total factor input and capital

National income (output)	Total factor input	Capital				
		Total	Inventories	Nonresidential structures and equipment	Dwellings	International assets
8.81	3.95	2.10	0.73	1.07	0.30	0.00

A.2.2. Growth in land and labor

Land	Labor					
	Total	Employment	Hours of work	Age–Sex composition	Education	Unallocated
0.00	1.85	1.14	0.21	0.14	0.34	0.02

A.2.3. Total factor productivity growth

Total (growth in output per unit of total input)	Advance in knowledge and innovation	Economies of scale	Improved resource allocation		Reduction of international trade barriers
			contraction of agricultural employment	Contraction of Nonagricultural self employment	
4.86	1.97	1.94	0.64	0.30	0.01

(*Continued*)

Table A.10: (*Continued*)

A.3. Sector specific estimates of total factor productivity growth, 1961–1995

Top ten (over 1961–1995 period) (%)			Bottom ten (over 1961–1995 period) (%)		
Sector	1961–1973	1961–1995	Sector	1961–1973	1961–1995
Air transportation	6.95	3.11	Water supply	−3.92	−2.12
Electric machinery	4.18	2.93	Other industries	−2.85	−2.05
Gas	2.86	2.36	Publishing	−2.32	−1.49
Trade	4.54	2.32	Agriculture	−2.24	−1.43
Precision machinery	3.39	2.19	Education	2.32	−0.63
Communications	1.79	2.01	Railway transportation	0.67	−0.59
Other mining (not coal)	5.45	1.73	Coal	−0.63	−0.52
Chemicals	2.91	1.65	Building and construction	−0.94	−0.34
Vehicles	2.47	1.53	Foods	−0.08	−0.29
Public services	3.91	1.46	Medical services	0.25	−0.22

B. Estimates for the growth in total factor productivity: Hong Kong, South Korea, and Taiwan, 1960–1999

Period	[1] Capital–income share	[2] Labor productivity	[3] Capital–labor ratio	[4] Total factor productivity (TFP) growth	[5] Contribution of TFP growth [4]/[2] (%)
		B.1.Hong Kong			
1966–1970	0.34	4.1	5.9	2.1	51
1970–1980	0.358	6.0	5.4	4.0	67
1980–1990	0.399	5.7	6.5	3.2	55
1990–1999	0.391	1.9	6.5	−0.7	−36
		B.2. South Korea			
1970–1980	0.478	3.6	9.6	−1.0	−27
1980–1990	0.429	6.2	8.7	2.5	40
1990–1999	0.389	4.4	8.6	1.1	25

(*Continued*)

Table A.10:   (*Continued*)

		B.3. Taiwan			
1960–1970	0.485	7.0	10.9	1.7	24
1970–1980	0.476	5.4	10.7	0.3	2
1980–1990	0.435	6.2	6.7	3.2	52
1990–1999	0.417	6.3	8.6	2.7	43

C. China

C.1. Growth accounting estimates for china, 1952-2005 contributions to growth of national domestic product (GDP)

C.1.1. Growth of output and inputs

		Average growth of inputs			
Period	Growth in GDP	Capital	Raw labor	Education-enhanced labor	Total factor productivity growth (TFP)
1952–2005	7.0	7.7	1.9	2.6	2.1
			1952–1978		
1952–1978	4.4	5.8	1.9	2.5	0.5
1952–1957	6.5	1.9	1.2	1.7	4.7
1957–1978	3.9	6.7	2.0	2.7	−0.5
1957–1965	2.4	5.2	1.5	2.1	−1.0
1965–1978	4.9	7.7	2.4	3.1	−0.2
			1978–2005		
1978–2005	9.5	9.6	1.9	2.7	3.8
1978–1985	9.7	9.2	3.4	4.5	3.2
1985–1990	7.7	6.9	2.5	2.9	3.1
1990–1995	11.7	9.1	1.4	1.9	6.7
1995–2000	8.6	10.5	0.9	1.6	3.2
2000–2005	9.5	12.6	1.0	1.8	3.1

C.1.2. Percentage shares of GDP growth attributable to

	Capital (%)	Education-enhanced labor (%)	Total factor productivity growth (TFP) (%)
1952–2005	47.7	21.4	30.9
1952–1978	56.3	32.7	11.0
1978–2005	43.7	16.2	40.1

(*Continued*)

Table A.10: (*Continued*)

C.2. Various estimates of total factor productivity growth, 1980s and 1990s, range [a]

Data used	1980s	1990s
National level GDP data	2.1–3.7 (4 estimates)	0.3–2.8 (4 estimates)
Provincial level GDP data	0.4–5.5 (4 estimates)	1.8–6.3 (3 estimates)
Industry level data	3.1–6.5 (2 estimates)	0.5–3.8 (2 estimates)

C.3. Estimates of total factor productivity growth in independent-accounting industrial enterprises, 1980–1996 [b]

Period	State owned enterprises	Collectively owned enterprises	Other domestic enterprises	Foreign invested companies
1980–1984	2.1	3.1	n.a.	n.a.
1984–1988	3.8	5.2	n.a.	n.a.
1988–1992	2.1	3.1	2.1	1.1
1992–1996	−1.1	4.3	3.1	0.7
1980–1996	1.7	3.9	n.a.	n.a.

[a] Some of the estimates for the 1980s cover the period from the late 1970s until the early 1990s. For the 1990s estimates for the second half of the decade tend to be lower than those for the first half of the decade.

[b] n.a. = not available.

Sources: For Panel A.1 p. 34 of Kim (2001). For Panel A.2 p. 98–99 of Denison and Chung (1976). For Panel A.3 pp. 173–174 of Nakajima *et al.* (2004). For Panel B p.36 of Kim (2001). For Panel C.1, p.839 of Perkins and Rawski (2008). For Panel C.2 p.416 of Bramall (2009). For Panel C.3 p.540 of Huang (2008).

post-1960 period, like Japan slowing down in the case of Hong Kong and Taiwan (giving manufacturers in these two jurisdictions a strong incentive to invest in China where labor costs were lower, wages rising with already achieved labor productivity gains in Hong Kong and Taiwan); and (5) total factor productivity growth was relatively slow in China during the heyday of the command and control economy, 1952–1978, picking up in the period after agricultural reforms and subsequent reforms associated with opening China up to foreign investment in manufacturing were introduced.

We can summarize these ideas concerning the pace of total factor productivity growth with the concept of an "arc of total factor productivity growth." When a country is absorbing and adapting a huge range of technologies from abroad the rate of total factor productivity growth is generally high. Moreover, as argued earlier, rapid absorption of foreign technology is typically associated with augmentation and physical capital accumulation. So during this phase total factor productivity growth tends to drift upward especially in newly established industries where the pace of technological adaptation is unusually rapid (e.g., in air transport, electrical machinery, and precision machinery in Japan between 1961 and 1973). At the same time in older more established industries total factor productivity growth may actually be negative during this phase (e.g., in agriculture, coal, and building construction) because the rate of growth in the augmentation of the factors of production actually outstrips the rate of growth of output. The aggregate level of total factor productivity growth is an amalgam of the individual sector total factor productivity growths (weighted through by the shares of the sectors in overall output). This is the dynamic during an upswing phase in the arc.

Eventually a follower country either catches up or at least closes the gap with the technological leaders in industry after industry, thereby dampening the rate of total factor productivity in all sectors. The pace of overall total factor productivity growth slackens overall as the downswing phase of the arc gains force.

During the long downswing phase — basically the fate of all economies once they make great strides in closing the technological gap with the leading economies — there is a strong incentive to seek opportunities for investment in other countries with lower wages (ones that do not enjoy the standard of living and hence the high wages associated with the more sophisticated technology and augmented labor of the home country). To some extent this is what happened in East Asia. A combination of absorbing foreign technology, accumulation, and augmentation of the factors of production drove up wages and eventually reduced the pace of total factor productivity growth — hence the rate of growth of per capita income — in Japan, South Korea, Taiwan, and Hong Kong by the late 1970s (see Table A.5). Naturally owners of capital, investors, in these countries began to look around for investment opportunities in their geographic neighborhood, namely in China where the market was huge and wages were far lower. At the same time Chinese leaders, realizing that the types of income per capita gaps evident for East Asia during the 1970s could not be perpetuated ad infinitum without inviting domestic political unrest realized the handwriting was on the wall. Some accommodation with the demands of foreign capitalists for relatively safe (that is not subject to Chinese nationalization) investment opportunities within China was called for. As a result Special Economic Zones were established along the Chinese coastline.

Endnotes

1. For details on national income accounting and a more extensive discussion concerning the practical difficulties encountered in estimating income see Mosk (2008: pp. 20–23 and pp. 353–367).

2. For Maddison's defense of his use of 1990 international Geary–Khamis dollars to compute levels of income per capita comparable across different time periods and different countries see Maddison (1998, 2006, 2007). Maddison's estimates appear in (or underlie figures appearing in) Tables A.2–A.6, and A.9 in this Appendix. While Maddison's assumptions and methodology in generating his estimates has been criticized, his figures are widely used in the economic development literature. This author believes that they are the most reliable currently available.

3. My approach differs from that employed by Bramall (2009). Bramall (2009) uses life expectancy as the principal gauge of the standard of living, improvements in life expectancy as the main calibrator of economic development gains.

Bibliography

Allen, F.; Qian, J. and Qian, M. (2008) "China's Financial System: Past, Present, and Future," in L. Brandt and T. G. Rawski (eds.) *China's Great Economic Transformation* (New York: Cambridge University Press).

Bell, L. (1992) "Farming, Sericulture, and Peasant Rationality in Wuxi County in the Early Twentieth Century," in T. Rawski and L. Li (eds.) *Chinese History in Economic Perspective* (Berkeley and Los Angeles: University of California Press).

Bell, L. (1999) *One Industry, Two Chinas: Silk Filatures and Peasant-Family Production in Wuxi County, 1865–1937* (Stanford: Stanford University Press).

Bian, M. (2005) *The Making of the State Enterprise System in Modern China* (Cambridge, MA: Harvard University Press).

Blackmore, S. (2001) "Evolution: The Human Brain as a Selective Imitation Device," *Cybernetics and Systems*, 32(1): 225–255.

Bo, Z. (2007) *China's Elite Politics: Political Transition and Power Balancing* (Singapore: World Scientific).

Bramall, C. (2009) *Chinese Economic Development* (New York: Routledge).

Brandt, L.; Hsieh, C. and Zhu, X. (2008) "Growth and Structural Transformation in China," in L. Brandt and T. G. Rawski (eds.) *China's Great Economic Transformation* (New York: Cambridge University Press).

Brandt, L.; Rawski, T.G. and Sutton, J. (2008) "China's Industrial Development," in L. Brandt and T. G. Rawski (eds.) *China's Great Economic Transformation* (New York: Cambridge University Press).

Brandt, L. and Sands, B. (1992) "Land Concentration and Income Distribution in Republican China," in T. Rawski and L. Li (eds.) *Chinese History in Economic Perspective* (Berkeley and Los Angeles: University of California Press).

Cai, F.; Park, A. and Zhao, Y. (2008) "The Chinese Labor Market in the Reform Era," in L. Brandt and T. G. Rawski (eds.) *China's Great Economic Transformation* (New York: Cambridge University Press).

Campbell, C. and Lee, J. (2004) "Mortality and Household in Seven Liaodong Populations, 1749–1909," in T. Bengtsson, C. Campbell, J. Lee, *et al.* (eds.) *Life Under Pressure: Mortality and Living Standards in Europe and Asia, 1700–1900* (Cambridge, MA: MIT Press).

Campbell, C. and Lee, J. (2005) "Deliberate Fertility in Late Imperial China: Spacing and Stopping in the Qing Imperial Lineage," California Center for Population Research On-Line Working Paper Series CCPR-041-05.

Chang, C. (1962) *The Income of the Chinese Gentry* (Seattle: University of Washington Press).

Chao, K. (1975) "The Growth of a Modern Textile Industry and the Competition with Handicrafts," in D. Perkins (ed.) *China's Modern Economy in Historical Perspective* (Stanford: Stanford University Press).

Chao, K. (1982) *The Economic Development of Manchuria: The Rise of a Frontier Economy* (Ann Arbor: Center for Chinese Studies).

Chen, X. (1991) "Chin's City Hierarchy, Urban Policy and Spatial Development in the 1980s," *Urban Studies*, 28(3): 341–367.

Chen, Y. (1983) *Chen Yun's Strategy for China's Development: A Non-Maoist Alternative* (Armonk, N.Y.: M. E. Sharpe, edited by N. Lardy and K. Lieberthal, translated by T. Mao and A. Du).

Cheng, L. (2003) *Banking in Modern China: Entrepreneurs, Professional Managers, and the Development of Chinese Banks, 1897–1937* (New York: Cambridge University Press).

China National Bureau of Statistics (2004) *China Statistical Yearbook 2004* (Beijing: China Statistics Press).

Ch'ü, T. (1962) *Local Government in China Under the Ch'ing* (Cambridge, MA: Harvard University Press).

Clark, G. (2007) *A Farewell to Alms: A Brief Economic History of the World* (Princeton: Princeton University Press).

Collier, P. (2007) *The Bottom Billion: Why the Poorest Countries are Failing and What Can Be Done About It* (New York: Oxford University Press).

Dawkins, R. (2006) *The Selfish Gene* (New York: Oxford University Press, reprint of original 1976 edition).

Denison, E. and Chung, W. (1976) "Economic Growth and Its Sources," in H. Patrick and H. Rosovsky (eds.) *Asia's New Giant: How the Japanese Economy Works* (Washington, D.C.: The Brookings Institution).

Diamond, J. (1999) *Guns, Germs, and Steel: The Fates of Human Societies* (New York: W.W. Norton & Company).

Duus, P. (1989a) "Japan's Informal Empire in China, 1895–1937," in P. Duus, R. Myers, and M. Peattie (eds.) *The Japanese Informal Empire in China, 1895–1937* (Princeton: Princeton University Press).

Duus, P. (1989b) "Zaikabō: Japanese Cotton Mills in China, 1895–1937," in P. Duus, R. Myers, and M. Peattie (eds.) *The Japanese Informal Empire in China, 1989–1937* (Princeton: Princeton University Press).

Easterly, W. (2002) *The Elusive Quest for Growth: Economists' Adventures and Misadventures in the Tropics* (Cambridge, MA: The MIT Press).

Elliot, M. (2001) *The Manchu Way: The Eight Banners and Ethnic Identity in Late Imperial China* (Stanford: Stanford University Press).

Elman, B. (2000) *A Cultural History of Civil Examinations in Imperial China* (Berkeley: University of California Press)

Elman, B. (2006) *A Cultural History of Modern Science in China* (Cambridge, MA: Harvard University Press).

Engelen, T. (2006) "Low Fertility in Premodern China: Positive, Preventive or Proactive Behavior?," *History of the Family*, 11(3): 125–134.

Fairbank, J. K. (1986) *The Great Chinese Revolution: 1800–1985* (New York: Harper & Row).

Faure, D. (1989) *The Rural Economy of Pre-Liberation China: Trade Expansion and Peasant Livelihood in Jiangsu and Gunagdong, 1870 to 1937* (New York: Oxford University Press).

Feuerwerker, A. (1977) *Economic Trends in the Republic of China, 1912–1949* (Ann Arbor: The University of Michigan).

Giersch, C. (2006) *Asian Borderlands: The Transformation of Qing China's Yunnan Frontier* (Cambridge, MA: Harvard University Press).

Hall, A. (1966) *The Scientific Revolution 1500–1800: The Formation of the Modern Scientific Attitude* (Boston: Beacon Press, reprint of original 1962 second edition).

Hannum, E.; Behrman, J.; Wang, M. and Liu, J. (2008) "Education in the Reform Era," in L. Brandt and T. G. Rawski (eds.) *China's Great Economic Transformation* (New York: Cambridge University Press).

Hirschmeier, J. (1964) *The Origins of Entrepreneurship in Meiji Japan* (Cambridge, MA: Harvard University Press).

Ho, P. (1959) *Studies on the Population of China, 1368–1953* (Cambridge, MA: Harvard University Press).

Hoffman, P. (2005) "Why Is It That Europeans Ended Up Conquering the Rest of the Globe? Prices, the Military Revolution, and Western Europe's Comparative Advantage in Violence" (unpublished manuscript).

Houston, R. (1988) *Literacy in Early Modern Europe: Culture and Education, 1500–1800* (New York: Longman).

Huang, C. (1990) *The Peasant Family and Rural Development in the Yangzi Delta, 1350–1988* (Stanford: Stanford University Press).

Huang, J.; Otsuka, K. and Rozelle, S. (2008) "Agriculture in China's Development: Past Disappointments, Recent Successes, and Future Challenges," in L. Brandt and T. G. Rawski (eds.) *China's Great Economic Transformation* (New York: Cambridge University Press).

Huang, P. (1985) *The Peasant Economy and Social Change in North China* (Stanford: Stanford University Press).

Huang, Y. (2008) "China" in A. K. Dutt and J. Ros (eds.), *International Handbook of Development Economics. Volume Two* (Northampton, MA: Edward Elgar).

Hunter, J. (2003) *Women and the Labour Market in Japan's Industrializing Economy: The Textile Industry Before the Pacific War* (New York: Routledge).

Jansen, M. (1975) *Japan and China: from War to Peace, 1894–1972* (Chicago: Rand McNally College Publishing Company).

Japan Ministry of Internal Affairs and Communications and Statistical Research and Training Institute (2009), "Historical Statistics for Japan" available at www.stat.go.jp/english/chouki (downloaded in February 2009).

Jones, S. (1972) "Finance in Ningpo: The 'Ch'ien Chuang,' 1750–1880," in W. Willmott (ed) *Economic Organization in Chinese Society* (Stanford: Stanford University Press).

Jordan, D. (1991) *Chinese Boycotts versus Japanese Bombs: The Failure of China's "Revolutionary Diplomacy," 1931–32* (Ann Arbor: The University of Michigan Press).

Junji, B. (1989) "Japanese Industrialists and Merchants in the Anti-Japanese Boycotts in China, 1919–1928," in P. Duus, R. Myers and M. Peattie (eds.) *The Japanese Informal Empire in China, 1989–1937* (Princeton: Princeton University Press).

Kim, J. (2001) "Total Factor Productivity Growth in East Asia: Implications for Future Growth" available online, downloaded in January 2009.

Klemm, F. (1964) *A History of Western Technology* (Cambridge, MA: The MIT Press).

Kueh, Y. (1995) *Agricultural Instability in China, 1931–1991: Weather, Technology, and Institutions* (New York: Oxford University Press).

Kuhn, T. (1962) *The Structure of Scientific Revolutions* (Chicago: University of Chicago Press).

Landes, D. (1998) *The Wealth and Poverty of Nations: Why Some Are So Rich and Some So Poor* (New York: W.W. Norton and Company).

Lee, J. and Campbell, C. (1997) *Fate and Fortune in Rural China: Social Organization and Population Behavior in Liaoning, 1774–1873* (New York: Cambridge University Press).

Lee, J. and Tan, G. (1992) "Infanticide and Family Planning in Late Imperial China: The Price and Population History of Rural Liaoning, 1774–1873," in T. Rawski and L. Li (eds.) *Chinese History in Economic Perspective* (Berkeley and Los Angeles: University of California Press).

Lewis, A. (1954) "Economic Development with Unlimited Supplies of Labor," *The Manchester School*, 22: 141–145.

Lewis, A. (1978) *The Evolution of the International Economic Order* (Princeton: Princeton University Press).

Li, L. (1981) *China's Silk Trade: Traditional Industry in the Modern World, 1842–1937* (Cambridge, MA: Harvard University Press).

Li, Y. (2001) *Chinese Bureaucratic Culture and Its Influence on the 19th-Century Steamship Operation, 1864–1885: The Bureau of Recruiting Merchants* (New York: The Edwin-Mellen Press).

Lin, A. (1997) *The Rural Economy of Guangdong, 1870–1937: A Study of the Agrarian Crisis and Its Origins in Southernmost China* (Houndmills, Basingstoke, Hampshire: Macmillan Press Ltd).

Liu, C. (2007) *Peasants and Revolution in Rural China: Rural Political Change in the North China Plain and the Yangzi Delta, 1850–1949* (New York: Routledge).

Lu, D. and Neilson, W. (eds.) (2004) *China's West Region Development: Domestic Strategies and Global Implications* (Singapore: World Scientific).

Lü, X. (2000) *Cadres and Corruption: The Organizational Involution of the Chinese Communist Party* (Stanford: Stanford University Press).

Lumsden, C. and Wilson, E. (1983) *Promethean Fire: Reflections on the Origin of Mind* (Cambridge, MA: Harvard University Press).

Ma, D. (2008) "Economic Growth in the Lower Yangzi Region of China in 1911–1937: A Quantitative and Historical Analysis," *The Journal of Economic History*, 28(2): 355–392.

Maddison, A. (1998) *Chinese Economic Performance in the Long Run* (Paris: Organisation for Economic Co-operation and Development, Development Centre Studies).

Maddison, A. (2006) *The World Economy: Volumes 1 and 2* (Paris: Organisation for Economic Co-operation and Development, Development Centre Studies).

Maddison, A. (2007) *Contours of the World Economy 1-2030 AD: Essays in Macro-Economic History* (New York: Oxford University Press).

Mallory, W. (1928) *China: Land of Famine* (New York: American Geographical Society).

Man-Cheong, I. (2004) *The Class of 1761: Examination, State, and Elites in Eighteenth-Century China* (Stanford: Stanford University Press).

Mann, S. (1987) *Local Merchants and the Chinese Bureaucracy, 1750–1950* (Stanford: Stanford University Press).

Marks, R. (1998) *Tigers, Rice, Silk, and Silt: Environment and Economy in Late Imperial South China* (New York: Cambridge University Press).

Mitchell, B.R. (2003) *International Historical Statistics: Africa, Asia & Oceania* (Houndmills, Basingstoke, Hampshire: Palgrave Macmillan).

Miyamoto, M. (2004) "Quantitative Aspects of Tokugawa Economy," in A. Hayami, O. Saitō, and R. P. Toby (eds.) *The Economic History of Japan: 1600–1990. Volume 1: The Emergence of Economic Society in Japan, 1600–1859* (New York: Oxford University Press).

Miyazaki, I. (1976) *China's Examination Hell: The Civil Service Examinations of Imperial China* (New York: John Weatherhill).

Mokyr, J. (2002) *The Gifts of Athena: Historical Origins of the Knowledge Economy* (Princeton: Princeton University Press).

Morgan, S. (2004) "Economic Growth and the Biological Standard of Living in China, 1880–1930," *Economics and Human Biology*, 2(2): 197–218.

Mosk, C. (1983) *Patriarchy and Fertility: Japan and Sweden, 1880–1960* (New York: Academic Press).

Mosk, C. (1995) *Competition and Cooperation in Japanese Labour Markets* (Houndmills, Basingstoke, Hampshire: Macmillan Press Ltd).

Mosk, C. (1996) *Making Health Work: Human Growth in Modern Japan* (Berkeley: University of California Press).

Mosk, C. (2001) *Japanese Industrial History: Technology, Urbanization and Economic Growth* (Armonk, NY: M.E. Sharpe).

Mosk, C. (2005) *Trade and Migration in the Modern World* (New York: Routledge).

Mosk, C. (2008) *Japanese Economic Development: Markets, Norms, Structures* (New York: Routledge).

Mosk, C. and Johannson, S. (1986) "Income and Mortality: Evidence from Modern Japan," *Population and Development Review*, 12: 415–440.

Müller, D.; Ringer, F. and Simon, B. (1987) *The Rise of the Modern Educational System: Structural Change and Social Reproduction, 1870–1920* (New York: Cambridge University Press).

Murphey, R. (1953) *Shanghai: Key to Modern China* (Cambridge, MA: Harvard University Press).

Myers, R. (1970) *The Chinese Peasant Economy: Agricultural Development in Hopei and Shantung, 1890–1949* (Cambridge, MA: Harvard University Press).

Myers, R. (1972) "The Commercialization of Agriculture in Modern China," in W. Willmott (ed.) *Economic Organization in Chinese Society* (Stanford: Stanford University Press).

Myers, R. (1982) *The Japanese Economic Development of Manchuria, 1932–1945* (New York: Garland Publishing, Inc.).

Myers, R. (1989) "Japanese Imperialism in Manchuria: The South Manchurian Railway Company, 1906–1933," in P. Duus, R. Myers and M. Peattie (eds.) *The Japanese Informal Empire in China, 1989–1937* (Princeton: Princeton University Press).

Nakagane, K. (1989) "Manchuko and Economic Development," in P. Duus, R. Myers and M. Peattie (eds.) *The Japanese Informal Empire in China, 1989–1937* (Princeton: Princeton University Press).

Nakajima, T.; Nomura, K. and Matsuura, T. (2004) "Total Factor Productivity Growth: Survey Report" (Tokyo: Asian Productivity Organization).

Ni, S. and Van, P. (2005) "High Corruption Income in Ming and Qing China," *Journal of Development Economics* 81(2): 316–336.

Parker, G. (1988) *The Military Revolution: Military Innovation and the Rise of the West, 1500–1800* (New York: Cambridge University Press).

Peattie, M. (1989) "Japanese Treaty Port Settlements in China, 1895–1937" in P. Duus, R. Myers, and M. Peattie (eds.) *The Japanese Informal Empire in China, 1989–1937* (Princeton: Princeton University Press).

Perkins, D. (1966) *Market Control and Planning in Communist China* (Cambridge, MA: Harvard University Press).

Perkins, D. (1969) *Agricultural Development in China, 1368–1968* (Chicago: Aldine Publishing Company).

Perkins, D. and Rawski, T. G. (2008) "Forecasting China's Economic Growth to 2025," in L. Brandt and T. G. Rawski (eds.) *China's Great Economic Transformation* (New York: Cambridge University Press).

Perkins, D. and Yusuf, S. (1984) *Rural Development in China* (Baltimore: The Johns Hopkins University Press for the World Bank).

Pinker, S. (2007) *The Language Instinct: How the Mind Creates Language* (New York: Harper Perennial Modern Classics, reprint of original 1994 edition).

Pomeranz, K. (2000) *The Great Divergence: China, Europe, and the Making of the Modern World Economy* (Princeton: Princeton University Press).

Poston, D. and Yaukey, D. (1992) *The Population of Modern China* (New York: Plenum Press).

Pritchett, L. (1997) "Divergence, Big Time," *Journal of Economic Perspectives*, 11(1): 3–12.

Rawski, T. G. (1979) *Economic Growth and Employment in China* (New York: Oxford University Press for the World Bank).

Rawski, T. G. (1989) *Economic Growth in Prewar China* (Berkeley: University of California Press).

Richerson, R. and R. Boyd (2005) *Not by Genes Alone: How Culture Transformed Human Evolution* (Chicago: The University of Chicago Press).

Riskin, C. (1975) "Surplus and Stagnation in Modern China," in D. Perkins (ed.) *China's Modern Economy in Historical Perspective* (Stanford: Stanford University Press).

Ronan, C. (1978) *The Shorter Science and Civilisation in China: An Abridgement of Joseph Needham's Original Text. Volume 1* (New York: Cambridge University Press).

Ronan, C. (1986a) *The Shorter Science and Civilisation in China: An Abridgement of Joseph Needham's Original Text. Volume 2* (New York: Cambridge University Press).

Ronan, C. (1986b) *The Shorter Science and Civilisation in China: An Abridgement of Joseph Needham's Original Text. Volume 3* (New York: Cambridge University Press).

Ronan, C. (1994) *The Shorter Science and Civilisation in China: An Abridgement of Joseph Needham's Original Text. Volume 4* (New York: Cambridge University Press).

Sachs, J. (2005) *The End of Poverty: Economic Possibilities for Our Time* (New York: The Penguin Press).

Schran, P. (1975) "On the Yenan Origins of Current Economic Policies," in D. Perkins (ed) *China's Modern Economy in Historical Perspective* (Stanford: Stanford University Press).

Schurmann, F. (1968) *Ideology and Organization in Communist China* (Berkeley and Los Angeles: University of California Press).

Shen, T.; Habicht, J.-P. and Chang, Y. (1996) "Effect of Economic Reforms on Child Growth in Urban and Rural Areas of China," *The New England Journal of Medicine*, 335(6): 400–406.

Sheridan, J. (1983) "The Warlord Era: Politics and Militarism Under the Peking Government, 1916–1928," in J. K. Fairbank (ed.) *The Cambridge History of China. Volume 12: Republican China, 1912–1949, Part 1* (Cambridge: Cambridge University Press).

Shimokawa, S. (2007) "The Labour Market of Body Weight in China: A Semiparametric Analysis," *Applied Economics*, 40(8): 1–20.

Skinner, G. W. (1995) "Marketing and Social Structure in Rural China" (Ann Arbor, MI: Association for Asian Studies).

Strauss, J. (1998) *Strong Institutions in Weak Polities: State Building in Republican China* (New York: Oxford University Press).

Sun, K. (1969) *The Economic Development of Manchuria in the First Half of the Twentieth Century* (Cambridge, MA: Harvard University Press).

Tawney, R. (1964) *Land and Labor in China* (Boston: Beacon Press reprint of original 1932 edition).

Taylor, G. (1980) *Japanese Sponsored Regime in North China* (New York: Garland Publishing reprint of original 1939 edition).

Thornton, P. (2007) *Disciplining the State: Virtue, Violence, and State-Making in Modern China* (Cambridge, MA: Harvard University Press).

Umeno, Y. (2008) "From Immigrants to Stayers: Micro-demography of a Historical Lineage in Sichuan, China," *The History of the Family*, 13(3): 268–282.

United Nations (2004) *Statistical Yearbook 2001* (New York: United Nations).

Walker, K. (1965) *Planning in Chinese Agriculture: Socialisation and the Private Sector, 1956–1962* (London: Frank Cass & Co.).

Wang, F. and Mason, A. (2008) "The Demographic Factor in China's Transition," in L. Brandt and T. G. Rawski (eds.) *China's Great Economic Transformation* (New York: Cambridge University Press).

Waswo, A. (1977) *Japanese Landlords: The Decline of a Rural Elite* (Berkeley: University of California Press).

Wilson, E. (1999) *Consilience: The Unity of Knowledge* (New York: Random House Vintage).

Wittner, D. (2008) *Technology and the Culture of Progress in Meiji Japan* (New York, Routledge).

World Bank (2002) *World Development Indicators 2002* (World Bank: Washington, D.C.).

Wray, W. (1989) "Japan's Big-Three Service Enterprises in China, 1896–1936," in P. Duus, R. Myers, and M. Peattie (eds.) *The Japanese Informal Empire in China, 1989–1937* (Princeton: Princeton University Press).

Yamamura, K. (1974) *A Study of Samurai Income and Entrepreneurship: Quantitative Analyses of Economic and Social Aspects of the Samurai in Tokugawa and Meiji Japan* (Cambridge, MA: Harvard University Press).

Yang, D. (1996) *Calamity and Reform in China: State, Rural Society, and Institutional Change since the Great Leap Famine* (Stanford: Stanford University Press).

Young, L. (1998) *Japan's Total Empire: Manchuria and the Culture of Wartime Imperialism* (Berkeley and Los Angeles: University of California Press).

Index